Friday 6:30 am - The Mix   Sunday 7pm The Mix

Suede

MW01518386

(ppl   nood)

NIGHT+DAY
LAS VEGAS

KOI - 702-454-4555
Planet Hollywood.

NOBU Sun 6th
702-693-
5ppl   5090
7:30pm

Planet Hollywood.
American Mile shops
ID: 91284704
Print voucher - 1st page.
10pm   8-8:30 pm pick up
tix + general admission

Premium outlet
F+S - 10-9pm 87 S south
Sun 10-8pm   grand
central
pkwy

PULSE GUIDES

Distributed in the United States and Canada by National Book Network (NBN).
First Edition. Printed in the United States. 30% postconsumer content.
Copyright © 2006 Greenline Publications, Inc. All rights reserved.
ISBN-10:0-9759022-8-8; ISBN-13:978-0-9759022-8-8

Credits

Executive Editor	Alan S. Davis
Editor	Anita Chabria
Contributing Editor	Christina Henry de Tessan
Lead Contributor	Patrick Green
Contributor	Adam Slutsky
Copy Editors	Kelly Borgeson, Gail Nelson-Bonebrake, Elizabeth Stroud
Maps	Chris Gillis
Production	Jo Farrell, Samia Afra

Photo Credits: (front cover, left to right) Les Byerley (martini), courtesy of MGM MIRAGE (Osteria del Circo and Bellagio Fountains); (back cover, left to right) courtesy of The Venetian Resort Hotel and Casino (Delmonico Steakhouse), courtesy of MGM MIRAGE (*La Femme* and Tabú) and Alan S. Davis (airport slots); (inside cover, top and bottom) courtesy of MGM MIRAGE, (middle) courtesy of Ivan Kane's Forty Deuce; (p.4) Mary Lou D'Auray.

Special Sales

For information about bulk purchases of Pulse Guides (ten copies or more), email us at bookorders@greenlinepub.com. Special bulk rates are available for charities, corporations, institutions, and online and mail-order catalogs.

NIGHT+DAY
the Cool Cities series from **PULSE**GUIDES

P.O. Box 590780, San Francisco, CA 94159
pulseguides.com

Pulse Guides is an imprint of ASDavis Media Group, Inc.

The Night+Day Difference

The Pulse of the City

Our job is to point you to all of the city's peak experiences: amazing museums, unique spas, and spectacular views. But the complete *urbanista* experience is more than just impressions—it is grown-up fun, the kind that thrives by night as well as by day. Urban fun is a hip nightclub or a trendy restaurant. It is people-watching and people-meeting. Lonely planet? We don't think so. Night+Day celebrates our lively planet.

The Right Place. The Right Time. It Matters.

A Night+Day city must have exemplary restaurants, a vibrant nightlife scene, and enough attractions to keep a visitor busy for six days without having to do the same thing twice. In selecting restaurants, food is important, but so is the scene. Our hotels, most of which are 4- and 5-star properties, are rated for the quality of the concierge staff (can they get you into a hot restaurant?) as well as the rooms. You won't find kids with fake IDs at our nightlife choices. And the attractions must be truly worthy of your time. But experienced travelers know that timing is almost everything. Going to a restaurant at 7pm can be a very different experience (and probably less fun) than at 9pm; a champagne boat cruise might be ordinary in the morning but spectacular at sunset. We believe providing the reader with this level of detail makes the difference between a good experience and a great one.

The Bottom Line

Your time is precious. Our guide must be easy to use and dead-on accurate. That is why our executive editor, editors, and writers (locals who are in touch with what is great—and what is not) spend hundreds of hours researching, writing, and debating selections for each guide. The results are presented in four unique ways: the *99 Best* with our top three choices in 33 categories that highlight what is great about the city; the *Experience* chapters, in which our selections are organized by distinct themes or personalities (Cool, Bachelor(ette), and Luxe); a *Perfect Plan* (3 Nights and Days) for each theme, showing how to get the most out of the city in a short period of time; and the *Las Vegas Black Book,* listing all the hotels, restaurants, nightlife, and attractions, with key details, contact information, and page references.

Our bottom line is this: If you find our guide easy to use and enjoyable to read, and with our help you have an extraordinary time, we have succeeded. We review and value all feedback from our readers, so please contact us at **feedback@pulseguides.com**.

At Burger Bar

From the Publisher

This book is dedicated to the memory of my uncle Morty, who taught me how to shoot craps at a very young age (he was also one of the nicest people I've ever known). By the time I was in college, I was ready to try the *real* thing—Las Vegas. Ever since, I've witnessed the ups and downs in the city's appeal, but every visit to Vegas has provided me with a fun-filled escape—and this, despite the fact that I've probably paid for a chandelier or two in many of the major casinos.

More than seven years ago, I published my guide to the 100 most fun events in the world, *The Fun Also Rises* (named after Ernest Hemingway's *The Sun Also Rises*, which helped popularize what has become perhaps the most thrilling party on earth, Pamplona's Fiesta de San Fermín, also known as the Running of the Bulls). Its success persuaded me that there were others who shared my interest in a different approach to travel. Guidebooks were neither exciting nor informative enough to capture peak experiences—whether for world-class events or just a night on the town.

Night+Day, the first series from Pulse Guides, presents the best that a city has to offer—hotels, restaurants, nightlife, and attractions that are exciting without being stuffy—in a totally new format. It's for Gen-Xers to Zoomers (Boomers with a zest for life), who know that if one wants to truly experience a city, the night is as important as the day.

Pulse Guides was created with one abiding principle: *Never settle for the ordinary.* I hope that a willingness to explore new approaches to guidebooks, combined with meticulous research, provides you with unique and significant experiences. Thank you for choosing **Night+Day** to help guide you through one of the world's most exciting cities, Las Vegas.

Wishing you extraordinary times,

Alan S. Davis

Alan S. Davis, Publisher and Executive Editor
Pulse Guides

P.S. To contact me, or for updated information on all of our **Night+Day** guides, please visit our website at **pulseguides.com**.

TOC

Lead Contributor

Patrick Green is a Los Angeles–based writer with Danny Ocean dreams and a Mike from *Swingers* reality. He is also the only known defendant to successfully use the "what happens in Vegas, stays in Vegas" defense in a court of law. When he's in Vegas, which is often, he can be found working on his "base coat" at The Hard Rock pool or teaching "class" at the old-school Peppermill. In between is anyone's guess. His nightlife reviews appear in **Night+Day** Los Angeles, Citysearch, Shecky's, and la.com. Check out his myspace page's blog, myspace.com/patrickgreen_la, for his latest tales, lies, and exaggerations on everything from the legacy of *Dolemite*, to the brilliance of Sergio Leone, to the many uses of peanut butter.

Contributor

Adam Slutsky ("Gambling Tips," p.177), who grew up in the Catskills with its myriad card rooms, was exposed to gambling at an early age. When most kids were playing Little League, Adam was learning about splitting aces and drawing for an inside straight. Rolling the bones, betting on bangtails, or taking the underdog plus the points—if it had to do with wagering you could safely bet the farm that Adam was involved. Today, that trend continues. Adam was the Las Vegas correspondent for *Chance: The Best of Gaming*, and is a frequent contributor to *Casino Player* and *Strictly Slots*. He also freelances for numerous major publications, covering a wide variety of subjects. When he's not working on a story, Adam can usually be found playing poker in one of America's card rooms or behind the wheel of a very fast automobile.

Acknowledgments

We've gotten suggestions from dozens and dozens of Vegas residents and visitors, without which this book could not have hit the mark. I'd like to thank, in particular, David Bodzin, Merdith Dalton, Leonard and Sophie Davis, Norine Dworkin, Dennis and Florence Forst, Lloyd Funtanilla, Jim and Gloria Hassan, Scott Rodder, Robert Ross, Alex Smith, Robbie Vergara, Chris Wessling, Amy Wittle, and Prema Zombari.
Alan S. Davis, Executive Editor

Introduction

Viva Las Vegas—America's most hedonistic playground. Each year, approximately 37 million people answer the sirens' call to cavort in the desert. As University of Nevada Las Vegas historian Hal Rothman likes to point out, that's more than visit Mecca. And without a doubt, Sin City is more fun.

Yes, Las Vegas has an allure that's at once cheesy and tacky, sophisticated and elegant. It is a city rich in dualities and contradictions: a successful tourist destination still grappling with a local identity; a den of sin that's largely run by Mormons; a stretch of jaw-dropping architectural spectacles standing in the middle of even greater natural desert beauty; a nonstop town that offers an incredible selection of relaxing and restorative spas. There's no such thing as restraint here. No doubt that's why Las Vegas continues to captivate our imagination the way few cities have.

Las Vegas: What It Was

So how did this strip of sand become one of America's ultimate destinations? Forget what you think you know about Las Vegas from Hollywoodized history. Long before the idea for the Flamingo even flickered through mobster Bugsy Siegel's brain, others had realized its enormous potential.

For starters, we can thank for the city's name the numerous traders traveling from New Mexico to California in the 1820s. When they wandered off the Old Spanish Trail, carved by missionaries in the 1700s, and discovered a lush, green area fed by mountain snowmelt and desert springs, they promptly noted it on their maps as *las vegas* (Spanish for "the meadows"). The name stuck.

Mormon missionaries from Salt Lake City were the first non-Indians to settle the area, establishing the Old Mormon Fort in 1855. But, beaten by the land and harsh conditions, they retreated three years later. (Eventually they returned, which is why Las Vegas has such a large Mormon population.) Not long after, silver was discovered and miners flooded in, hoping for riches. Lead was also discovered nearby and some miners even prospected for gold around the Colorado River.

But it wasn't until the late 1800s that the groundwork was laid to make Las Vegas an actual city. At the time, railroad magnate and U.S. senator William Clark was building tracks from Salt Lake City to Los Angeles, and Las Vegas made an ideal depot to replenish fuel and water.

On May 15, 1905, Las Vegas became a city when 110 acres of land were auctioned off to hopeful citizens in what is now downtown Las Vegas. In fact, Jackie Gaughn's Plaza Hotel stands on the site where the auction was held and where the old Union Railroad depot once stood. By 1911, Las Vegas was incorporated as a city; at the time, it had 800 residents and occupied fewer than 20 square miles. The city continued to grow, but it was the 1930s, '40s, and '50s that shaped modern Las Vegas.

Indeed, 1931 turned out to be a landmark year: Gambling was legalized; the waiting period for divorce was shortened from six months to six weeks, making Nevada the most divorce-friendly state in the union; and construction began on the Hoover Dam, which eventually supplied Las Vegas (and the surrounding Southwest) with the water and power it needed to fuel the mega-resorts to come.

World War II, according to UNLV historian Gene Moehring, made it clear that Las Vegas' destiny lay in gambling and tourism. In preparation for the first stage of the war—the initial assault in Africa—thousands of troopers training in the early '40s were stationed around Arizona, California, and southern Nevada—the only places hot enough and rugged enough to resemble Africa. And on weekends, those soldiers poured into Las Vegas for much-welcomed R & R. Las Vegas still has a military connection. Nellis Air Force Base, the now-closed nuclear test site where the military tried out new hardware, is nearby, as is the secret Area 51, where some people believe alien remains snatched from Roswell are hidden.

Developers quickly seized on Las Vegas' potential as a vacation destination. The first hotel built on the old Los Angeles Highway, which eventually became Las Vegas Boulevard or the Strip, was the El Rancho. A pioneer of sorts, the sprawling 100-acre ranch-style resort was the first to be constructed away from downtown and the rail lines. Forward-thinking developers opted instead for proximity to the highway, which they correctly believed would be key to leisure travelers. (The El Rancho was long ago consumed by fire, but the lot where it stood, on Las Vegas Boulevard across from the Sahara Hotel & Casino, still stands empty.) More hotels followed in quick succession: The Hotel Last Frontier opened in 1942, then Bugsy Siegel's famous Flamingo in 1946. The Strip was born.

Glamour begets glamour, and in no time Las Vegas became showbiz central, as the nightclub cabaret scene intersected with Hollywood and the rise of television. Legendary casino showrooms at the Sands, Dunes, Sahara, Tropicana, Stardust,

> **Indeed, 1931 turned out to be a landmark year: Gambling was legalized.**

Hacienda, New Frontier, and Riviera featured performers like Frank, Dino, Sammy, and the rest of the Rat Pack. Don Rickles, Rich Little, Danny Thomas, Milton Berle, Red Skelton, and Debbie Reynolds rotated through the legendary showrooms. So did Barbra Streisand and Elvis, who bombed initially before being hailed as the King. Even Ronald Reagan (well before becoming president) did a stint as a song-and-dance man at the Last Frontier.

Many of those once-famous showrooms in their once-famous resorts are long gone (or gone to seed). The Landmark's destruction was spectacularly captured in the camp film *Mars Attacks*. The Sands (though actually destroyed post-production) was the scene of a fiery air crash in *Con Air*. And thousands turned out to watch the implosions of the Dunes (now the site of The Venetian), Hacienda (now Mandalay Bay), and Aladdin (rebuilt as the Aladdin) hotels.

Key Dates

1829 Spanish explorers find springs and dub them *las vegas*, Spanish for "the meadows."

1855 Mormons create first settlement.

1905 Land auction begins development of city.

1931 Gambling is legalized.

1935 The Hoover Dam opens.

1937 The Strip, then part of Highway 91, gets pavement.

1941 El Rancho, the first Strip hotel, and El Cortez, the first downtown casino, open.

1946 Famed mobster Benjamin "Bugsy" Siegel opens the Flamingo Hotel.

1977 Clark County gaming revenues reach the $1 billion mark.

1989 Steve Wynn builds the first of his mega-resorts, The Mirage.

1993 The Luxor with its laser beam of light opens on October 15. Treasure Island opens 12 days later.

1998 The Bellagio Hotel opens as the most expensive hotel ever built at a cost of $1.7 billion.

2005 Las Vegas celebrates turning 100.

Las Vegas: What It Is

Visionary Steve Wynn polished up Las Vegas' image and turned it from a punch line into a playground. In 1989, Wynn opened the first destination mega-resort in Vegas. The Mirage dazzled guests with its innovative (now ubiquitous) Y-shaped construction, accommodations, classy casino, and tourist-friendly attractions like the Dolphin Habitat, which doubles as a serious research facility. Next, he constructed Treasure Island, followed by the luxurious Bellagio, whose jaw-dropping dancing fountains have

Night+Day's Las Vegas Urbie

Night+Day cities are chosen because they have a vibrant nightlife scene, standard-setting and innovative restaurants, cutting-edge hotels, and enough attractions to keep one busy for six days without doing the same thing twice. In short, they are fun. They represent the quintessential *urbanista* experience. This wouldn't exist but for the creativity and talents of many people and organizations. In honor of all who have played a role in making Las Vegas one of the world's coolest cities, Pulse Guides is pleased to give special recognition, and our Urbie Award, to one individual or organization whose contribution is exemplary.

THE URBIE AWARD: George Maloof Jr.

Casino mogul and proud bachelor George Maloof Jr. epitomizes the "work hard, play hard" mantra that fuels Las Vegas. Maloof Jr., known as much for his business savvy as for his Playboy Playmate girlfriends, is a Steve Wynn for a new generation, living every bachelor or single businessman's fantasy in both the boardroom and the bedroom.

Maloof Jr. is the visionary tycoon behind The Palms Resort and, some would say, the brains behind the billion-dollar Maloof family empire, which includes the NBA Kings, the WNBA Monarchs, a beer distributorship, a film production company, and a record label. He parlayed the sale of the family's Fiesta Hotel and Casino into the $270 million Palms in 2001. His goal was simple: Return the "sin" to Sin City.

"I wanted to create a place that represented, to me, the real reason people came to Las Vegas," Maloof Jr. has said, "That's to come and party and have fun."

While competitors focused on families and older folks, the Palms catered to the MTV generation, especially the hot, young, rich, and famous, using his family's crossover connections to draw stars from the NBA, NFL, Hollywood, and hip-hop worlds. His first stroke of genius was allowing MTV to film its popular reality show *The Real World* here in 2002. The move put The Palms on the pop culture map.

His latest venture (thus far) is the Palms' 40-story Fantasy Towers, with the first Playboy Club in over 25 years. The $600 million expansion is a huge risk for the grandson of a Lebanese immigrant.

"As they say in poker, 'All in,'" has said Maloof, a former late-night gambler in his college days at UNLV. "We're all in."

no doubt surpassed the vintage "Welcome to Fabulous Las Vegas" sign as the city's icon.

As he made over Las Vegas, and even stamped his signature on the town with the new $2.7 billion Wynn Las Vegas on the site where the Sands once stood, Steve Wynn sparked a building boom that's still going strong today. Each resort on the Strip tries to keep up and "out-new" the last one. When The Venetian's Canyon Ranch SpaClub became the largest spa in town, the Bellagio chose to redesign its own spa. When Mandalay Bay added a boutique wing of suites called THEhotel, Caesars built the Augustus Tower, a modern, "de-themed" suites-only section of the resort. And this growth doesn't even begin to touch upon the convention facilities being added, or how Vegas is booming in the world of pop culture.

> Often called an adult's Disneyland, Vegas truly offers more ways to spend your money than ever before.

In 1993, the Travel Channel brought Texas Hold 'Em poker and the World Poker Tour to mainstream media. Now, you can't flip stations on your TV without hearing the words "I'm all in." The poker craze swept the nation, and now casinos up and down the Strip are reopening flashy poker rooms. But poker isn't the only thing on TV—the world got to see the renovation of the Golden Nugget through the show *Casino*, go backstage at Bally's, and follow the rise and fall of Vegas showgirls in *Jubilee!*, and then there was the train wreck, *Caesars 24/7*, which actually took away from the established reputation of the palace on the Four Corners. America doesn't have its own all-gambling channel, but we're not far from it. All the exposure of Las Vegas on TV has online travel websites humming with traffic and sales on flights and vacation packages to Glitter Gulch.

However, if you don't gamble, it's no problem. The genius marketing staffs behind Sin City are turning Las Vegas into a destination playground for anyone and everyone. Those who don't roll the bones come for the celebrity chefs, hopping night life, and, of course, to party in such a way that they can live up to the city's motto—"What happens in Vegas, stays in Vegas." Often called an adult's Disneyland, Vegas truly offers more ways to spend your money than ever before.

As the business landscape of Las Vegas changes, so does the skyline. Nearly 30 condo projects have been proposed on and around the Strip. A few years down the road, The Stratosphere won't be the only super high-rise tower in the sky. Whether you want to call it the Manhattanization of Las Vegas, or the South Beachification of the Strip, Vegas is reinventing itself—again. The mega-resorts, while still a dynamic part of Vegas, are so last century. Sin City in the new millennium envisions itself as a Strip teaming with high-rise condos, luxury lofts, and all-inclusive communities. It aspires to be both the home and the playground of the Hollywood glitterati, the affluent young, and moneyed jet-setters. Las Vegas is where the action is, and it's constantly imagining new ways to keep its run going. While the façade may be in constant flux, the core of Vegas has remained constant: From its pioneer days until today, Sin City's heart has always been about having fun.

Welcome to Fabulous Las Vegas!

THE 99 BEST of LAS VEGAS

Who needs another "Best" list? You do—if it comes with details and insider tips that make the difference between a good experience and a great one. We've pinpointed the 33 categories that make Las Vegas exciting, magnetic, and unforgettable, and picked the absolute three best places to go for each. Whether you live in Las Vegas or are just visiting, these are the ultimate ways to indulge in Sin City.

After-Hours Clubs

#1–3: This is the land of "What happens in Vegas, stays in Vegas," and it's more a rule than an option to play late. We're talking late-late. David Letterman is off the air and in bed before these places get grooving.

Drai's*
Barbary Coast, 702-737-0555 • Bachelor(ette)

The Draw: Even though it's in the nearly laughable Barbary Coast, everyone—taxi drivers, locals, and especially veteran clubbers wanting to rub up with Hollywood types—knows Drai's is the "it" spot for hot, late-late-night fun.

The Scene: Before midnight, it's a romantic French restaurant—after midnight, it becomes a sizzling club. If you're looking for a lounge full of beautiful people that's still hopping at 5am, this is it. *Wed-Sun midnight-dawn.* C≡

Hot Tip: It's rumored that this is a hookup spot for couples who are looking to find a third.

Empire Ballroom
3765 Las Vegas Blvd. S., South Strip, 702-415-5283 • Bachelor(ette)

The Draw: Small by Sin City standards (it only holds 1,300 people), this place pulls in a young, tireless crowd that loves its DJs as much as it does dancing into the dawn.

The Scene: Before 3am, Empire is a hipster venue with an old-school, Art Deco vibe, perfect for watching live shows like Prince and the Killers in an intimate setting. After 3am, it's the hottest after-hours scene in Vegas. *Club: Fri-Sat 10pm-2am. After-hours: 3am-close.* C≡

Hot Tip: On Thursday night, after-hours bottle service begins at $150—a bargain by Vegas standards and an easy way through the separate VIP entrance.

Seamless
4740 S. Arville St., East Flamingo, 702-227-5200 • Cool

The Draw: A relative newcomer on the after-hours scene, Seamless has won devoted followers with a very steamy vibe that goes well into the next day.

The Scene: Before 4am, this is a topless joint with dancers strutting on a glass catwalk, and even on the bar. But at 4am, staff comes out to move furniture off the hardwood floors, opening up the space for dancing, and the catwalk rises up to the ceiling. Suddenly, it's a chic nightclub that draws youthful patrons from nearby hot spots like Rain. *24/7.* C≡

Hot Tip: Be sure to check out both the bathrooms and the roof. The roof (on the parking garage) offers 360-degree views of the city. The unisex bathrooms have a different kind of view if you're not careful: The clear glass stalls turn opaque only when you lock the door.

Best   All-Night Eats

#4–6: Forget 24-hour-restaurant stereotypes: greasy spoons, waitresses named Mabel, and health-code violations. Pre-dawn dining in Vegas is just like any other meal here. Think video poker, sexy servers, and star-worthy food.

California Pizza Kitchen
The Mirage, 702-791-7357 • Bachelor(ette)

The Draw: Also known as CPK, this is what Californians call comfort food. People come for the thin-crust pizzas and big chopped salads.

The Scene: This is an "open" restaurant (no walls to separate it from the surrounds), set toward the front of the hotel, nestled right next to the Race and Sports Book. It's popular with hotel guests as well as visitors. If The Mirage is hosting a World Poker Tournament, you're likely to find a few professional poker players as well. *Sun-Thu 11am-midnight, Fri-Sat 11am-2am.* $ =

Hot Tip: If you're dining alone or as a twosome, head to the front and volunteer to sit at the counter to avoid a long wait.

Grand Lux Café
The Venetian, 702-414-3888 • Bachelor(ette)

The Draw: In an elegant space with high ceilings, tiled floors, big roomy booths, and "patio seating" on the casino level, you can expect classic Continental fare and monster portions—it's owned by the Cheesecake Factory.

The Scene: The Grand Lux Café serves both guests of The Venetian and hungry tourists and conventioneers. Dinnertime seating can be pretty packed and loud, so if you want to hear what your companions are saying, go for the late-night eats anytime after 10pm. *24/7.* $ B=

Hot Tip: Big booths mean parties of eight or ten won't have trouble getting a spot together, and the pu-pu platter is a fun dish to share.

Mr. Lucky's 24/7
The Hard Rock, 702-693-5000 • Bachelor(ette)

The Draw: Mr. Lucky's serves up great American diner food when you don't want the pomp and circumstance of high-end Vegas restaurants or typical hotel cafe food. This is the coolest 24-hour coffee shop—with comfort food and rock-'n'-roll style.

The Scene: Come during the graveyard shift and you'll find some stumblers on the tail end of partying, or starving after a Joint show. Other than that, you'll mostly find Hard Rock hotel guests—meaning L.A. hipsters and other stylish kids. Hunker down in a faux tiger-skin booth for some award-winning chicken soup, burgers, or über-yummy milkshakes. *24/7.* $ =

Hot Tip: Ask for the super-lucky, off-the-menu special: an 8-ounce New York steak, three grilled shrimp, a baked potato, and a salad.

Bars with a View

#7–9: Las Vegas' neon splendor is most impressive at night when the city truly sparkles. With flashing Technicolor lights and quick-changing digital marquees, the four-mile stretch of Las Vegas Boulevard known as the Strip was recently named the nation's only urban scenic byway.

Ghostbar

Palms, 702-938-2666 • Cool

The Draw: Palms is known for being a catch-all of celebrities, and the Ghostbar is one of its more in-vogue areas to see and be seen.

The Scene: Fashionistas ride the elevators up to the 55th floor to dance high above the Las Vegas Valley. First-timers gather around the square of Plexiglas looking down to the ground below. Don't be surprised if you see a girl-on-girl make-out session on the dance floor. *Nightly 8pm-3am.* C☰

Hot Tip: Dining at the Palms' Alizé gains you automatic entrance to Ghostbar.

Mix Lounge

THEhotel, 702-632-9500 • Cool

The Draw: This swanky ultra lounge on the 64th floor of THEhotel has the view of all views.

The Scene: This mile-high club offers sexy décor and sweeping Strip views, luring in a fun, 30-something crowd. Wall-to-wall black leather furnishings and deep red lighting set a sensual mood, complemented by a cozy outdoor patio. *Nightly 5pm-3am, Wed until 4am.* C☰

Hot Tip: Wednesday is "service industry night," when the small dance floor really heats up and the bar stays open an extra hour.

Voodoo Lounge

The Rio, 702-252-7777 • Cool

The Draw: High atop The Rio, the Voodoo provides a fantastic vantage point of the entire Strip from its stepped-back position on Flamingo Road.

The Scene: This black arts–inspired lounge is adorned with real talismans and fluorescent designs that glow in the blacklight, the better to show off the trendy young crowd. Choose indoor viewing from floor-to-ceiling windows or, on windless days, check out the terrace. *Nightly 5pm-4am.* C☰

Hot Tip: The view is best enjoyed with a Witchdoctor, the Voodoo's rum-loaded signature cocktail.

THE 99 BEST

Best

Brasseries

#10–12: Vegas likes to think of itself as a worldly city. It collects international icons (the Eiffel Tower, Lake Como) the way some people collect matchbooks. While some attempts are bigger on kitsch than class, when it comes to French food, the town has hit the mark with a slew of upscale, très authentic spots.

Bouchon

The Venetian, 702-414-6200 • Luxe

The Draw: This is chef Thomas Keller's (Nor-Cal's French Laundry and Bouchon and the Big Apple's Per Se are his) foray into Glitter Gulch, and it's already won awards for Best New Restaurant on the Strip, Best French, Best Restaurant on the Strip, and Best Restaurant.

The Scene: It's French cafe simple-chic here, with high ceilings, pretty tiled floors, and a well-heeled crowd that knows café Americano from espresso. *Daily 7-10:30am, 5-10:45pm; lunch Sat-Sun noon-2:30pm. $$* B≡

Hot Tip: In warm weather, ask for patio seating, and while dinner here is a delight, it's also one of the best breakfast scenes in the city.

Daniel Boulud Brasserie

Wynn, 702-770-3300 • Luxe

The Draw: People come to Daniel Boulud for what it isn't—a look-at-me dining experience with a media-hungry celebrity chef. There is no obvious flash here. It's about one of the best meals in Vegas, in the company of the well bred.

The Scene: It's all calm sophistication in this earth-toned gem on the lower level of Wynn. From the food to the clientele, you'll be impressed. *Nightly 5:30-10:30pm. $$$$* B≡

Hot Tip: The burger is as good as its hype, but the steak au poivre is no slouch.

Mon Ami Gabi

Paris Las Vegas, 702-944-4224 • Cool

The Draw: Even locals make the trip to the Strip to dine on the patio of this French gem, just across the street from The Bellagio's fountains.

The Scene: For dinner or lunch, you'll find a buzzing, happy crowd munching on mussels, burgers, and crepes—all while people-watching the masses on Las Vegas Boulevard. *Mon-Thu 11:30am-11pm, Fri-Sat 11am-midnight, Sun 11am-11pm. $$* ≡

Hot Tip: Summer in Vegas hits triple digits—if you lunch on the patio, make sure you get an umbrella-covered table near the misters.

Burlesque

#13–15: The burlesque revival started a few years ago in L.A., but it just had too much of a Vegas flair not to find its way onto the Strip. Today, you can't throw a G-string without hitting some new, old-fashioned tease show. But this isn't your grandpa's peel-and-pose. No, this is a modern take on an old art, and it's lots of fun.

Ivan Kane's Forty Deuce
Mandalay Bay, 702-632-9442 • Cool

The Draw: It's sultry striptease without the potential sleaze factor of a typical topless club, brought to you by one of L.A.'s top nightlife impresarios.

The Scene: Many guests of Mandalay Bay, Four Seasons, and THEhotel gather around the cozy tables for a late-night drink and a smile before heading back to their rooms. Women love it as much as men. *Thu-Mon 10:30pm-4am, Fri-Sat and Mon after-hours until 6am.* C≡

Hot Tip: Stage-front seats are by far the best, but you'll have to reserve with bottle service to get one.

Pussycat Dolls Lounge
Caesars Palace, 702-731-7110 • Cool

The Draw: Often called the city's best burlesque, this Hollywood troupe makes even jaded guests purr.

The Scene: Hipsters and Caesars VIPs getting ready for a night out at nearby PURE stop here for a warm-up, or after dancing for a cooldown. Performances are only three minutes long, but they take place every half hour, and sometimes feature celebrity guests. *Tue-Sat 8pm-4am. First show at 10:30pm, and every 30 minutes thereafter.* C≡

Hot Tip: You can access the nightclub PURE directly from inside this lounge.

Tangerine
Treasure Island, 702-894-7580 • Bachelor(ette)

The Draw: A fun bar that's easy to get into, it boasts an outdoor patio with front-row seats to the spicy action of the *Sirens of TI* show, which runs every hour and a half from 7pm.

The Scene: The lounge glows with orange neon under-lights on the bar. Twenty- and 30-somethings ready to use the "What happens in Vegas ..." motto come here for drinks and carousing. *Tue-Sat 6pm-4am, patio 5:30pm-midnight.* C≡

Hot Tip: Watch out for TI Siren Allison, the brunette bombshell. She likes to pinpoint a victim in the audience and tease and shake her butt at him during her performance.

Celebrity-Spotting Hotels

Best

#16–18: Hollywood stars have lit up the Vegas scene since before the Rat Pack roamed these streets. With L.A. only a few hours away, it's no wonder the city's a popular getaway for the rich and glamorous. While Vegas isn't that big, celebrity Vegas is even smaller. For a glimpse of your favorite actors, wander over to one of the hotels that new Hollywood likes to call home.

The Hard Rock

4455 Paradise Rd., East Flamingo, 702-693-5000 • Bachelor(ette)

The Draw: Action, action, action—and we're not talking about cards. Cooler-than-thou 20-somethings come for the shows at the Joint, to soothe their hangovers while looking at bikini-clad beautiful people on Rehab Sundays, and for sushi at Nobu any night of the week.

The Scene: L.A. hipsters and those who love them make a party come to life everywhere any day—from the bar in the middle of the casino, to upstairs in the penthouse suite with Vegas's first bowling alley.

Hot Tip: Heaps of A-listers live like rock stars at the club Body English on the weekends. Take a peek in the private parlor room to see who's there.

Palms

4321 W. Flamingo Rd., West Flamingo, 702-942-7777 • Bachelor(ette)

The Draw: Since its opening, George Maloof Jr.'s Palms has been all about the who's who being right here. And that's still what brings the crowds. It's hosted MTV's *The Real World*, BRAVO's *Celebrity Poker Showdown*, and now it's kicking it up another notch with the Fantasy Tower, including the Playboy Mansion suite, the Playboy Club, and a Playboy lingerie store.

The Scene: Paris Hilton and Tara Reid dance at the Ghostbar while Dennis Rodman and current pro basketball players party in the Hardwood Suite in the Fantasy Tower.

Hot Tip: The Playboy Club is a current hot spot in Vegas, and has old-school bunnies complete with tails—but the new club Moon on the top level of the Fantasy Tower, with its retractable roof, also is a raging scene.

Wynn Las Vegas

3131 S. Las Vegas Blvd., North Strip, 702-770-7000 • Luxe

The Draw: It's the hotshot on the Strip, with the biggest price tag. Everybody wants to see Steve Wynn's latest, and see who else is there.

The Scene: You'll find all kinds at Wynn, from professional poker players to high-rolling Asian imports. The décor is nothing like Wynn's last bit of genius at The Bellagio. No, the style is barely explainable, kind of like an opulent circus set in a garden.

Hot Tip: The celebs like the floating table at Okada, Wynn's sushi joint, but you can't sit down for less than $1,200.

Cirque Shows

#19–21: Cirque du Soleil dominates Glitter Gulch entertainment, and for good reason. Founded in Quebec in 1984, it has grown into a global phenomenon. It first hit Vegas with *Mystère* in 1994, and since then has taken over the town with one great show after another.

The Beatles: "Love" Cirque du Soleil
The Mirage, 702-792-7777 • Cool

The Draw: The latest offering from Cirque du Soleil is a psychedelic treasure trove of both favorite and unreleased songs from the Fab Four.

The Scene: This is Vegas' hottest ticket, and crowds have drawn celebrities, tourists, and locals alike to the new, specially built theater. If you're a fan of the Beatles, this is a whole new way of experiencing their music. *Thu-Mon 7:30pm and 10:30pm.* C≡

Hot Tip: Extra dates are sometimes added to the schedule. Check the website (mirage.com/entertainment/entertainment_cirque_du_soleil.aspx) for updates, and plan on purchasing long before you arrive in Vegas.

Kà
MGM Grand, 702-796-9999 • Cool

The Draw: The fourth Cirque to open in Vegas, *Kà* blows away audiences as much for its trademark theatrics as for its amazing stage—a custom-built contraption that moves in almost every direction.

The Scene: *Kà*, whose name refers to the Egyptian idea that each person has a spiritual double that follows him or her through life, draws crowds from every walk. You'll find families (mostly at the early show), theater aficionados, and even hipsters sprinkled in between. *Tue-Sat 6:30pm and 9:30pm.* C≡

Hot Tip: *Kà* has the strongest story line of the Cirque shows, so if plot is important to you, choose this one. And consider a front-row center seat to really experience the action.

O
The Bellagio, 702-693-7722 • Luxe

The Draw: Cirque du Soleil's most ambitious performance features a company of synchronized swimmers, divers, aerialists, and clowns who create an astonishing feast for the eyes with bendy, twirly, twisty, how-on-earth-is-that-possible acrobatics above, in, and below the water stage.

The Scene: The 10,000-square-foot stage can be transformed into a million-and-a-half-gallon pool to handle the show's water acrobatics. The scene is a mix of those staying in the hotel, as well as theater-savvy fun seekers. *Wed-Sun 7:30pm and 10:30pm.* C≡

Hot Tip: The best seats are at mid-level, allowing easy viewing of the stage as well as overhead antics.

Best

Destination Spas

#22–24: Maybe you need to detox from last night's indulgences, or maybe you just deserve a break. Las Vegas spas run the gamut from simple to posh, and have a cure for every complaint. Be warned: Just because a spa is in a fancy hotel doesn't mean it's great (some don't live up to the hype), but these deliver the goods.

Canyon Ranch SpaClub
The Venetian, 702-414-3600 • Cool

The Draw: Canyon Ranch is a wellness brand known around the globe, and this Vegas version keeps the high standards alive.

The Scene: With a three-story rock-climbing wall, dozens of exercise classes from yoga to salsa, a well-appointed workout facility, and chic spa facilities, this oasis on the fourth floor of The Venetian draws in a sophisticated crowd that knows its spas. *Daily 5:30am-10pm.*

Hot Tip: Try the mango sugar scrub to get an all-over glow before heading out for the night.

MGM Grand Spa
MGM Grand, 702-891-3077 • Cool

The Draw: This is truly a connoisseurs' spa with rich wood floors, ultra-plush lounge chairs, and even a menu that recommends treatments for your level of spa experience, from neophyte to been-there-done-that.

The Scene: Away from the casino chaos at the back of the hotel near the pool, this Zen-inspired space draws relaxation junkies with signature services like its Amazon Rainforest Ritual—which combines massage, scrubs, wraps, and general bliss. *Daily 6am-8pm.*

Hot Tip: This spa is strictly for MGM guests on the weekends. Also, for Skyloft guests, MGM has a 24-hour spa facility available.

Paris Spa by Mandara
Paris Las Vegas, 702-946-4366 • Bachelor(ette)

The Draw: Mandara is the Sanskrit word for calm, and finding that state of serenity is what brings a suave set to this urban oasis.

The Scene: Brightly colored Gauguinesque wall murals combine with dark wicker furniture, stone, and Balinese wood elements for an ethereal and relaxing environment. *Sun-Thu 7am-7pm, Fri-Sat 7am-9pm.*

Hot Tip: Mandara does couples treatments right, with specially designed duo rooms complete with their own lounges, whirlpools, double-headed showers, and personal attendants.

Fine Dining

#25–27: Fine dining in Vegas has soared to new heights in recent years with an influx of high-profile chefs from around the globe. While not all of them actually staff their often-eponymous kitchens, without a doubt some of the most exciting and innovative meals in the world can be found on the Strip.

Aureole (G)
Mandalay Bay, 702-632-9500 • Luxe

The Draw: With its 42-foot wine tower complete with flying "wine angels," chef Charlie Palmer's elegant, hushed establishment draws crowds as much for the spectacle as the food.

The Scene: Refined and quiet (but not too quiet), Aureole pulls sophisticated diners looking for a memorable culinary experience. It's also a great spot for romance, especially the patio-side tables in the "swan court." *Nightly 5:30-10pm. $$$$* B –

Hot Tip: If you didn't reserve well ahead, consider dining à la carte in the charming bar area, where there are a few non-reservation tables.

Bradley Ogden* (G)
Caesars Palace, 702-731-7731 • Cool

The Draw: Ogden, who made his name at California's Lark Creek Inn, is known for using the freshest, mostly organic ingredients to create sumptuous New American dishes. Add that to a sleek yet welcoming space, and the allure is undeniable.

The Scene: You'll see jeans and you'll see little black dresses. Any approach seems to work in the stylish, earth-toned space. Whatever the outfit, the crowd itself is a mix of foodies who know Ogden's rep, hungry neophytes drawn in by the central location, and pre- and post-show crowds from the nearby Céline Dion and Elton John shows. *Sun-Thu 5-11pm, Fri-Sat 5pm-midnight. $$$$* B –

Hot Tip: The booths along the wall are the prime seats, and if you just want something light, the bar has its own menu.

Nob Hill (G)
MGM Grand, 702-891-7337 • Cool

The Draw: Chef Michael Mina of San Franciso is lauded for his seafood, but Nob Hill proves he knows comfort food, too.

The Scene: Mina has a loyal following of knowledgeable foodies, but the restaurant also draws a mixed crowd headed to and from Cirque du Soleil's *Kà*. It's also a popular special-occasion spot for locals. *Nightly 5:30-10:30pm. $$$$* B =

Hot Tip: The room can get noisy even when it's not crowded. Opt for a booth for a bit more privacy, and definitely don't miss the lobster pot pie and excellent mac and cheese.

Best

Free Attractions

#28–30: It's not every city that lets you watch the world's largest fountain show, experience a pirate battle, and get close to a wild animal or two—all within a half-mile walk, and all for free. Vegas is nothing if not packed with spectacles, each one vying to be more outlandish than the last.

Bellagio Fountains
The Bellagio, 702-946-7000 • Luxe

The Draw: Day or night, The Bellagio's fountain show inspires some of the most romantic moments on the Strip. The choreographed water and lights spectacular is nothing less than stunning.

The Scene: Weekdays and weeknights have less of a crowd, which makes for a quieter environment in front of Bellagio's Lago di Como. On weekends, the sidewalks are packed with loud revelers hitting the scene between bars and clubs well into the dawn. *Every 30 minutes, Mon-Fri 3-8pm, Sat-Sun and holidays noon-8pm. Every 15 minutes, nightly 8pm-midnight.*

Hot Tip: Share a gelato with your sweetheart while waiting for the fountain show. There is a stand just inside The Bellagio doors at street level that serves a few beverages and tasty Italian ice cream.

Sirens of TI Show
Treasure Island, 702-894-7111 • Bachelor(ette)

The Draw: It doesn't get any more campy-fabulous than this Vegas spectacle, complete with barely clad babes of both sexes battling it out with fireworks and cannons.

The Scene: Crowds gather on the sidewalk and around the *TI Sirens* set to gawk as the ladies of legend sing for their reluctant suitors to come and party. *Nightly at 7, 8:30, 10, and 11:30pm.*

Hot Tip: Watch the show with a drink in hand from the balcony of Tangerine.

Venetian Hotel
The Venetian, 702-414-1000 • Luxe

The Draw: If you've never been to Italy, then this will seem a lot like it.

The Scene: Gondoliers, singing and slowly paddling, whisk tourists up and down chlorinated canals, through the shopping scene inside or along the Strip outside, while tourists marvel at the impressive frescoed walls and marble-patterned floors of the lobby.

Hot Tip: Private gondolas ($60 inside and $50 outside) are the best way to get the full experience. Otherwise, it's four to a boat for shared rides with strangers. And if you really love those waterways, a special wedding gondola allows you to get married during your journey. *Gondola hours: Sun-Thu 10am-11pm, Fri-Sat 10am-midnight.*

Gay Bars and Clubs

#31–33: Las Vegas can be a surprisingly conservative town when you get off the main drags, but when you're in the party zone, there is no shortage of gay-friendly fun. While certain places are definitely alternative-lifestyle destinations, you'll almost always find a mixed crowd on the dance floor.

Freezone

601 E. Naples, Airport, 702-794-2310 • Bachelor(ette)

The Draw: Fun events and friendly staff keep this a favorite.

The Scene: The scene varies as the events change, but just a little. This club is known for having a welcoming, no-pretensions staff and a big restaurant that's often packed (although better food can be found elsewhere). Friday night is drag night, and on Sundays and Mondays, there's Gay Karaoke. It's a small venue with only 255 occupancy, but there is rarely a cover. *24/7.* ☰

Hot Tip: Tuesday night is Ladies' Night with a "Lick Her Bust Beer Bust!" party.

Gipsy

4605 S. Paradise Rd., Airport, 702-731-1919 • Bachelor(ette)

The Draw: The longest-running gay dance club in Vegas has a very loyal and high-energy following.

The Scene: Mostly gay men and a few women who love to dance crowd the floor and gyrate to techno, pop, and disco. This place is so popular that it's hard to get a drink on the weekends. *Wed-Mon 9pm-3am.* Ⓒ☰

Hot Tip: If you like Gipsy, wander next door to the new and long-anticipated 8-1/2 Ultra Lounge & Piranha Night Club, brought to you by the same owners.

KRAVE

3667 S. Las Vegas Blvd., Center Strip, 702-836-0830 • Bachelor(ette)

The Draw: It's easy to get to and located right on the Strip at Aladdin/Planet Hollywood, making it a big draw for visitors.

The Scene: You'll find a lively mix of both local and tourist gay men and women, with some straights who are comfortable with everyone. It's one large room with a sunken dance floor surrounded by booths, lounges, and tables. KRAVE owner Sia Amiri calls it "omni-sexual." A lot of thought went into this plush theater-nightclub hybrid. *Nightly 11pm-dawn.* Ⓒ☰

Hot Tip: Catch the *Fashionistas* show Mon-Sat at 8pm. This gender-blending erotica spectacle has been getting rave reviews.

Best ## Golf Courses

THE 99 BEST

#34–36: Think you've got better odds of shooting a hole-in-one than rolling a natural seven? Vegas has some of the world's top golf courses, designed by legends with no expense spared, on acres and acres of lush fairways.

Bear's Best

11111 W. Flamingo Rd., West Flamingo, 702-804-8500 • Cool

The Draw: Legendary golfer and course designer Jack Nicklaus presents 18 of his favorite holes from around the world, including some from private clubs and far-flung resorts like PGA West Resort, Cabo del Sol, Desert Highlands, Desert Mountain, and Castle Pines.

The Scene: Tee off way out west on Flamingo Road, in the foothills of the Red Rock Mountains. Golfers will enjoy the views and a variety of uphill and down-hill holes. *Daily 6:30am-sunset.* $$$

Hot Tip: Have lunch in the Clubhouse Grill, decorated with Nicklaus memorabilia from his long and illustrious career.

Reflection Bay Golf Club

Lake Las Vegas, 702-740-4653 • Bachelor(ette)

The Draw: Named on *Golf Magazine*'s "Top Ten You Can Play" as well as *Golf Digest*'s "Top 100 Public Golf Courses" and "Best New Upscale Public Course" lists and *Golf for Women's* "50 Best Courses for Women," this 7,261-yard, par-72 Jack Nicklaus course provides breathtaking views of Lake Las Vegas.

The Scene: Course highlights include three waterfalls and plays around arroyos and water—five holes are located along one and a half miles of Lake Las Vegas. *Daily 6:30am-sunset.* $$

Hot Tip: Check out the Flick Game Improvement School, a premier golf instructional school formed by Jack Nicklaus and Jim Flick.

Shadow Creek

3 Shadow Creek Dr., North Las Vegas, 702-791-7161 • Luxe

The Draw: It's the most exclusive course in town—from Steve Wynn, of course.

The Scene: Despite being in the desert, you'll feel like you're in the mountains. Sixteen thousand rounds are played here each year, including a few by Michael Jordan, Reggie Jackson, Michael Douglas, George Clooney, and Matt Damon. *Daily 6:30am-sunset.* $$$$ ($500 per round)

Hot Tip: Don't go on windy days—Wynn built the course near a pig farm (you can imagine the aroma).

Gourmet Buffets

#37–39: The all-you-can-eat buffet: You know you love it, shameful as such gluttony is. Since Las Vegas' humble beginnings as a railroad town, local hoteliers have lured bargain-hunters with dirt-cheap eats. But a steady rise in celebrity chefs has elevated the city's culinary profile, including the buffet, to gourmet.

The Buffet

Wynn Las Vegas, 702-770-3340 • Luxe

The Draw: The name Wynn is synonymous with luxury in Vegas, and this simply named buffet is no exception. From the room to the food, it's top quality.

The Scene: Divided into smallish, garden-themed spaces, The Buffet has a more intimate feel than some of its competition. Food is served from 17 stations, each specializing in a type of cuisine, from seafood to meats to regional offerings like Indian and Chinese. The menu changes daily. *Sun-Thu 8am-10pm, Fri-Sat 8am-10:30pm.* $$$ ▣

Hot Tip: Avoid the tables with benches—they aren't as comfortable as the chairs. And save space for dessert—the crème brûlées are oversized and worth the splurge.

The Buffet at Bellagio

The Bellagio, 702-693-7111 • Luxe

The Draw: It is hailed as the best buffet in town and was the first one to go gourmet. It's not uncommon to find Kobe beef, tandoori game hen, or white miso soup on the menu, which includes king crab legs.

The Scene: People come from all hotels to try this buffet, and there are long, Disneyland-style lines to get in. It's common to wait more than an hour, but once inside, you'll find the surroundings in line with the rest of the resort: stylish but comfortable upscale Italian. *Mon-Thu 8am-10pm, Fri-Sun 8am-11pm.* $$$ ▣

Hot Tip: This buffet has a rare full bar inside.

Sterling Brunch

Bally's, 702-967-7999 • Luxe

The Draw: The surroundings are anything but grand, but it's an impressive buffet, with high-quality selections of sophisticated dishes such as broiled Maine lobster, sushi, rack of lamb, and Japanese baby octopus.

The Scene: Even hard-core foodies come here. But while Sterling's sweets and savories are amazing, décor is nothing special. No glitz, no glam, just conventional white-tablecloth fine dining. *Sun 9:30am-2:30pm.* $$$ ▣

Hot Tip: Forgo traditional buffet mainstays. Instead, go for the endless mounds of caviar and Perrier-Jouët champagne.

Best | High-Roller Dining

#40–42: In Vegas, there's fine dining, and then there's high-roller dining. "What's the difference?" you ask. The limit on your credit card, we answer. There are few places on earth where you can drop four figures on dinner, and Vegas has more than its share. Expect world-renowned chefs, the best, most exotic ingredients, and rooms designed to rival the food's "wow" factor.

Alex at Wynn (G)
Wynn, 702-770-3300 • Luxe

The Draw: It's the most elegant restaurant at Wynn, with a celebration of haute French cuisine that has already earned it a five-diamond rating by AAA—making it one of only three restaurants in Las Vegas with this award.

The Scene: Sophisticated big spenders wearing evening attire and businesspeople on limitless expense accounts enter in-house designer Roger Thomas' rendition of a luxe theater inspired by Louis XIV. The candelabra at the entrance provides a glowing welcome before you descend the presentation staircase into the main room. Pay attention to the chairs—their legs are modeled after those of Mr. Wynn's German shepherd, Paulo. *Nightly 5:30-10:30pm.* $$$$ 🔲

Hot Tip: In warm weather, request a terrace table overlooking the Lake of Dreams, or for a very memorable night, nab the chef's table, which seats eight.

Joël Robuchon at The Mansion (G)
MGM Grand, 702-891-7358 • Luxe

The Draw: Chef Jöel Robuchon has been called the Chef of the Century, and this is his first restaurant outside France. Foodies are swooning.

The Scene: There's no riffraff at the Mansion. The crowd is gourmands and those looking for bragging rights. While the space has both the elegance and grandeur of a mansion, it pleases connoisseurs with the intimacy of a dining room for only 64. The tasting menus have 6 or 12 courses, but it is possible to order à la carte. *Nightly 5:30-10:30pm.* $$$$ 🔲

Hot Tip: Save room, because the waiter will come out with a trolley of petits fours for you to sample, even if you've already had dessert.

Restaurant Guy Savoy (G)
Caesars Palace, 702-731-7286 • Luxe

The Draw: It's very simple: Savoy is the newest celebrity chef on the Strip, and has a worldwide reputation as one of the hottest assets in any kitchen.

The Scene: A-list cool cats and Caesars VIPs take over the second floor of the Augustus Tower where Savoy has brought his three Michelin-star talent to Glitter Gulch. Dining here is as much about being seen as it is about the food. *Wed-Sun 5-10:30pm.* $$$$ 🅱🔲

Hot Tip: Ask for a table with a view of the Roman Plaza, and make reservations well in advance as the room seats only 75.

Live Music

#43–45: Old Vegas boasted Elvis and Frank Sinatra. These days the fans are screaming for U2, the Rolling Stones, Coldplay, or the Killers. No matter what you've got on your MP3 player, these stages rotate the acts to make sure everyone has a reason to get their groove on in Sin City.

House of Blues*
Mandalay Bay, 702-632-7601 • Cool

The Draw: A modern legend, it boasts an intimate stage, a state-of-the-art sound system, supreme sight lines, and a diverse selection of bands.

The Scene: Located below the House of Blues restaurant, this small club has a roughhewn wood décor with wild art from the Deep South that provides an ideal backdrop for grooving to folks like Social Distortion, B.B. King, Goo Goo Dolls, Stone Temple Pilots, and Howie Day. *Nightclub: Wed-Mon 9pm-3am. Restaurant: Sun-Thu 7:30am-midnight, Fri-Sat 7:30am-1am. Showtimes vary, call for schedule.* C☰

Hot Tip: Come Monday nights for Rockstar Karaoke, and sing with a live rock band behind you. Or come feed your soul at the Sunday Gospel Brunch, with delicious Southern food.

The Joint
The Hard Rock, 702-693-5066 • Bachelor(ette)

The Draw: The Joint features only the hottest new bands and frequently grabs rock-'n'-roll superstars like David Bowie, Metallica, Alanis Morrissette, Green Day, Santana, and Matchbox20, to name a few.

The Scene: Whoever the band is, the small auditorium-style concert venue will be packed with die-hard fans. *Showtimes vary, call for schedule.* C☰

Hot Tip: Get VIP tickets and sit in the balcony, which is a little less crowded and has its own bar and restrooms.

MGM Grand Garden Arena
MGM Grand, 702-891-1111 • Cool

The Draw: The biggest concerts in town play here, and it hosts championship fights. The Rolling Stones, U2, Bruce Springsteen, Billy Joel, Coldplay, Britney Spears, Madonna, Aerosmith, Lenny Kravitz, Cher, the Eagles, and Barbra Streisand have all rocked here.

The Scene: This arena has 16,800 seats and is modeled after Madison Square Garden in New York. *Showtimes vary, call for schedule.* C☰

Hot Tip: Parking can sometimes be difficult. If you're not staying at the MGM, leave your car at your hotel and take The Deuce (the local shuttle) up the Strip to get there.

Best | Meet Markets

#46–48: Did you come to Vegas to put its "What happens in Vegas" slogan to the test? Everyone is here for a good time, and one thing's for certain: This is a city where it's easy to make new friends. For a night.

Center Bar
The Hard Rock, 702-693-5000 • Bachelor(ette)

The Draw: Looking for a California girl or boy? This is your spot.

The Scene: The hot young 20-somethings look better than the black-leather-clad cocktail waitresses. Located in the center of the casino, it's an odd place for a bar, but why not when you want to see and be seen? *24/7.* Ⓒ☰

Hot Tip: Check the schedule of The Joint to see what types of people will likely be partying here. And don't miss dancing at nearby Body English.

Centrifuge Bar
MGM Grand, 702-891-1111 • Bachelor(ette)

The Draw: This bar has a little bit of everything that makes Vegas great. Plasma screens play sports, pretty patrons lounge on banquettes and in black and red chairs, and cocktail waitresses in tiny leather uniforms keep the booze flowing.

The Scene: In a round space at the center of MGM, you'll find a buzzing scene heavy on classic rock (think Lynyrd Skynyrd and Aerosmith) and friendly patrons of all ages. Every half-hour the bar staff—men and women—hop up on the counter for a little bump and grind, just to keep the action lively. *Sun-Fri 4pm-4am, Sat noon-4am.* Ⓒ☰

Hot Tip: Try the chai martini, a mix of vanilla Stoli and chai tea. It's delicious.

rumjungle
Mandalay Bay, 702-632-7408 • Bachelor(ette)

The Draw: It's over-the-top Vegas at its best. You don't have clubs like this at home, even if home is L.A. or New York.

The Scene: Outside the bar, you'll find a line of excited young fashionistas already working their come-on eyes. Inside, you'll find displays of fire and water with Latin, Caribbean, and African music beating late into the night (or morning), while go-go dancers set the primal vibe in cages above the dance floor. There is a mind-boggling number of rums and exotic drinks, so be sure to take advantage of the vast array of options. *Sun-Thu 11pm-2am, Fri-Sat 11pm-4am.* Ⓒ☰

Hot Tip: The food isn't stellar, but if you get there for dinner before 10pm, you'll avoid the cover and much of the long line. Dinner is served beginning at 5:30pm nightly.

Mega-Nightclubs

#49–51: Las Vegas nightclubs offer an unparalleled combination of spectacle, design, and entertainment, with club impresarios bringing the theatrics of mega-shows into a scintillating dance environment—some of these spots cost upwards of $20 million to open. The scene is sensual, sophisticated, and mysterious, and full of decadence, debauchery, and beautiful people.

Jet
The Mirage, 702-791-7111 • Bachelor(ette)

The Draw: This chic nightclub on the Strip was designed by the trend-setting style magicians at Light Group, and upscale partiers are flocking here in droves.

The Scene: VIPs have their own entrance outside, but even those who enter from inside The Mirage get the red carpet treatment. The foyer glows with candlelight, and dance lovers move from room to room depending on their musical tastes. Rock, hip-hop, and house are played beneath a state-of-the-art light and sound system. This is a big place and a constant party. *Fri-Sat and Mon 10:30pm-4am.* C≡

Hot Tip: If the bar has a line, keep moving. There is one in every room.

PURE
Caesars Palace, 702-731-7873 • Cool

The Draw: The best of the A-list party here. Are you hip enough?

The Scene: The lounge is split into three areas with a different DJ and sound system in each room. VIPs have their own Red Room with private bar. The ultimate outdoor dance floor is on the terrace and can be seen at a distance from the Strip. Loungers with table service have private draped booths. *Fri-Sun and Tue 10pm-dawn.* C≡

Hot Tip: Indulge yourself—get a private cabana for your party and sit outside while you watch the lights and people on the Strip.

Studio 54
MGM Grand, 702-891-7254 • Cool

The Draw: An updated tribute to its New York namesake, this tri-level space caters to a fun-loving crowd with lots of entertainers and disco favorites.

The Scene: Clubbers from their 20s to 40s dance among a veritable carnival of performers—from go-go dancers to wall walkers. The music changes more to house and hip-hop as the hours tick by. *Tue-Sat 10pm-dawn.* C≡

Hot Tip: Take an art break: A gallery here has celebrity photos from famed '70s paparazzo Felice Quinto, taken at the original Studio 54.

Best

Mexican Restaurants

#52–54: When the heat on the Strip feels like a furnace and your luck is running cold at the tables, there's really only one solution: margaritas. From rare Mezcals to good old Cuervo, Vegas understands the south-of-the-border cure, and it's not so bad with the food either. You'll find far more than tacos—it's all about creative concept cuisine served in stylish spaces.

Border Grill

Mandalay Bay, 702-632-7403 • Cool

The Draw: Celebrity chefs Susan Feniger and Mary Sue Milliken whip up fantastic Mexican fare in a fun environment.

The Scene: Tequila flows freely even at lunch as Mandalay Bay guests and fans of the Border Grill empire munch on updates of classic Mexican and Latin American favorites inside and out on the patio. *Mon-Thu 11:30am-10pm, Fri 11:30am-11pm, Sat 11am-11pm, Sun 11am-10pm.* $$$ ▣

Hot Tip: In good weather, ask for patio seating and you'll feel like you're in sunny Mexico.

Diego*

MGM Grand, 702-891-3200 • Bachelor(ette)

The Draw: Hot reds and pinks and cool tequilas make this the hippest Mexican spot in town.

The Scene: Diego is a bubbly locale designed with fun in mind. A good-looking, lively crowd of mixed ages fills the vibrant space nightly, searching for great margaritas and innovative Mexican fare. *Nightly 5:30-10pm.* $$ ▣

Hot Tip: Stick around after dinner on weekends, when Diego transforms into a high-energy club.

Isla Mexican Kitchen*

Treasure Island, 702-894-7349 • Cool

The Draw: Spicy food and more types of tequila than you can shake a worm at are served up in a stylish, casual setting with wood floors and vibrant artwork.

The Scene: The food is good—especially the guacamole made tableside—but from the moment you're greeted by a "tequila goddess," you'll know that the main attraction here is having fun with the young, trendy crowd. *Wed, Fri, and Sat 4pm-midnight, Sun-Tue and Thu 4-10:30pm; bar daily 11am-4pm.* $$ ▣▣

Hot Tip: All tequilas are not created equal. Let the very sexy Diosa Tequila (Tequila Goddess) introduce you to one of the exotic offerings from the well-stocked bar.

Nightclubs

#55–57: In the past decade, Las Vegas has transformed its club scene into one of the hottest on the planet with a slew of high-design concept spaces created to lure in A-listers and celebs. Led by local impresarios The Light Group, this trend has raised the stakes for what it means to open a new hot spot in Glitter Gulch.

Body English

The Hard Rock, 702-693-7000 • Bachelor(ette)

The Draw: Body English is well known for its sexy ambience and ability to woo the celebrity elite.

The Scene: Once you get past the long line, you'll find a saucy split-level club with Hollywood hipsters and music lovers dancing to hip-hop and house. There is an upper deck where voyeurs can watch the dancers below. After-hours ends somewhat early here at 4am on weekends, but regulars also love Sunday nights for the "Sunday School"–themed events that come complete with big-name DJs and drink specials. *Fri-Sun 10:30pm-4am.* C≡

Hot Tip: Check in with NapkinNights.com to see if it can help get you around the lines and onto the guest list. And note: The clientele here changes depending on who is playing The Joint—fans come by after shows.

Light

Caesars Palace, 702-693-7111 • Luxe

The Draw: It's considered one of the top clubs on the Strip—and one of the toughest to get in—and consistently draws visiting A-listers and celebrities.

The Scene: Past the surly bouncers, up one level, and down a candlelit hallway is an intimate club scene filled with very pretty young things enjoying bottle service at the few tables, and dancing the night away to house and hip-hop. *Thu-Sun 10:30pm-4am.* C≡

Hot Tip: If you're in a group of guys, you have only a very slim chance of getting in without reserving bottle service.

Tao Nightclub

The Venetian, 702-388-8588 • Cool

The Draw: Everyone who's anyone comes here sometime.

The Scene: VIPs actually use the VIP skyboxes, and the atmosphere is hip Zen. The more trend-conscious margin of conventioneers who don't mind braving the lines, or buying their way in, drink and dance amid the Vegas A-list. It's mostly beautiful people and those who love them, with a little something to please everyone. *Nightly 5pm-5am.* C≡

Hot Tip: There is exclusive Tao valet service in front of The Venetian.

Best

Pool Scenes

#58–60: Summer sizzles in Vegas and temperatures soar to well over 100 degrees. Nearly every casino resort has a pool where you can cool off, but these retreats go the extra mile to make sure you know the parties don't have to stay in the club.

Mandalay Beach

Mandalay Bay, 702-632-7777 • Bachelor(ette)

The Draw: An outdoor "island" stage set inside Mandalay Bay's pool area draws huge crowds to weekend concerts.

The Scene: Mandalay Bay's pool is a guests-only affair except on summer weekend nights, usually Fridays, when Mandalay Beach hosts concerts that are more party than show, drawing acts like Pat Benatar and Los Lonely Boys. *Mid-Apr–mid-Sep 8am-7pm, mid-Sep–late-Oct 9am-7pm, Nov 9am-5pm. Closes mid-Nov. Showtimes vary. $$*

Hot Tip: Nude tanning is allowed during the day at the Moorea Beach Club, Mandalay Bay's exclusive pool area.

Palms Casino Resort Pool

Palms, 702-942-7777 • Bachelor(ette)

The Draw: Spring 2006 brought an even bigger, even better two-acre pool to the Palms. George Maloof refuses to let his resort get stale or the celebs get bored. The old Skin Pool Lounge reigned supreme as the hot pool party, but the new pool at the Palms is an even hipper scene of wetness.

The Scene: Those older than 35 or wearing their cellulite in the open seem out of place at the Palms, though its chic minimalist décor and three bars are draws for anyone looking for fun. To get your chill on at the pool, make sure you stay at the Palms—its parties are not always open to the public. *Mar–Oct 9am-6pm. $$*

Hot Tip: Splurge on the coveted private bungalows.

Rehab at Hard Rock

The Hard Rock, 702-693-5000 • Bachelor(ette)

The Draw: Whether you're hungover or not, this is the best place to be on a Sunday afternoon. The Hard Rock has one of the most happening pools in Las Vegas, and although it's prescribed to cure the damage done the night before, Rehab is its own fresh party with hotties of all kinds attending.

The Scene: L.A. hipsters and beautiful locals with connections chill out by the lagoon with cocktails. Palm trees provide some shade, and modern music jams keep the scene kicking while revelers play in the pool. This is the best daytime party in Vegas, by far. *Sun noon-8pm. $$*

Hot Tip: HardRockHotel.com has a webcam on its pool so you can check out the action ahead of time.

Quiet Bars

#61–63: Even go-go-go Las Vegas has its sophisticated low-key places, far from humming machines, roaring sports crowds, and blaring techno music. Tucked away in hotel corners, these spots provide perfect privacy for sealing any kind of deal, whether of the Wall Street or romantic variety.

Charlie Palmer Steak*
The Four Seasons, 702-632-5120 • Luxe

The Draw: This is the ultimate post-dinner retreat where you can enjoy good conversation with cigars and cognac.

The Scene: Located inside The Four Seasons, this mahogany-lined lounge with its soft leather sofas, gorgeous oil paintings, and piano puts you in the mind of a manly society club. *Nightly 5pm-12:30am.* ☐

Hot Tip: On Friday and Saturday evenings, the bar features live entertainment, and this being a celebrity haunt, you never know who might turn up. One night Billy Joel strolled in to tickle the ivories in an impromptu concert that delighted the handful of guests who happened to be there.

Fontana Bar
The Bellagio, 702-693-7989 • Luxe

The Draw: This is a perfect getaway for a quiet cocktail after huffing it on the Strip all day, and it has a fabulous view.

The Scene: A supper-clubby lounge off the main casino, this circular, sophisticated room boasts plush furnishings framed by a rotunda-style ceiling. There's also patio seating with misters to cool you down, and a prime view of Bellagio's lake and the dancing fountains. *Mon-Thu 5:30pm-2am, Fri-Sat 1pm-2am.* ☐☐

Hot Tip: The patio fills up for fountain-watching. Go well before showtime, and try some chocolate-dipped strawberries and champagne while you wait.

Napoleon's Champagne Bar
Paris Las Vegas, 702-946-7000 • Cool

The Draw: You'll find an impressive list of champagnes with at least ten different kinds by the glass, featuring everything from Freixenet to Cristal, along with such devilishly decadent desserts as chocolate-dipped fruit and truffles.

The Scene: This champagne-bar-cum-jazz-club has a European-style bar with dark wood and a crimson interior with vintage sofas, giving it a cozy feel. Spending an hour here with its upscale clientele will make you feel like you've crossed the pond and returned to the old world. A pianist plays daily 5-8pm. *Sun-Thu 4pm-2am, Fri-Sat 4pm-3am.* ☐

Hot Tip: If you're really looking for peace, avoid Friday and Saturday nights when dueling pianos take over and make it a very lively spot.

Best

Regional Dining

#64–66: Whether you're after fine dining or fast food, Vegas undoubtedly has something to tempt your palate. Despite its desert setting, this city is a culinary world tour, where virtually every taste on the planet can be sated.

Commander's Palace

Aladdin/Planet Hollywood, 702-892-8272 • Cool

The Draw: It's a touch of Crescent City in the heart of Sin City—high ceilings, chandeliers, and Southern hospitality.

The Scene: The elegant setting and old-school reputation draw a mature and sophisticated crowd out to sample legendary dishes like turtle soup and bananas Foster (created at the New Orleans original branch of this restaurant). *Mon-Fri 9-11am, 11:30am-2pm and 5:30-10pm, Sat-Sun 10:30am-2pm and 5:30-10pm.* $$$$ B≡

Hot Tip: Opt to sit in the wine room if you're looking for privacy or romance, and don't miss the 25-cent martinis at lunch.

Emeril's New Orleans Fish House

MGM Grand, 702-891-7374 • Cool

The Draw: With its brick and wood dining room, oval seafood bar, and "outdoor" patio surrounded by a quaint New Orleans–style wrought-iron fence, this seafood restaurant on MGM's Studio Walk is a wonderful counterpoint to the "bam" chef's sleek and understated steakhouse at The Venetian.

The Scene: The ambience is more charming than sophisticated, but less formal than other celebrity-chef spots, and the fish is front and center. Signature dishes include barbecue shrimp and Atlantic salmon, sole, yellowfin tuna, and a clam chowder so rich you could stand a spoon up in it. *Daily 11am-2:30pm, 5:30-10:30pm; seafood bar 11:30am-10:30pm.* $$$ B≡

Hot Tip: Save room for the banana-cream pie drizzled with caramel.

Mesa Grill

Caesars Palace, 702-650-5965 • Cool

The Draw: Iron Chef Bobby Flay cooks up contemporary Southwestern specialties in a fun, lively environment.

The Scene: Flay designed the room himself, including the giant rotisserie that holds court in the center. Because of its central location in Caesars, it draws a mixed crowd of passersby, those going to nearby shows such as Elton John, and die-hard Flay fans. They have one thing in common—they're looking for a good time. *Mon-Fri 11am-2:30pm and 5-11pm, Sat-Sun 10:30am-3pm and 5-11pm.* $$ B≡

Hot Tip: Flay is only behind Mesa's stoves one weekend a month. Call ahead and ask when he'll be there if you want to see the Food Network star at work in the open kitchen.

Shows

#67–69: Las Vegas is out to give New York a run for its money when it comes to Broadway-worthy shows. Sure, they may be abbreviated here, but admit it, you get bored after the 15th song anyway. And what Vegas lacks in duration, it makes up for in spectacle, with newer theaters, bolder stunts, and bigger names.

Blue Man Group
The Venetian, 702-414-1000 • Bachelor(ette)

The Draw: This long-running favorite continues to enthrall audiences with its trio of blue dudes playing rhythms and performing comedy skits.

The Scene: A crowd of mixed ages can barely sit still during the percussion-heavy, slapstick show that has the audience laughing and tapping its toes from start to finish. *Nightly 7:30pm and Sat 10:30pm.* C≡

Hot Tip: This performance is high on audience interaction. Sit front and center in the "poncho section" if you're into taking part, or on the balcony if you prefer a little bit of distance.

Elton John: The Red Piano
Caesars Palace, 702-731-7110 • Luxe

The Draw: These are extremely coveted tickets. Elton has been named Vegas' "Best All-Around Performer," among other accolades.

The Scene: Caesars' VIPs and middle-aged lite-rock fans (both sexes) come to pay homage to the rock-'n'-roll legend. *The Red Piano* is an unforgettable performance that sails through the course of his career and continues to sell out shows on Céline's off nights. *Tue-Wed and Fri-Sun 7:30pm. Showtimes change seasonally, call for schedule.* C≡

Hot Tip: It's worth it to get a seat up front. John addresses the audience frequently and reaches out to some of them.

La Femme
MGM Grand, 702-891-7777 • Luxe

The Draw: *La Femme* brings the French reverence for sensuality and the famed Parisian sense of style to Las Vegas—all 13 dancers in this show are members of the original Paris troupe.

The Scene: With its intriguing play of light on skin, this artsy import from the Crazy Horse in Paris is so tasteful, blending eroticism with classic and modern dance, you could almost take Granny to see it without offending her delicate sensibilities. *Nightly 8:30pm and 10:30pm; must be 21.* C≡

Hot Tip: Don't worry about missing any goodies—every seat is a winner in this tiny cabaret theater.

Best

Sports Books

#70–72: Super Bowl Sunday, the Final Four, the World Series: If you're in Vegas on a big day, find a good sports book and enjoy the action on and off the field. Sports books offer all kinds of exotic wagering that goes way beyond who's going to win and who's going to lose. If you can dream it, you can usually bet on it.

Bellagio Sports Book
The Bellagio, 702-693-7111 • Luxe

The Draw: One of the classiest sports books in Vegas, it's also one of the most comfortable. If you don't want your own individual desk with TV, then have your friends join you in a leather booth. When the room is not showing a big game, this is a great place to have a private business meeting.

The Scene: It's located next to the sexiest poker room in Las Vegas, so don't be surprised if you run into some of the Texas Hold 'Em pros you've seen on TV. As you might expect, it's fully packed whenever there's a big game, especially the Super Bowl or March Madness. *24/7.*

Hot Tip: The bar by the sports book is a good place to look for some high-rent action—of the "companionship" kind.

Caesars Palace Sports Book
Caesars Palace, 702-731-7110 • Cool

The Draw: When men find a sports book they like, they stick with it. And after they've been to Caesars, there's no going anywhere else.

The Scene: With sports books, it's not about who's there, it's about how big the screens are. Caesars has six 12-by-15-foot oversized screens, a 20-by-50-inch LED board, and twelve 50-inch plasma screens. There are 140 seats and a 12-inch flat screen at each of the tables. Caesars pioneered horse-racing simulcasts from Aqueduct back in the '80s (prompting every other casino to follow). *24/7.*

Hot Tip: This place throws killer Super Bowl parties.

Wynn Las Vegas Sports Book
Wynn, 702-770-7800 • Luxe

The Draw: This is the newest sports book on the Strip, and Steve Wynn did it right. One travel writer was heard to say, "If I had to die in a sports book while rooting for my team, this would be the place."

The Scene: Yes, there are great big giant screens and a bar, but trust us, you want to sit down—the yellow leather chairs are heavenly. And each is stationed at a desk with its own TV monitor. Even if you just need a break from walking around the casino, try the chairs. *24/7.*

Hot Tip: This is a good place to watch, but not necessarily the best one for placing bets. If you want to make big bets, look elsewhere for better odds.

Steakhouses

#73–75: Not so long ago, Las Vegas' only gourmet option was the steakhouse, reflecting either its Western heritage or the need to provide a decent, easy-to-prepare meal to hordes of visitors—without a cadre of top chefs. Much has changed, but a good piece of meat is still part of the classic Vegas experience, and these days, you'll find yourself in a stylish, sophisticated spot while enjoying it.

Charlie Palmer Steak*
The Four Seasons, 702-632-5120 • Luxe

The Draw: It's got an old-school feel with class to spare.

The Scene: Four Seasons guests and those in the know come to this elegant, clubby enclave for steaks and more served in formal style. *Nightly 5-10:30pm.* $$$ ⊟

Hot Tip: Top cuts may be the big draw here, but don't miss the excellent shellfish platter for a starter.

Delmonico Steakhouse
The Venetian, 702-414-3737 • Luxe

The Draw: A favorite of those with discerning tastes, for both its upscale atmosphere and its excellent food. It's the kind of place you return to more than once.

The Scene: Served in a sophisticated and soothing setting for a cultivated crowd, with large oak doors, vaulted ceilings, and a petite grand piano, the food impresses with dishes like Creole broiled gulf shrimp and pepper crusted dry-aged beef sirloin. *Sun-Thu 11:30am-2pm and 5:30-10:30pm, Fri-Sat 11:30am-2pm and 5:30-11pm.* $$$$ B⊟

Hot Tip: Don't miss the Parmesan Truffle Chips.

Prime Steakhouse
The Bellagio, 702-693-8484 • Luxe

The Draw: Uber-chef Jean-Georges Vongerichten enthralls diners who've followed his career through Café JoJo and Vong and Jean-Georges in New York City. He has ten signature sauces, and the menu is complemented with a large selection of French wines and bold American reds.

The Scene: Steak lovers and romantics dine beneath Baccarat chandeliers in a 1930s-style speakeasy. This is a highly elegant chophouse in a league of its own. *Nightly 5:30-10pm.* $$$$ B⊟

Hot Tip: Request a seat on the garden patio.

Best

Strip Clubs

#76–78: Strip clubs have gone upscale in recent years, with national behemoths like Scores raising the bar. But strip club aficionados know that it's more than size that matters—these spots deliver all the goods, right to your lap.

Palomino Club
1848 Las Vegas Blvd. N., North Las Vegas, 702-642-2984 • Bachelor(ette)

The Draw: It's one of the oldest strip clubs in Vegas and one of the few that has a full bar mixed with full nudity.

The Scene: This Wild West bordello-style club (think red, red, red) has burlesque on the main stage downstairs and unparalleled lap dances in the lounge upstairs. A bit seedy, but did we mention full nudity and full bar? *Nightly 5pm-5am.* C≡

Hot Tip: Complimentary (car) rides to and from the club are available; just call Palomino to schedule a pickup.

Sapphire Gentlemen's Club
3025 Industrial Rd., North Strip, 702-796-6000 • Luxe

The Draw: A $26 million renovation turned the former Sporting House fitness club into a very different kind of hard-body showcase. The owners claim this 24-hour strip-o-rama, where upwards of 300 gals take it off nightly, is the largest in the world.

The Scene: Black-gowned hostesses direct you through the marbled entrance to the giant main dance room for a prime view of hotties shaking it on the raised stages and at tables all around. A hundred dollars and a drink will get you three private dances in the less-trafficked VIP lounge. *24/7.* C≡

Hot Tip: Buy some private time with your favorite beauty in the plush skyboxes, furnished with comfortable couches, an entertainment center and bar, and a full view of what's happening below.

Spearmint Rhino
3340 S. Highland Dr., North Strip, 702-796-3600 • Cool

The Draw: Rumored to have some of the hottest dancers in Sin City, this topless spot is packed with both women and male patrons, giving it a high-energy vibe.

The Scene: This is not a locals' joint; the customers here are tourists. This upscale gentleman's club is a chain with clubs around the world that draws dancers from all nationalities and races. *24/7.* C≡

Hot Tip: The food here is decent (think steaks, chicken wings, and nachos).

Sushi Restaurants

#79–81: "Sushi in the desert?" you ask. This ain't Utah, we say. Vegas has the cash to fly it in so fresh it's still gasping for air. Mix that with world-renowned sushi masters, and get ready to experience Japanese food at its arid peak.

Nobu (G)

The Hard Rock, 702-693-5090 • Cool

The Draw: There's sushi, and then there's Nobu Matsuhisa's sushi. Opened in 1999, Las Vegas Nobu, which earned a four-star rating from Mobil, is one of the brightest stars in Matsuhisa's stellar culinary empire.

The Scene: The Hard Rock brings its own kind of cool to the typical Nobu scene. The high energy of the crowd, packed with beautiful people, is the perfect foil to the room's Zen décor of muted tones, abstract bamboo trees, and rock and water walls. *Nightly 6-11pm.* $$$$ B=

Hot Tip: Try Nobu's famous spicy sashimi, Kobe beef carpaccio, thinly sliced whitefish sashimi, and beef with foie gras. For dessert, opt for the warm chocolate soufflé.

Shintaro (G)

The Bellagio, 702-693-8141 • Luxe

The Draw: Come for the remarkable décor: a huge, gorgeous jellyfish tank, backlit in brilliant colors. As the jellyfish float, they look like lava lamps.

The Scene: Less scene, more serene. The main dining room features teppanyaki tables where chefs play with fire, performing tricks while they cook for a well-heeled clientele. It's an elegant experience. *Nightly 5:30-10:30pm.* $$$ B❘=

Hot Tip: The chef whips up unique and creative rolls according to what's in season; ask for the daily special. Also, request a lake-view table when booking.

Sushi Roku

Caesars Palace, 702-733-7373 • Cool

The Draw: A new(ish) hipster hangout on the Strip, Sushi Roku is a sibling to the popular L.A. line of haute Japanese restaurants.

The Scene: Because of its location in the Forum Shops, Sushi Roku's diners are mostly tourists, but still the cool kids of the bunch. As you'd expect, the busiest nights are Friday and Saturday between 7:30 and 10pm. Lunches are fairly quiet, with only the main room and the sushi bar open. *Sun-Thu 11am-11pm, Fri-Sat 11am-midnight.* $$$ B=

Hot Tip: If you'd like to sit on the floor, ask for one of the zashiki tables. They can even accommodate a party of up to 15 people. For a view of the Strip, ask to be seated in the back of the restaurant.

Best

Texas Hold 'Em Poker Rooms

#82–84: Texas Hold 'Em, the "Cadillac of poker games," is at the forefront of the recent poker boom. Now every hotel casino that's worth its chips has reopened, remodeled, or built a poker room to satisfy every card shark and bandwagon fish in town.

Bellagio Poker Room
The Bellagio, 702-693-7290 • Luxe

The Draw: The Bellagio is the current epicenter of the poker universe. Rarely will you see the room not buzzing with some of the game's biggest names.

The Scene: For fans, it's worth a stop here, just for the stargazing. The legendary "Big Game" is on seven nights a week in a glass room perfect for voyeurs. All games at most limits are offered, but you will nearly always have a wait, sometimes over an hour long, to get a seat. *24/7.*

Hot Tip: For more stargazing, stop by the Sports Book bar next door. Most nights, you can catch some of poker's brightest stars (like the ones you'd recognize from TV) taking a break from the action, or just chilling out.

Mirage Poker Room
The Mirage, 702-791-7291 • Bachelor(ette)

The Draw: Once the hub of the poker world, this stalwart still offers great action. Daily tournaments offer good value and get good-sized fields. All games are on offer, but call ahead, as the lists can get quite long.

The Scene: Many of poker's old guard and top players still come here, and never left for the newer Bellagio experience, so beware—the average caliber of talent may be higher than it appears. *24/7.*

Hot Tip: The Mirage hosts a very cool "Heads Up" tournament series, which is a great way to have fun while working on your game. Call for info.

Wynn Las Vegas Poker Room
Wynn, 702-770-7800 • Luxe

The Draw: One of Las Vegas' newest and most hyped poker rooms, the Wynn is a high-tech, comfy place to play. It includes a nice perk for hotel guests—you can put your name on a list, then monitor your position through the TV in your room.

The Scene: It's the absolute snapshot of today's live poker scene. Plenty of young players wearing baseball caps and sunglasses mix with conventioneers, and people who are playing "just for fun." Games are offered at many levels, but call first unless you are looking for small buy-in, no-limit hold 'em, or limit hold 'em at 10/20 level or under, which are always available. *24/7.*

Hot Tip: Daily tournaments get good-sized fields that are full of newer players. Satellites (available in the morning) offer a chance to win your way into the bigger tourney.

Thrill Rides

#85–87: Vegas is one wild ride after another. One spin, roll, or shuffle you're up and the next you're down. Adrenaline junkies looking for that same rush away from the gambling tables can find it at these thrill rides, which are just as exciting and much less risky.

The Big Shot
The Stratosphere, 702-382-4466 • Bachelor(ette)

The Draw: Get a taste of weightlessness with the four Gs of force on this awesome ride way up in the desert sky.

The Scene: Teenagers and daredevils take the elevator all the way up The Stratosphere Tower. At 921 feet, the Big Shot shoots you 160 feet into the air in 2.5 seconds with a force equal to what astronauts feel as they rocket into space. *Sun-Thu 10am-1am, Fri-Sat noon-2am.* $

Hot Tip: Skip Stratosphere's roller coaster, the High Roller. It pokes along at a mere 35 mph.

Flyaway Indoor Skydiving
200 Convention Center Dr., North Strip, 702-731-4768 • Bachelor(ette)

The Draw: This is a quick hit of almost-airplane jumping just off the Strip.

The Scene: In a slightly seedy warehouse-looking building, you'll don a mostly clean jumpsuit and launch yourself over a giant DC-3 propeller, which is pushing out winds of up to 120 mph. Classy? No. Fun? Yes. And more difficult to master than you would think. *Classes run every half hour. Daily 10am-7pm.* $$$$

Hot Tip: The wind tunnel is available for private rental. $1,200 will get you a group of ten in there for an hour.

Manhattan Express
New York-New York, 702-740-6969 • Bachelor(ette)

The Draw: Hands down the best roller-coaster on the Strip, the Manhattan Express twists and turns around the hotel's simulated New York skyline.

The Scene: Kids of all ages (including adults) line up to careen through a 144-foot drop, a stomach-churning loop, and a 540-degree spiral that mimics the tuck and roll of a Navy jet fighter. *Daily 10:30am-midnight.* $

Hot Tip: If one ride is not enough, consider an all-day pass for $25.

Best

Trendy Tables

#88–90: In a city built on revelry and recreation, a red-hot scene is often more valued than a four-star dinner. These restaurants might not be the brightest jewels in Las Vegas' culinary crown, but they certainly are the most fashionable.

Mix in Las Vegas*
THEhotel, 702-632-9500 • Cool

The Draw: World-renowned chef Alain Ducasse's Vegas venture is a stunning mix of culinary art, cutting-edge design, star sightings, and breathtaking views of the Las Vegas Strip.

The Scene: Soaring high in the sky on the top floor of Mandalay Bay's THEhotel is this retro-futuristic astral-lounge and restaurant. The white-on-white Jetsons décor matches the white-hot scene as the well-heeled and well-connected gather to break bread as well as hearts. *Nightly 6-11pm.* $$$$ ≡

Hot Tip: The much-desired outdoor balcony tables offer one of the best views of the entire Las Vegas Valley.

N9NE*
Palms, 702-933-9000 • Cool

The Draw: Owner Michael Morton's (son of the legendary Arnie Morton of Morton's Steakhouse) trendy reinvention of the American steakhouse is one of the juiciest hot spots in town.

The Scene: The sleek, contemporary interior combines Las Vegas crass (neon-lit caviar and champagne bar, pumping house music) and Chicago's finest carnivore classics (prime rib, filet mignon, Kobe burger). The Maloof brothers and the ubiquitous Hugh Hefner are known to entertain their famous friends here, so be sure to call ahead. *Mon-Thu 5-11pm, Fri-Sun 5-11:30pm.* $$$$ B≡

Hot Tip: N9NE lures the ladies in with a pre-set bachelorette package ($70 per woman) that includes dinner and dessert as well as complimentary VIP entry to Rain nightclub.

Tao Asian Bistro*
The Venetian, 702-388-8338 • Cool

The Draw: Tao is one of the hottest nightclubs, lounges, and restaurants on the Strip, consistently drawing a pretty, ready-to-party crowd.

The Scene: Think big. The restaurant alone seats 400 stylish fun-seekers, fueling up for a night of debauchery, while a 20-foot Buddha guards over the dining room. This is a great place to come for a lively scene, but don't expect culinary genius. *Sun-Thu 5pm-midnight, Fri-Sat 5pm-1am.* $$$$ ≡

Hot Tip: Ask your server for help getting past Tao Nightclub's velvet rope. They'll give you a line pass, but you'll still have to pay the cover.

Ultra Lounges

#91–93: Steadily refining Las Vegas with a sophisticated, sexy, and distinctly modern scene, ultra lounges are the new hangout of the jet set. Stunning and elegant, these chic dens are the ideal place to recline with a glass of Cristal (unless you're boycotting it with Jay-Z) and hang with the beautiful people.

Caramel
The Bellagio, 702-693-8300 • Luxe

The Draw: It's the place in The Bellagio to drink if you don't want to dance or be seen with the gambling blue-hairs who frequent the Baccarat Bar.

The Scene: The crowd has a mix of ages, but all are a bit on the snobbier side. It's not your velvety kind of lounge, but the sofas are comfortable and make for good wall posts if you want to keep tabs on any celebs who are present. *Nightly 5pm-4am.* ≡

Hot Tip: If you meet up with someone you'd like to get romantic with, take a short stroll to the Fontana Bar, where the outside patio is the best spot to watch the romantic Bellagio Fountain Show.

Lure
Wynn, 702-770-3375 • Luxe

The Draw: This is a true lounge space, with lots of toffee leather banquettes and plush chairs to idle away the night in comfort.

The Scene: Clubbers from nearby Tryst and sophisticated cocktail sippers relax in this chic, modern space with a friendly vibe. *Tue-Sat 9pm-close.* C ≡

Hot Tip: The fire pit on the back patio is the perfect spot to meet new friends.

Tabú
MGM Grand, 702-891-7129 • Cool

The Draw: Meld Jeffrey Beers' architectural expertise with the special-effects artistry of Roger Parent, former art director for Cirque du Soleil, and the result is a mind-blowing interior that shifts and changes throughout the night.

The Scene: The center bar, with its rotating iridescent liquor towers, is a virtual projection screen with images floating by under your drinks, captivating a hip young crowd. *Nightly 9pm-7am.* C ≡

Hot Tip: Sneak away to the Tantra Room: It's a beautiful egg-shaped area with its own ice bar that looks out onto the action from a slight distance.

Best Vintage Vegas

#94–96: Sin City wasn't always about megaplex-theme casino hotels, Canadian circus shows, and fat-ankled family fun. It had class, sass, and a seedy underbelly that's still prevalent in downtown. To get some insight into what old-school Vegas was really like, check out these vintage venues.

Fremont Street Experience
Fremont St. (between Main St. and Las Vegas Blvd.), Downtown • Luxe

The Draw: Dance to free bands, cruise for souvenirs beneath the neon signs, and check out the $17 million Viva Vision.

The Scene: A lively pedestrian walkway, and the heart of vintage Vegas, Fremont Street is surrounded by old-school resorts including The Vegas Club, The Plaza, Main Street Casino, Fitzgerald's, Four Queens, and the shiniest gem—The Golden Nugget. Binion's, respected as the home of the World Series of Poker until 2005, still hosts a popular poker room as well.

Hot Tip: This is neon heaven. The Neon Museum has two outdoor galleries here that can be seen 24/7. The first is in front of Neonopolis on the south side near the Horse and Rider, and the other is on the 3rd Street cul-de-sac adjacent to The Fremont Street Experience canopy.

Liberace Museum
1775 E. Tropicana Ave., North Las Vegas, 702-798-5595 • Luxe

The Draw: Check out the flashy legacy of "Mr. Showmanship," a true icon.

The Scene: This museum covers two buildings filled with piano and car galleries, and costume and jewelry collections. See a re-creation of Liberace's Palm Springs bedroom; his red, white, and blue Rolls-Royce; and a cape that was designed to be just like one of King George V's coronation robes. *Mon-Sat 10am-5pm, Sun noon-4pm.* $

Hot Tip: Some say Liberace's ghost has been seen at Carluccio's Tivoli Gardens, a restaurant that he used to own just off the Strip.

21 Historic Markers
Various locations along Fremont and Main Sts., Downtown • Luxe

The Draw: To celebrate the Las Vegas Centennial in 2005, the Historical Marker Initiative selected 21 sites that best signified the creation and evolution of Vegas. Start downtown in front of The Plaza at the intersection of Fremont and Main, the site of the 1905 land auction where the first train depot was built.

The Scene: The markers explain everything from neon and atomic testing to hookers. Our favorites: block 16 at North First Street between Ogden and Stewart, which was notorious for prostitution until 1942; Gaming and Helldorado at First and Fremont; and the Railroad Cottages at Second (now Casino Center) to Fourth, and Garces to Clark.

Hot Tip: Find a list of the markers on the website lasvegas2005.org.

Wedding Chapels

#97–99: It's a snap to get married in Vegas, just ask Britney. No blood test or waiting period required. Heck, you don't even have to be sober. The Clark County Marriage License Bureau is open daily 8am to midnight (it recently ended its 24-hour service on weekends and holidays). If a chapel is too conservative, consider getting hitched on a roller-coaster, or simulcast it on the internet.

Little Church of the West

4617 S. Las Vegas Blvd., South Strip, 702-739-7971

The Draw: It's one of the oldest chapels in Las Vegas (opened in 1942) and the only one on the National Register of Historic Places.

The Scene: The minister will give a beautiful, traditional 30-minute ceremony (you can provide your own vows) for up to 75 guests. *Daily 8am-midnight.*

Hot Tip: On a nice day, exchange vows in Little Church's outdoor gazebo.

Little White Wedding Chapel

1301 S. Las Vegas Blvd., North Strip, 702-382-5943

The Draw: This is where Britney Spears had that oops wedding, and several other celebrities have tied the knot here, including Michael Jordan, Paul Newman, Ricki Lake, Mickey Rooney, and Frank Sinatra. Whether you want a drive-through wedding, the requisite singing Elvis ceremony, or something more adventurous involving a helicopter—this place has it.

The Scene: This 50-year-old chapel does 35,000 weddings a year. On Saturdays and holidays, brides wearing everything from cutoffs to couture are a dozen deep at the counter waiting for room in one of the eight chapels. *24/7.*

Hot Tip: For the ultimate kitsch wedding, exchange vows in the drive-through chapel, adorned with cupids and angels and cherubs, and request Elvis to sing "Love Me Tender" or "Viva Las Vegas."

Viva Las Vegas Wedding Chapel

1205 S. Las Vegas Blvd., North Strip, 702-384-0771

The Draw: Las Vegas' only bed and breakfast—really just a motel with a cute diner offering self-serve coffee and muffins—is a total kitsch-a-rama, featuring Austin Powers, *Star Trek*, Gothic, Egyptian, and gangster-style wedding ceremonies and motel rooms that continue the fantasy.

The Scene: The Mission-style main chapel (seating 100) has Spanish tiles, a wood-beamed ceiling, and cathedral-style stained-glass windows. The Little Chapel (seating 36) is adorned in French vanilla satin, with a luminous burgundy tile floor. Both offer a free webcam to allow you to share this special day. *Daily 8am-midnight.*

Hot Tip: Book the E & P (Elvis and Priscilla) honeymoon suite, which boasts a genuine 1965 Pepto-pink Cadillac that's been turned into a queen-size bed.

THE LAS VEGAS EXPERIENCE

The Strip isn't that long, but it is diverse. So strut into the Las Vegas of your choice with one of three themed itineraries: *Cool* (p.50), *Bachelor(ette)* (p.78), and *Luxe* (p.106). Each is designed as a special invitation to a unique style of enjoying Sin City. The experiences will put you in the right place at the right time—the best restaurants, nightlife, and attractions. Whether you're looking to indulge in a decadent meal created by a celebrity chef, or party with A-listers at one of the hottest clubs, you'll find what you need to know right here.

Cool Las Vegas

Benjamin "Bugsy" Siegel had a vision for Las Vegas from the time he first laid eyes on this dusty stretch of nothing. That dream matched his style—suave, smooth, but totally without restraint. By the time Sinatra and the Rat Pack hit Glitter Gulch, there was no doubt that this city was cool. It knew something about our deepest, darkest desires, and even more about how to fulfill them. Today, Vegas serves up lifestyle fantasies with a healthy dose of irony, making it all the more fun to go off the deep end. So grab your entourage and get ready. In this version of Vegas, you're the star.

Note: Venues in bold are described in detail in the listings that follow the itinerary. Venues followed by an asterisk ( ) are those we recommend as both a restaurant and a destination bar.*

Cool Las Vegas:
The Perfect Plan (3 Nights and Days)

Perfect Plan Highlights

Friday

Cocktails	Red Sq.*, Foundation Rm.
Dinner	N9NE*, Tao*, Red Sq.*
Nighttime	House of Blues*, Forty Deuce, Ghostbar
Late-Night	Tao Nightclub, Scores, Peppermill Lounge

Saturday

Morning	Hoover Dam, Maverick Helicopter Tour, Grand Canyon
Lunch	Burger Bar, Border Grill
Afternoon	Moorea Beach Club, spa, Art of Shaving, Guggenheim Hermitage
Dinner	Bradley Ogden*, 808, Mesa Grill
Nighttime	PURE, Shadow: A Bar
Late-Night	Pussycat Dolls, Voodoo Lounge, Spearmint Rhino

Sunday

Morning	Bear's Best golf, Royal Links, Mandalay shops, Forum shops
Lunch	Mon Ami Gabi, R Bar Café*
Afternoon	Shark Reef, Richard Petty, Caesars Palace Poker Rm.
Cocktails	Mix Lounge, Island Lounge
Dinner	Mix, Nob Hill, Seablue
Nighttime	*Love*, *Kà*, Mix Lounge Tabú, Studio 54
Late-Night	Seamless

Morning After

Brunch	Commander's Palace

Hotel: THEhotel

Friday

7pm Start your weekend with a drink at either of these very hot, very different spots: **Red Square*** or The **Foundation Room**. If it's the latter, you'll need to be a big spender and shell out $500 for four-day membership to the private club—but it's worth it for the A-list experience. It's not surprising to find the rock stars who are on the bill later at House of Blues warming up with a few cocktails here. But if it's pure, egalitarian fun you're after, take the party into Red Square.

8:30pm Dinner Tonight's about the trendiest spots in town. Palms has a very sultry steak joint—**N9NE***, where the beautiful people like to hang out. Just as hot is dining beneath the 20-foot Buddha at The Venetian's **Tao Asian Bistro***—ask your waiter for a pass to skip the line into the adjoining club. Or stay close to home at **Red Square***, where it's a headless statue of Lenin that lords over the place.

10:30pm If you're a music lover, grab the schedule for **House of Blues*** at Mandalay Bay. Some shows start earlier in the night, so plan accordingly. If you're after something saucier, it's time for **Ivan Kane's Forty Deuce**, where you'll find a group of talented ladies doing classic burlesque. This is a show both men and women will enjoy. For a different kind of view—and a stylish crowd of fun seekers—make your way to **Ghostbar** on the 55th floor of the Palms. It's one of Sin City's most exclusive scenes, backed by gorgeous views of the Strip.

1am Whether you dined at Tao or not, the attached **Tao Nightclub** is a hot dance spot you don't want to miss. If you'd rather watch the groove and grind than take part, hop a cab to **Scores**. It's enormously popular in New York, so it got a warm welcome in Vegas, despite the plethora of topless clubs in the city.

3am It's not Vegas without a bit of kitsch. Try your lounge lizard act at **Peppermill Fireside Lounge**. Wander through the dingy diner into the retro haven in back, grab a banquette, and tell one of the black-gowned cocktail waitresses what you're drinking, baby.

Saturday

8am Get up early and get out of town. Have a rental car delivered to your front door, and head toward Hoover Dam (see p.172), about 40 minutes away on Highway 93. While you can drive across the span, it's better to park and walk across to get a feel for the 726-foot-tall modern

wonder. But if the dam isn't spectacular enough, take a **Maverick Helicopter Tour** to the Grand Canyon instead. Its "Indian Territory" trip combines the flight with a H2 Hummer tour on the canyon's rim. You'll visit areas unavailable to regular guests. But it's definitely for early birds—it starts at 7am.

1:30pm Lunch Back on the Strip, you won't find a better burger than at the **Burger Bar**. Sure, some of the menu seems a bit chichi, with Kobe beef and truffles, but it does a great classic cheeseburger as well, and each booth has its own sports-playing TV. Or go for tasty Mexican at **Border Grill**, also in Mandalay Bay.

3pm **Moorea Beach Club** is the place to go for a bit of relaxation in the sun. This private portion of the Mandalay pool area is ultra-luxe, with comfy chaises and posh cabanas. Or, for a shot of culture, check out the **Guggenheim Hermitage** at the Venetian for a quick hit of world-class art.

5pm If you need to take relaxation to another level altogether, you won't go wrong at **Canyon Ranch SpaClub** in The Venetian, where the massages will make you forget all of your cares. **Spa Mandalay** also offers up some of the best lounging facilities in Glitter Gulch, along with exotic treatments like a Fijian Sugar Scrub, perfect preparation for a night on the town. Gentlemen, consider a relaxing break at the **Art of Shaving**, where you'll get the full hot-towel treatment and old-fashioned service.

7:30pm Wander into **Fifty Five Degrees Wine+Design**, the bottle shop with a few sleek seats in the back where you can enjoy a glass of wine from the large list. You could also warm up in the bar of **Bradley Ogden***, where comfy chairs complement sophisticated drinks.

9pm Dinner **Bradley Ogden*** in Caesars is a delicious and refined spot, all light wood and soft colors, where you'll find innovative California cuisine. For seafood with a bit of flash, head to **808**, where a sophisticated crowd dines in a cozy, modern space. If fun is just as important as the food, try **Mesa Grill**: Food Network star Bobby Flay has created an open-air restaurant where the buzz is as good as the tequila.

11:30pm Head over to the celebrity favorite **PURE**. It's one of the hardest club lines in Vegas to pass, so guarantee your entry by ordering VIP bottle service, and plan on staying late. For a more mellow but no less fun scene, it's time for a cocktail at the tantalizing **Shadow: A Bar**, where dancers behind a screen tease patrons with their gyrating silhouettes.

1:30am It's time to reveal some of the sin in this city. Indulge your senses in a titillating show by the **Pussycat Dolls**. Photographs of celebrity guest performers such as Paris Hilton, Christina Aguilera, and Charlize Theron adorn the red walls. Burlesque performances only last a few minutes, but happen every half hour. Or hop a cab to The Rio and head up to **Voodoo Lounge**, where you can sip cocktails overlooking the Strip, and mingle with a lively late-night crowd.

3am Say yes to **Spearmint Rhino**, a high-energy, upscale strip club. This is not the kind of place a man wants to bring a date.

Sunday

10am Time to swing some iron. **Bear's Best**—the legendary Jack Nicklaus golf course—will challenge even the most devoted players. **Royal Links,** a par-72 course, is another great option. If shopping is more your style, browse the stores in **Mandalay Place**. This intimate space has hipster spots like Fornarina, alongside decadent shops like the **Chocolate Swan**. Then grab a cab and get dropped off at the **Forum Shops**, where you'll find treasures—from sexy lingerie at **Agent Provocateur** to stylish shoes at **Taryn Rose**—guaranteed to help max out your credit card.

12:30pm Lunch An al fresco feast with great people-watching sounds appealing: Try **Mon Ami Gabi**, a favorite with both locals and visitors for its patio right above street level on the Strip. **R Bar Café*** is also a stylish place for a cocktail and a bite to eat. Enjoy

COOL

oysters on the half shell, or try the Dungeness crab pot au feu or delicious hamachi ceviche.

2pm Belly full of sushi, head down to **Shark Reef** and watch all kinds of sea creatures, including 12 types of sharks, as they swim above and around you. If shark sightings are too tame, get behind the wheel of your very own race car. Cab it to the **Richard Petty Driving Experience**, where you can live out your NASCAR fantasies.

5pm Wander into **Caesars Palace Poker Room**, where you'll find some of the best players any time of day. To catch a ballgame, try **Caesars Palace Sports Book**.

7pm Time for cocktails and an amazing view straight down the Strip. Take the elevators up to **Mix Lounge** at THEhotel, where you can recline on outdoor couches 64 floors up. For a more down-to-earth experience, get your drinks at **Island Lounge** and watch the casino action begin to heat up for the night.

8:30pm Dinner Dinner at **Mix,** Alain Ducasse's sleek white restaurant, is an affair to remember, especially if you can snag one of the outdoor tables with views out to the Las Vegas Valley. Or try one of celebrity chef Michael Mina's spots: **Nob Hill** at the MGM for yummy comfort classics like lobster pot pie, or elegant **Seablue** for a Mediterranean touch.

10:30pm It's not Vegas without a show. The hottest one in town right now is *Love*, the Beatles-inspired Cirque. *Kà*, another acrobatic adventure by the Canadian troupe, is also a top pick. Or, if you dined at Mix, head back over to **Mix Lounge**, where the late-night scene gets very lively.

1am Are you looking for a sophisticated lounge scene or a flat-out party? Either way, Vegas can deliver. At **Tabú**, you'll find a sexy, urbane clientele sipping cocktails and reclining on sofas. At **Studio 54**, it's about the hot DJ tunes, barely costumed dancers, and packed dance floor.

4am **Seamless** is one of Vegas' most alluring after-hours scenes, and it's just starting up at 4am—so get ready, you're not going home anytime soon.

The Morning After
End your Vegas weekend with a classic touch: brunch at **Commander's Palace**, where you'll find Southern favorites like turtle soup and crab cakes—and lots of stiff cocktails.

Cool Las Vegas:
The Key Neighborhoods

Center Strip is the center of the action. The Four Corners, where Las Vegas Boulevard intersects with Flamingo Road, is the place to be. Bellagio anchors one corner, Caesars Palace another, Paris/Bally's the third, and Flamingo and Barbary Coast the fourth. Just to the south is The Aladdin/Planet Hollywood. You can't go wrong here.

East Flamingo If you travel on Flamingo Road east of Las Vegas Boulevard, you'll find The Hard Rock Hotel & Casino, which caters to an L.A. hipster crowd. Farther east is where locals like to gamble, but the area holds little allure for visitors.

North Strip Wynn is where you'll likely land on the north end of the Strip. The Stratosphere stands tall a bit farther down, with the rest of the area marked by older hotels like the Stardust and the New Frontier—meaning it's the least buzzing stretch of the Strip.

South Strip When it comes to cool, Mandalay Bay is the soul of the south Strip, but Excalibur, the emerald-green MGM, The Luxor, the Four Seasons, THEhotel at Mandalay Bay, New York-New York, and Monte Carlo also house numerous trendy restaurants and scorching nightlife scenes, making this a lively area.

Summerlin is the "master" planned community—on land once owned by Howard Hughes—12 miles west of the Strip. Its suburban streets are home to the Red Rock Casino, and some of the area's wealthiest residents.

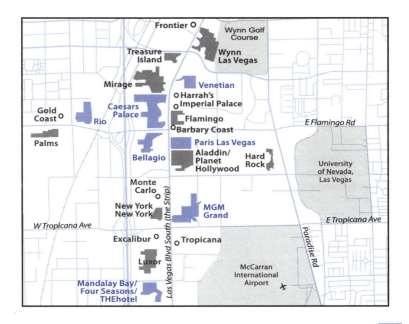

Cool Las Vegas:
The Shopping Blocks

Caesars Forum Shops

Cruising this temple of the retail gods—Vegas' original mega-mall and some say still its best—is as much fun for the color-shifting atmosphere and Roman theme as for the shops themselves. It's hard not to walk around with your head back, craning at the ceiling, which seems to move as you do. But pull your eyes down to mortal level if you don't want to miss some of Sin City's most fashionable stores. *Sun-Thu 10am-11pm, Fri-Sat 10am-midnight.* 3500 S. Las Vegas Blvd., 702-893-4800, forumshops.com

Agent Provocateur If a Provocateur purchase doesn't spark a few fantasies, your man needs Viagra. It's high-quality, inspirational lingerie. (p.74) 702-696-7174, agentprovocateur.com

Nanette Lepore Flirty and fun, Nanette Lepore specializes in suits, dresses, and tops that are whimsical, but not too girly-girly for grown-ups. 702-893-9704, nanettelepore.com

Taryn Rose An orthopedic surgeon turned footwear guru, Rose opened her first Beverly Hills boutique a few years ago. Hollywood took notice, and now her designs, from vintage-inspired to contemporary, are coveted. (p.77) 702-732-2712

Thomas Pink From classic to hip, Pink's is about men's shirts and ties from one of London's most beloved names. 702-696-1713, thomaspink.co.uk

Fashion Show Mall

It's huge, with seven flagship stores, from Neiman-Marcus to Saks to Bloomingdales, and a giant multimedia display outside that makes it seem futuristic. Beware: You could spend a whole day here. *Mon-Fri 10am-9pm, Sat 10am-8pm, Sun 11am-6pm.* 3200 S. Las Vegas Blvd., 702-369-8382, thefashionshow.com

Deetour Mid-priced trendy brands like Seven jeans, Miss Sixty, and Juicy Couture. 702-894-9898

Diesel It's been around a while, so this label is becoming the granddaddy of hipster fashion, but that doesn't mean it's even a little passé. 702-696-1055

Talulah G Founded by a native New Yorker, this boutique (now with three Vegas locations) claims to have brought a fashionista sensibility to the desert. We buy it, literally, with brands like Michael Kors and True Religion. 702-737-6000, talulahg.com

Mandalay Place

Located on a bridge between Mandalay Bay and the Luxor, Mandalay Place is the new cool kid on the shopping block. It's still high end, but with less pretension than other malls and more emphasis on interesting stores over ones with big-name recognition. With only about 40 businesses, it has an intimate feel. *Sun-Thu 10am-11pm, Fri-Sat 10am-midnight.* 3950 S. Las Vegas Blvd., 702-632-7777

The Chocolate Swan This sweet-tooth's paradise, known for its truffles, is a great place for a coffee and a pick-me-up while cruising the stores; take a box home as an edible souvenir. 702-632-9366, chocolateswan.com

Fifty Five Degrees Wine + Design Sleek and almost intimidating, this wine shop boasts Vegas' best selection, created by the wine master behind Aureole. Head to the tasting bar in back. 702-632-9373

Five Little Monkeys So you left your own little monkeys at home, and now you feel guilty. Sort of. Bring home a toy or gift from here, and you're sure to be quickly forgiven. 702-632-9382, 5littlemonkeys.com

Fornarina You'll find fun, hip fashions and great shoes here. 702-215-9300, fornarina.com

COOL

Cool Las Vegas:
The Hotels

Caesars Palace • Center Strip • Classic (3,348 rms)
Like Wayne Newton, the Rat Pack, Tom Jones, and Bobby Darin, the AAA four-diamond Caesars, immortalized in films like *Electric Horseman* and *Rain Man*, remains an enduring Las Vegas icon. In 2005, the ever-expanding hotel added its newest tower of rooms, the Augustus Tower, which are now by far the best the facility has. Its gold and marble interior, soaring columns, vaulted ceilings, spouting fountains, and replicas of classic Greek and Roman sculptures (like Michelangelo's *David* and the *Winged Victory at Samothrace* out front) are as impressive today as they were when it first opened in 1966. While most of the cheesier elements have been toned down in favor of more sophisticated décor—though the costumed centurions remain—Caesars lives on as a classic symbol of eye-popping extravagance. It has always catered to high rollers, and boasts some of the nicest accommodations on the Strip. Standard rooms are spacious (starting at 550 square feet) and elegant. Bathrooms have marble floors, deep Jacuzzi tubs, double vanities, TV speakers, and phone lines. Before hitting the casino, check out the bronze statue of Caesar at the main entrance—rubbing his finger is said to bring luck. $$$$ 3570 S. Las Vegas Blvd. (Flamingo Rd.), 702-731-7110 / 800-634-6001, caesars.com

Mandalay Bay Resort and Casino • South Strip • Contemporary (3,200 rms)
Mandalay Bay is a mysterious chameleon-like resort always turning into whatever you want it to be. Tucked inside a lush tropical entrance on the south end of the Strip, this grand destination resort occupies 60 acres of land. It is the center of a three-hotel complex that includes the Four Seasons and THEhotel. Its guests vary as much as its attractions. There are the well-heeled mature couples who actually stay in the hotel and appreciate the high caliber of the traditional tropical room design, families who come to enjoy the highly guarded Mandalay Beach with wave pool, and Gen X and Gen Y nightlife lovers partying at rumjungle and House of Blues. More recently, MB has become a dining destination for culinary connoisseurs sampling the celebrity chefs of the new Vegas. Aureole (p.116), Fleur de Lys (p.119), Red Square (p.65), 3950 (p.66), China Grill (p.61), Charlie Palmer (p.117), and Mix (p.63) are all stars on the Sin City restaurant scene. All rooms have floor-to-ceiling windows, and the best rooms overlook the pools. The top room class is the Mandalay Suites, which have an additional room, while the Junior and Executive suites don't. If you want a good view of the Strip, ask for a room on the 20th floor or higher. $$$ 3950 S. Las Vegas Blvd. (Mandalay Bay Rd.), 702-632-7777 / 877-632-7000, mandalaybay.com

MGM Grand • South Strip • Modern (5,034 rms)
Though it's soon to be overtaken by other Strip resorts in the throes of expanding, for the moment the MGM Grand reigns as the largest hotel in the country. Living up to its name, everything here is on a grand scale. The hotel is still emerald—giving off a beautiful glow at night—but that's the last remnant of the former Wizard of Oz décor, jettisoned when it adopted its more glamorous City of Entertainment theme, celebrating classic Hollywood. Even the signature lion

that once stood guard over the hotel's entrance has been replaced with a more stylish, 45-foot, 100,000-pound bronze cat at the corner of Tropicana Avenue and Las Vegas Boulevard. The 16,000-seat Grand Arena hosts pro basketball, hockey, and rodeo events and concerts like the Rolling Stones, Sting, and the Backstreet Boys. In 2000, the MGM Grand completed an $85 million renovation in which every one of the rooms was redone. With their Art Deco furnishings, the new spaces are meant to replicate an MGM Studio bungalow from the golden age of Hollywood. Like many other spots on the Strip, MGM has also recently added offerings to lure sophisticated travelers with a modern aesthetic. In the West Wing rooms, you'll find TVs in the bathroom mirrors and Bose radios, all in a sleek, minimalist décor. In the ultra-plush Skylofts (p.113), which occupy the top two floors of the hotel, you'll get a two-story setup with floor-to-ceiling windows and every amenity, including a personal, 24-hour butler—along with a whopping 1,440 square feet. $$ 3799 S. Las Vegas Blvd. (Tropicana Ave.), 702-891-1111 / 800-929-1111, mgmgrand.com

THEhotel • South Strip • Modern (1,117 rms)
Don't laugh at the name: This place is a cut above the rest. Crisp Gen Xers—and their parents—who aren't concerned with telling people they're "at the Four Seasons" find an instant haven in this boutique wing of Mandalay Bay, where every room is a modern suite that's larger than any other standard room on the Strip. At a generous 725 square feet, they include luxury accommodations such as a living room, a desk with business facilities, and three plasma TVs, one of which is in the bathroom. Staying at THEhotel entitles you to access at the Mandalay Beach, Mandalay Spa, and their pools, in addition to THEbathhouse Spa and fitness center on its own side of the complex. It has its own sleek entrance, registration area, parking, and valet. But it's the easy access to all of the Mandalay Bay dining and entertaining amenities that makes THEhotel so popular. It also owns one of the best views of Las Vegas at Mix restaurant (p.63) and Lounge (p.69) 64 floors up. Chef Alain Ducasse has already been honored with the prestigious Mobil Travel Guide Four-Star Award for his classic French and American fare. Ask for a corner room called a V-Suite, which is a little bit larger and has a panoramic view of the Strip. Rooms are assigned the day of arrival, but you can ask for the highest floor available upon booking. $$ 3950 S. Las Vegas Blvd. (Mandalay Bay Rd.), 702-632-7800 / 877-632-7800, mandalaybay.com

Cool Las Vegas:
The Restaurants

Augustus Café • Center Strip • Continental
Usually visitors that come to Vegas wind up eating at their casino's cafe, but they never tell anyone about it. Not at Caesars. In the new Augustus Tower, the cafe that overlooks the Roman Plaza is something to rave about—especially for breakfast. Enjoy pumpkin pancakes with maple glazed pecans and pumpkin spiced butter, coconut pound cake French toast, or vanilla poached apricot crepes. Those looking for the usual fare will be happy with gussied-up egg dishes, frittatas, and, believe it or not, biscuits and gravy. The warm apple cider doughnuts are a rare treat, too. It's open 24 hours and has individual lunch, dinner, and late-night menus in addition to breakfast. *24/7.* $$ ▤ Caesars Palace, 702-650-5920, caesars.com

BOA Steakhouse • Central Strip • Steakhouse
An offshoot of the swank and fabulous L.A. steakhouse by the same name, BOA has quickly established its own identity in Las Vegas. Located on the third floor of the Forum Shops, the interior is futuristic-sleek, with driftwood trees throwing their twisted arms up toward amber lighting. Despite the buzzing, atmospheric interior that's popular with celebs, savvy conventioneers, and even locals, the best seating is on the outdoor patio, which offers views of the southern Strip toward the Bellagio. The friendly, fun scene and this view would be enough to make BOA a standout, but add in excellent steaks, each with its own choice of rub or sauce (think blue cheese or the signature J-1 concoction) and you have one of the city's top joints for a juicy piece of meat. *Sun-Thu noon-10pm, Fri-Sat noon-midnight.* $$$ Ⓑ▤ Caesars Forum Shops, 702-733-7373, boasteak.com

Border Grill • South Strip • Mexican
Best Mexican Restaurants Those *Too Hot Tamales* from the Food Network, chefs Susan Feniger and Mary Sue Milliken, established an outpost of their popular Border Grill restaurants alongside Mandalay Beach and promptly started scooping up awards for their spicy fare. It's easy to see why. The space, designed by architect Josh Schweitzer and decorated with Su Huntley and Donna Muir's playful wall murals, serves up gourmet Mexican food that has its roots in dishes culled from street vendors, backyard barbecues, and beachside taco stands. You'll find ceviches, generous salads, tacos, and quesadillas, and standout entrées like slow-roasted pork with cilantro and onions, and gaucho steak, a 16-ounce rib eye stuffed with serrano peppers. Be sure to save room for dessert—the Oaxacan mocha chocolate cake and the tres leches torte are muy delicioso. You expect to find ample tequila in a Mexican restaurant, but Feniger and Milliken go a step further, not only stocking more than a dozen well-known brands, but also listing a slew of additional tequilas and some mezcal that are perhaps known only to aficionados. *Mon-Thu 11:30am-10pm, Fri 11:30am-11pm, Sat 11am-11pm, Sun 11am-10pm.* $$$ ▤ Mandalay Bay, 702-632-7403, bordergrill.com

Bradley Ogden* • Center Strip • American (G)

Best Fine Dining This award-winning chef's upscale eatery boasts farm-fresh California cuisine in a casually elegant ambience, with chairs cloaked in soft, subtle grays and square wood columns giving it a natural feel. The crowd is as sophisticated as the food—most diners here come for destination dining. San Francisco's Bradley Ogden is a Bay Area legend, garnering national acclaim and high-profile culinary awards with his hearty, organic dishes culled from boutique American farmers. The 140-seat interior is divided into three intimate dining areas, including a relaxed bar and lounge where you can grab a ground steak burger, seared big-eye tuna, or Barron Point oysters before heading out to a show or club. The booths along the wall are the prime seats (ask for a booth in the "30s"), while larger parties covet the booths in the front window, which seat five. The seasonal menu includes the Humboldt Fog blue cheese soufflé, triple-seared Kobe steak, and Alaskan ivory salmon. The ever-expanding, all-American wine list includes more than 900 labels. Beware: Farm-fresh ingredients don't come cheap—entrées can hit $180 here. *Sun-Thu 5-11pm, Fri-Sat 5pm-midnight.* $$$$ B⊟ Caesars Palace, 702-731-7731, larkcreek.com

Burger Bar • Mandalay Bay • American

Few know about this gem hiding within the shopping hall called Mandalay Place between the Mandalay Bay and the Luxor. It's not a super-sized restaurant with lots of glitz like we've come to expect from Vegas eateries. Nope, this is a simple joint where you can get a damn good burger and a cold draft beer in the company of casual, like-minded company. Sports games play on plasma TVs behind the long bar and throughout the restaurant, and each booth has its own mini-screen. Sure, there are some eccentric burgers, like the Rossini burger made from Kobe beef with foie gras and shaved truffles, and named after the 19th-century Italian composer ($90), or the Surf and Turf burger made from Black Angus with grilled half lobster and grilled green asparagus on plain bun ($24), but that's just celebrity chef Hubert Keller showing off. You can choose your own toppings, or have a classic American cheeseburger with Ridgefield farm beef ($12). *Sun-Thu 10:30am-11pm, Fri-Sat 10am-3am.* $$ B⊟ Mandalay Bay, 702-632-9364, fleurdelyssf.com

Canaletto • Center Strip • Italian

The tastemakers behind the Il Fornaio restaurant chain take their authentic yet affordable tastes of Northern Italy to a new level with this panoramic two-story eatery. The Venetian's indoor St. Mark's Square re-creation is a perfect complement to chef and Venice native Luigi Bomparola's repertoire of regional recipes. A charming, 300-seat patio leads to a stunning open kitchen, decked out in 16-foot ceilings, hardwood floors, and marble trimmings. A more intimate upstairs dining area offers views of the faux Grand Canal and the gondolas passing below. The tasty and reasonably priced menu caters to a casual, mixed crowd that is looking for an easy meal, and is rich in risotto, gnocchi, and polenta selections—but the wood-fired pizzas, poultry, and seafood dishes are the most popular. *Mon-Thu 11:30am-11pm, Fri-Sun 11:30am-midnight.* $$$ ≡ The Venetian, 702-733-0070, venetian.com/dining/canaletto.cfm

China Grill • South Strip • Chinese

Part of the popular China Grill restaurant chain, which has outposts in hip cities like New York and South Beach, this Vegas version also specializes in authentic Asian-inspired cuisine, served family-style for sharing. It has a gimmicky retro-modern atmosphere that draws a fashionable, casual crowd and hotel guests in equal numbers. *Sun-Thu 5-11pm, Fri-Sat 5pm-midnight.* $ B≡ Mandalay Bay, 702-632-7404, chinagrillmgt.com

Commander's Palace • Center Strip • Creole
Best Regional Dining Open since 2000, this bayou-style brasserie is decorated with a dark wood interior and distressed tile floors, and has separate dining rooms. The Wine Room has a large fireplace and to-the-ceiling shelves stacked with bottles of vino. The Garden Room, like the parlor of a great Southern plantation, has a crystal chandelier and fabric-draped ceiling, and offers good views onto the Strip. Fans of the original New Orleans Commander's Palace will find many of their favorite dishes on the menu, such as the turtle soup, the crab cakes (made with a half-pound of crab meat), and the light-as-air, melt-in-your-mouth beignets. But chef Carlos Guia also whipped up some only-in-Las-Vegas dishes, like the crispy barbecued alligator and the grilled filet served over Andouille-roasted smashed new potatoes. *Mon-Fri 11:30am-2pm, Sat-Sun 10:30am-2pm; nightly 5:30-10pm.* $$$$ B≡ Aladdin/Planet Hollywood, 702-892-8272, commanderspalace.com

Craftsteak • South Strip • Steakhouse (G)
Chef Tom Colicchio (of New York's Craft and Gramercy Tavern) is the latest James Beard Award–winning kitchen god to toss his toque into the Vegas dining scene. A super-sized copy of the original Craft (named for Colicchio's emphasis on the craft of cooking), Craftsteak focuses on simply prepared prime cuts of beef, like Kobe-style skirts and hangars, porterhouses, and strips, served home-style on Bernardaud china and Frette linens. It draws a savvy, fashion-conscious crowd, along with a fair share of foodies. Even vegetarians will have plenty to eat here, with the menu's astonishing array of mushrooms, as well as a list of vegetable sides that go well beyond creamed spinach and baked potatoes. The $39 market menu is an amazing value, offering four courses for what you'd normally pay for a single entrée. And given that it was developed under the guidance of former Gramercy Tavern wine guru Paul Grieco, Craftsteak's wine and spirits list is a mix of the well-known and esoteric and what it claims is the largest Scotch collection in Nevada. *Nightly 5:30-10:30pm.* $$$$ ≡ MGM Grand, 702-891-7318, mgmgrand.com

808 • Center Strip • Fusion
Foodies gripe that many of the celebrity chefs who've set up Las Vegas outposts rarely show their faces, but chef Jean-Marie Josselin makes a point of spending at least a week every month here to oversee his Euro–Pacific Island kitchen. Josselin has created a simple space accented with dark wood, an aquarium with red coral, and a copper conduit ceiling. Tucked in a casino corner, it draws passersby, but most patrons are sophisticated diners who've planned ahead. Start with the deconstructed ahi roll—a sumptuous tower of ahi tartare, avocado, crab ceviche, sushi rice, and white truffle dressing. The New Wave Bento Box—which wins for most creative presentation—is filled with six bite-size morsels sequestered in their own cubbies. For main courses, the wok-charred mahi-mahi over Asian stir-fried vegetables with lime ginger beurre blanc is stellar, and the lobster stir-fry is always a favorite. For four tops, table 53 straight back from the entrance is the best seat. For duos, tables 33 and 34 along the glass partition are the most sought-after, while the two tops on the far side of this glass wall are more private. *Nightly 5-11pm.* $$$ B⊐ Caesars Palace, 702-731-7604, caesars.com

Emeril's New Orleans Fish House • South Strip • Cajun

Best Regional Dining We'll spare you the "Bam!" jokes. If you haven't seen chef Emeril Lagasse on his famous trademark TV show, we're at least certain you've heard the name. This long-running Vegas favorite showcases his Creole and Cajun roots, while throwing an Asian influence in the mix to keep things interesting, so you find items like a nori-wrapped yellowfin tuna, along with pecan-crusted Texas redfish. There's also a seafood bar if you want to keep things light or are dining solo. The setting has been updated, with a water theme incorporating bright blue booths and flowing metal sculptures. For the best people-watching, nab a table on the indoor "patio" on the MGM studio walk, but be warned—it gets noisy. One thing that hasn't changed too much is the mostly reasonable prices—an increasing rarity in celebrity-owned Vegas spots. *Daily 11am-2:30pm, 5:30-10:30pm, seafood bar: 11:30am-10:30pm.* $$$ B☰ MGM Grand, 702-891-7374, emerils.com

Isla Mexican Kitchen* • Center Strip • Mexican

Best Mexican Restaurants Chef Richard Sandoval focuses on fresh at this Treasure Island Mexican hangout. From the exotic guacamoles (think lobster and corn combos) made tableside to Mexican meatballs, there's sure to be something on the menu that the average Mexican joint doesn't have. The crowd here is young, trendy, and often made up of groups of singles getting ready for a night on the town—maybe even next door at Tangerine. That singles scene might have something to do with the tequilas here—a vast selection with some very rare bottles. No matter what draws patrons in, the casual-chic room with a blue tiled wall, colorful modern artwork, and simple wood tables is a fun spot to lounge away a few hours. *Wed, Fri, and Sat 4pm-midnight, Sun-Tue and Thu 4-10:30pm; bar daily 11am-4pm.* $$ B☰ Treasure Island, 702-894-7349, treasureisland.com

Joe's Seafood, Prime Steak & Stone Crab • Center Strip • Seafood

The lively patio at this Miami transplant is a favorite spot of Friday power-lunchers. Like its Florida parent, this Joe's is famous for its delicious fresh stone crab (seafood is flown in daily) and sides like creamy mashed potatoes and creamed spinach. If you're not after fish, the menu also has thick, bone-in steaks. It's a masculine spot with a clubby atmosphere—lots of dark wood and deep booths, the best seats if you can get them—and a busy bar that offers a variation of the lunch menu at dinner (in the main restaurant, it's a dinner-only affair). *Sun-Thu 11am-11pm, Fri-Sat 11am-midnight.* $$$ B☰ Caesars Palace, 702-792-9222, icon.com/joes

Mesa Grill • Center Strip • Southwest

Best Regional Dining Iron chef Bobby Flay, a favorite star of the Food Network, is the mastermind behind this busy and lively Southwestern-themed spot. Located near the Sports Book, it's not the best place to go if you're looking for quiet or a romantic ambience, but it is a great spot for a festive meal with a buzzing crowd. Flay fans are often the margarita-at-lunch crowd, and they flock to the earth-toned room to try his spicy concoctions, and rave about items like the pork tenderloin. *Mon-Fri 11am-2:30pm, 5-11pm, Sat-Sun 10:30am-3pm, 5-11pm.* $$ B☰ Caesars Palace, 702-650-5965, mesagrill.com

Mix in Las Vegas* • South Strip • French

Best Trendy Tables When the occasion calls for a big first impression, head to Mix. Whether you start off at the Lounge next door (see *Cool Nightlife*, p.69, for details), or head straight for Alain Ducasse's Mobile Four Star Award–winning restaurant, the chic décor and sweeping view of the Las Vegas Valley will surprise even the most

callused traveler. Dine on Ducasse's signature dishes, executed by chef Bruno Davaillon. Customers—as cool as the modern white interior—rave about the roasted Maine lobster "au curry," the sautéed salmon with caviar and sea urchin, and the popular elbow pasta with black truffle, ham, and Gruyère cheese. A meal at Mix is certainly an indulgence, and the floor-to-ceiling windows 64 floors above the Strip will take your breath away. Both the restaurant and lounge have become fast favorites among Vegas lovers. If you can't score an outdoor table (on a warm night), then opt for one of the white, egg-shaped booths. *Nightly 6-10:30pm.* $$$$
≣ THEhotel, 702-632-9500, alain-ducasse.com

Mon Ami Gabi • Center Strip • French

Best Brasseries Mon Ami Gabi, romantic and low-key by Vegas standards, is one of the few restaurants with Strip-side terrace seating. On spring days, you can sit on the patio and watch the traffic on the main drag from your cafe table, shaded by a big red canvas umbrella. House specialties include flaky pastries, omelets, and French onion soup. Unlike many places on Las Vegas Boulevard, Mon Ami Gabi is as much a locals' scene as a favorite among experienced Vegas visitors who want something special without the hype of the celebrity-chef destinations. *Mon-Thu 11:30am-11pm, Fri-Sat 11am-midnight, Sun 11am-11pm.* $$ ≣ Paris Las Vegas, 702-944-4224, monamigabi.com

N9NE* • West Flamingo • Steakhouse

Best Trendy Tables In a city full of steak and seafood places, N9NE holds its own with its slick contemporary décor and prime aged beef served Chicago-style. Makes sense since the owners, Michael Morton (son of Morton's steakhouse founder Arnie Morton and brother to Hard Rock creator Peter Morton) and Scott DeGraff—best friends since they were nine, hence the name—hail from Chicago, where they opened the original N9NE in 2000. Classic starters include caviar by the ounce, chilled shellfish platters (piled with shrimp, crab legs, lobster, oysters, and clams), and sashimi. Noting that "all steaks can surf," executive chef Brian Massie (who earned his chops at the New York and Vegas outposts of Charlie Palmer Steak and Aureole) will pair any of his cuts with Alaskan crab legs or lobster. If it's just the scene you're after, sit yourself down at the champagne and caviar bar, which holds court in the center of the room. *Mon-Thu 5-11pm, Fri-Sun 5-11:30pm.* $$$$ B≣ Palms, 702-933-9000, n9negroup.com

Nob Hill • South Strip • Seafood (G)

Best Fine Dining This is the sister restaurant to Michael Mina's seafood place, Aqua at Bellagio. It's sedate décor, hardwood floors, and roomy, sequestered booths done in leather are a tribute to the eponymous San Francisco neighborhood, and help to draw a mature crowd looking for a fine meal without the flash of other top spots. Mina imports seasonal fresh foods from the City by the Bay to create his Californian dishes, including yellowfin tuna carpaccio, pumpkin soup, seared Atlantic cod steak, roast filet of beef rossini, and shark. Try lobster pot pie, chock-full of two pounds of Maine lobster, and his dry-aged Colorado lamb tasting, featuring different cuts like rack, chop, boneless loin, and grilled leg. *Nightly 5:30-10:30pm.* $$$$ B≣ MGM Grand, 702-891-7337, michaelmina.net

Nobu • East Flamingo • Sushi (G)

Best Sushi Restaurants Nobu, named after its creator, chef Nobu Matsuhisa, is on the tip of sushi lovers' tongues when asked about the best sushi in town. And judging from the way the reservations fill up, it's one of Sin City's trendiest tables, too. Decorated like Nobu in New York with minimalist Zen-like detail, the 214-seat dining room is filled with hipsters and business associates, both of whom dress in smart-casual attire. There are also 16 seats at the sushi bar for when you've forgotten reservations and still need a Nobu fix. The Omakaze (chef's menu) is legendary. At the very least, do not finish your meal without ordering the yellowtail sashimi with jalapeños. Iron Chef Masaharu Morimoto gets co-credit for the mastery of this restaurant and is a champion sushi chef in his own right. *Nightly 6-11pm.* $$$$ B= The Hard Rock, 702-693-5090, hardrockhotel.com

Postrio • Central Strip • Fusion
Postrio is Wolfgang Puck's charming Mediterranean-meets-Asian-meets-American cafe. Dine inside or al fresco under the pretty faux-Italian sky where the people-watching is as intriguing as the food. The menu runs the gamut from gourmet pizzas to lamb chops to Chinese duck. Patrons here are a mixed lot, mostly drawn from shoppers wandering the Canal shops, and guests of The Venetian looking for a break from the casino floor. *Daily 11:30am-11pm.* $$ B= The Venetian, 702-796-1110, wolfgangpuck.com

R Bar Café* • South Strip • Seafood
R Bar at the foot of Mandalay Place is a fine resting spot after shopping, before a big gambling spree, or even just to chill out before a fancy dinner. Whether you have a simple taste for beer and a shrimp cocktail, or you're more likely to ponder over a list of ten different kinds of oysters, R Bar has you covered. The oyster list changes daily, and the wine menu has 350 bottles to choose from. No need to wear your Sunday best, it's casual here. *Sun-Thu 5-11pm, Fri-Sat 5pm-midnight.* $$ = Mandalay Bay, 702-632-9300, rmseafood.com

Red Square* • South Strip • Continental
Red Square is a very hot club, which makes it surprising that the food is so good. Continental fare like filet mignon is given Russian touches, and caviar flows as freely as the vodka. See *Cool Nightlife,* p.71, for details. *Sun-Thu 5pm-2am, Fri-Sat 5pm-3am.* $$$ = Mandalay Bay, 702-632-7407, mandalaybay.com

Restaurant RM • South Strip • Seafood
New Yorker Rick Moonen was lured away from his Big Apple restaurant to open this Mandalay Bay outpost, making it one of the few places that actually has the rock-star cook working in the kitchen. RM is designed to feel like the interior of a plush yacht, with soft blues and golden wood. The prime seats are the semi-walled booths, which provide a very private feel while still offering up a few views of the room. There's also a long wooden bar in a separate room good for solo dining. The food features very fresh seafood, from tuna to bass, prepared in inventive ways. Downstairs from this elegant spot, you'll find its more casual cousin, R Bar Café. *Nightly 5:30-10:30pm.* $$$$ B= Mandalay Bay, 702-632-9300, rmseafood.com

Seablue • South Strip • Seafood
Celebrity chef Michael Mina doesn't just have one restaurant in Vegas, he has three. The James Beard Award winner earned his fame for his Michael Mina restaurant in San Francisco, and brought two more to the MGM Grand. Seablue is the newest of the jewels and inspires diners with Mediterranean dishes and shellfish selections that rotate daily. The fish is flown in from all over the world. Guests are encouraged to eat family style, and the small plates are arranged in

five categories based on preparation: raw, marinated, steamed, batter-fried, and crusted. The tables for two can get crowded with all these little dishes, so request a larger booth if possible. The atmosphere is lively (the music can get downright loud), and the interior design modern. Come for fun, but not a quiet conversation (though the dining room on the right is a bit less noisy). *Nightly 5:30-10pm.* $$$$ B≡ MGM Grand, 702-891-3486, michaelmina.net

Sushi Roku • Center Strip • Japanese
Best Sushi Restaurants If the Palms or Hard Rock seem too far off the Strip to go to party with hipsters, try Sushi Roku. Located on the Terrace Level in the Caesars Forum Shops, this Japanese crib that became popular in L.A. is just as hot in Vegas. Expect a buzzing modern Zen dining room with shopping bags tucked under the tables. Those who've been to Sushi Roku come back for more and bring their friends. The best seats in the house are in the back with a view of the Strip, or at the zashiki tables right on the floor. It has a full bar, and can be booked for private parties. *Sun-Thu 11am-11pm, Fri-Sat 11am-midnight.* $$$ B≡ Caesars Palace, 702-733-7373, sushiroku.com

Tao Asian Bistro* • Center Strip • Asian Fusion
Best Trendy Tables This hot Vegas spot is part of the "Asian City" that includes Tao Nightclub and Tao Lounge—in all taking up more than 40,000 square feet of space at The Venetian. It's all about the scene here, with a giant golden Buddha holding court over the dim dining room, and A-list celebrities noshing and heading upstairs to the nightclub. The menu covers everything Asian, from Thai to Korean, but don't come here for a gourmet experience or fine service. Even with a reservation, you'll probably have a wait at the bar, followed by an average meal. But you're coming for the scene, and if you're lucky, your server can give you a VIP pass to skip the long line to the club. *Sun-Thu 5pm-midnight, Fri-Sat 5pm-1am.* $$$ ≡ The Venetian, 702-388-8338, taolasvegas.com

3950 • South Strip • Steakhouse
What's black and white and red all over? Mandalay Bay's AAA four-diamond steakhouse with a décor that's as sharp as the knives you'll use to slice into your porterhouse. A boutique steakhouse (with just 88 seats), 3950 boasts suede booths, red leather walls, purple benches, zebra flooring, and polished steel triangular plates stamped with the restaurant's name—a slick reminder of the resort's address. While you wait for a table, hang in the lounge and watch the black-tipped reef sharks and bonnetheads swim by on the flat-screen virtual aquarium that beams images from the tanks at Shark Reef into the restaurant. Chef Scott McCarter, who earned his chops at Treasure Island and Mirage and regularly cooks for the athletes and VIPs at the Olympic Games, is known for his lobster bisque. Other standouts include the portobello Napoleon and seared foie gras appetizers, rack of lamb and pan-seared Chilean sea bass entrées, along with an expected selection of filets, strips, and chops. For dessert, toss out your calorie counter and dig into the High Brow Banana Split, a house specialty made with caramelized bananas and Tahitian vanilla, dark chocolate, and strawberry ice creams. *Nightly 5-11pm.* $$$$ B≡ Mandalay Bay, 702-632-7417, mandalaybay.com

Cool Las Vegas:
The Nightlife

The Beatles: "Love" Cirque du Soleil • Center Strip • Show

Best Cirque Shows This odd, yet seemingly inevitable collaboration celebrates the musical legacy of the Fab Four through the stunning visual imagery of Cirque du Soleil. Using the master tapes at Abbey Road Studios, Beatles producer Sir George Martin and his son Giles create a panorama of sound by weaving together snippets of more than 130 original and unreleased Beatles songs. The rock-'n'-roll poem attempts to interpret the lyrics of classics such as "Strawberry Fields Forever" and "Come Together" through dance and imagery, while marking the first and only time the Beatles' music has been authorized for a theatrical production. The Mirage's new custom-built theater, featuring 360-degree seating, is a perfect fit for the show's surround sound and digital video projections. *Thu-Mon 7:30pm and 10:30pm.* C☰ The Mirage, 702-792-7777, mirage.com

Bradley Ogden*• Center Strip • Bar/Restaurant

Earth tones and comfy seats make this a great place for a pre-dinner drink and a gourmet snack. See *Cool Restaurants,* p.61, for details. *Sun-Thu 5-11pm, Fri-Sat 5pm-midnight.* C☰B— Caesars Palace, 702-731-7731, larkcreek.com

Cherry • Summerlin • Nightclub

If you're coming to Cherry, you've got to check out the men's bathroom. It's not often that the john is a high point of a club scene, but Cherry is the exception. Wander down the long mirrored hallway that serves as an entrance, past the giant sculpture of brilliant red cherries by artist Takashi Murakami, and head into the lav, where you'll be met by bright red glass urinals shaped like a pouting pair of woman's lips. That kind of excess and whimsy can be found throughout this off-Strip hot spot located in the Red Rock Casino Resort and Spa. The creation of nightlife guru Rande Gerber, Cherry occupies coveted real estate next to the pool, and has retractable doors that open to connect the two areas in warm weather. On lazy summer weekends, the club hosts a pool party complete with cabana bottle service. The red theme dominates the 8,500 square-foot space, with red leather walls, crimson glass, and fire-engine booths ringing the oval room—what's not red is covered in walnut or chrome. Cherry attracts a sophisticated but low-pretension crowd. *Wed-Sat 10pm-5am.* C☰ Red Rock Resort, 11011 W. Charleston Blvd. (215 W. Freeway), 866-767-7773 / 702-797-7180, redrocklasvegas.com

Drop Bar • Henderson • Bar/Lounge

Here's a chill-and-chat nightlife alternative to the see-and-be-seen scene at the swanky Whiskey Bar. Sheer curtains shield the circular-shaped bar from the surrounding casino's bells and whistles, almost making you forget you're smack dab in the middle of Green Valley Ranch Resort's game pit. The modern, minimalist, retro-futuristic décor features dark wooden floors, snowflake chandeliers, and sleek white leather chairs and couches. Laid-back locals and trendy tourists looking to get away from the Strip indulge in cocktails and conversations as down-tempo grooves set a casually cool vibe. *24/7.* ☰ Green Valley Ranch Resort, 702-617-7777, greenvalleyranchresort.com

Foundation Room (at the House of Blues*) • South Strip • Lounge
Find a way to get into the Foundation Room on the 43rd floor of Mandalay Bay, step out onto the patio deck, and you will find yourself looking at one of the most stunning views of the Las Vegas Strip. It is connected to the House of Blues, and many of the bands playing downstairs come up afterward to party. Though it's known to be members-only, the public can get in for a cover charge late Monday nights (starting at 11pm, $30 cover, strict 21-and-up policy with a dress code). You can also buy a temporary, four-day membership for $500. Those staying at Mandalay Bay, THEhotel, and the Four Seasons also get passes on occasion—ask the concierge. Once inside, it's a cavernous chain of dining rooms and lounges decorated in an East Asian theme. It's a mixed crowd of very A-list men and women of all ages, all united in their quest for a good time. *Mon-Fri 5pm-late, Sat-Sun 3pm-late. Mon at 11pm open to public.* C☰ Mandalay Bay, 702-632-7601, hob.com

Ghostbar • West Flamingo • Nightclub
Best Bars with a View You have a better chance of drawing a royal flush than getting into this swank, space-agey lounge that claims to be on the 55th floor (since forties are unlucky in Asian cultures, the hotel skips those floors; it's actually on the 43rd). But don't let that stop you from trying. On windless days, the terrace provides a great view of the Strip, and much is made of the transparent floor that lets you see all the way to the ground below. That the see-through panel is only shoulder-width wide (if that) is a bit disappointing. But it's still a little freaky to stand there, looking down. Inside, with its all-white décor, three walls of floor-to-ceiling windows, and ghostly mascot on the ceiling, Ghostbar is popular with the L.A. crowd and *Real World* devotees determined to be seen partying in a place featured on MTV. One way to beat the lines is to show up unfashionably early, then nurse a few cosmos until the crowd picks up around 11pm, or dine at Alizé, which guarantees entry and is great. Hotel guests can show their room keys between 8pm and 9pm and have the cover disappear. You might consider going up for a drink, getting your hand stamped for re-entry, then having dinner and breezing back in at a more fashionable hour. *Nightly 8pm-3am.* C☰ Palms, 702-938-2666, n9negroup.com

House of Blues* • South Strip • Nightclub/Live Music
Best Live Music House of Blues needs little introduction. The famous chain is well-established as a stomping ground for hot bands, but also has a good restaurant with a great Sunday Gospel Brunch. See *Bachelor(ette) Restaurants,* p.89, for details. *Nightclub Wed-Mon 9pm-3am; restaurant Sun-Thu 7:30am-midnight, Fri-Sat 7:30am-1am; gospel brunch Sun 10am and 1pm.* C☰ Mandalay Bay, 702-632-7601, hob.com

Island Lounge • South Strip • Lounge
This open bar in the center of the Mandalay Bay casino is a great spot to rest up with a cocktail and watch the action unfolding around the hotel. There is often live music, from rock to jazz, and a mixed crowd of all ages looking for a break. Like the name suggests, there is an island theme going on here, and the house specialty is tropical drinks. For those looking for something a bit more exciting than an umbrella on their rum, rumor has it that this is a good place to meet working girls. *24/7.* ☰ Mandalay Bay, 702-632-7777, mandalaybay.com

Ivan Kane's Forty Deuce • South Strip • Nightclub

Best Burlesque Following the success of the L.A. original, it only seemed natural that Ivan Kane would open up a burlesque nightclub in Las Vegas. Relax with a swank cocktail in front of the stage, and get ready for dancers to seduce you all night long. Designed to feel like a vintage speakeasy, Forty Deuce is located on the casino level of Mandalay Bay next to the escalator to Mandalay Place, not far from the corridor to THEhotel. General ticketed entry is standing-room only, but there is seating for those who purchase bottle service. *Thu-Mon 10:30pm-4am, Fri-Sat and Mon after-hours until 6am.* C☰ Mandalay Bay, 702-632-9442, fortydeuce.com

Kà • South Strip • Show

Best Cirque Shows *Kà* is the fourth Cirque du Soleil to come to Las Vegas and has quickly become a favorite among show fans. It's an epic tale of two twins embarking on an Asian adventure that crosses sea and land. But like all Cirque endeavors, it's less about the story than the stunning visual experience, with acrobatics, pyrotechnics, music, and performance dance (although to be fair, it is the most plotted of the Cirque endeavors). You'll find some behind-the-scenes information on the website about the technical side of the production, but just know the Cirque puts exceptional amounts of blood, sweat, and megabucks into designing this theater and presentation. *Tue-Sat 6:30pm and 9:30pm.* C☰ MGM Grand, 702-796-9999, cirquedusoleil.com

MGM Grand Garden Arena • South Strip • Live Music

Best Live Music This arena is the place for most of Las Vegas' super-sized events. Designed after New York's Madison Square Garden, it has 16,800 seats and has hosted concerts for the Rolling Stones, Bette Midler, Madonna, Cher, Paul McCartney, Elton John, and Bruce Springsteen, among others. Floor seats A to E are the closest you can get to the stage, but you'd be pretty happy to get tickets in the Lower Level sections 1 to 12, too. *Prices and showtimes vary.* C☰ MGM Grand, 702-891-1111, mgmgrand.com

Mix Lounge • South Strip • Ultra Lounge

Best Bars with a View Even those who are afraid of heights will be impressed by the view at Mix, 64 floors above the Strip. Located at THEhotel at Mandalay Bay, this is a swank lounge with sweeping views out to the western Las Vegas valley. The large bar with black leather sofas and chairs looks out at Sin City through the floor-to-ceiling windows. Though it'll seem like there's not a bad seat in the house, most people want to be outside on the patio with their low seats and votive-lit tables. There are a few romantic cocoon tables by the center bar and a VIP area upstairs. The crowd is a sophisticated mix of in-the-know conventioneers, hip locals, and high rollers. The outside deck is reserved for VIP service after 10:30, and the lounge changes to more of a dance scene at midnight when resident DJ Adam Webb turns it up. If you're looking to show off to a business partner or lover, this place will score you some points. *Nightly 5pm-3am, Wed until 4am.* C☰ Mandalay Bay, 702-632-9500, mandalaybay.com

Napoleon's Champagne Bar • Center Strip • Bar Lounge

Best Quiet Bars This European-style bar is a perfect spot to get away from the noise of the casinos, or to take a meeting in a refined setting away from the conference halls of Paris and Bally's. It's usually quiet in the afternoons except during happy hour when a crowd gathers for the free sandwich that comes with your first drink, and on weekend nights when dueling pianos take over and the scene gets lively. Sink back in the leather chairs and sip from one of the variety of champagnes while the pianist plays into the evening. *Sun-Thu 4pm-2am, Fri-Sat 4pm-3am.* ⬛ Paris Las Vegas, 702-946-7000, parislasvegas.com

N9NE* • East Flamingo • Restaurant/Bar
This sexy steak joint doubles as a great cocktail lounge, filled with a stylish crowd. See *Cool Restaurants,* p.64, for details. *Sun-Thu 5-10pm, Fri-Sat 5-11pm.* ⒸⒷ▤ Palms, 702-933-9000, n9negroup.com

Peppermill Fireside Lounge • North Strip • Lounge
It's kitschy-fabulous to the extreme, dripping with blue and magenta neon, mir-rored walls, a firepit where gas flames bubble through too-blue water, gown-wearing waitresses, and fake bougainvillea creeping over every surface. In short, everything you need to make it feel just right to be drinking Scorpions at 10am. But the Peppermill is no wannabe—this is the real deal, having cultivated cool since opening in 1972. Hipster locals cried foul when it plastered seemingly every square inch of its dark, smoky, make-out lounge interior with music-video-playing plasma screens, but we say, bring it on. This is a spot where there is no such thing as excess. It was also one of Sinatra's favorite late-night hangouts (and was featured in *Casino* and *Showgirls*), and it still has a sexy vibe, excel-lent for illicit canoodling on red banquettes. *24/7.* ▤ 2985 S. Las Vegas Blvd. (E. Desert Inn Rd.), 702-735-4177, peppermilllasvegas.com

Playboy Club • West Flamingo • Nightclub
Geriatric gigolo Hugh Hefner teamed up with the kings of Vegas, the Maloof brothers, to open up the first Playboy Club in 20 years. The multifaceted venue located on the top three levels of the Palms' jaw-dropping, $600 million Fantasy Towers is a bunny-brand bonanza. The Playboy pantheon features a restaurant, store, casino, and Moon nightclub, which has a retractable roof. World-renowned glam rock fashion designer Roberto Cavalli updated the spanking-new (pun intended) Bunny costumes, so longtime Playboy "article-reading" fans won't be disappointed. *Daily 8pm-4am.* Ⓒ▤ Palms, 702-942-7777, palms.com

PURE • Center Strip • Nightclub
Best Mega-Night Clubs An ultra-hip nightclub that's ultra-hard to get into. There are two lines to enter, those for mixed groups, and those just for girls. You figure out who gets in faster. It's a two-level club with three rooms. The first level pumps hip-hop and current chart music, while DJs spin techno and house music elsewhere. The dance floor is a bit tight and hard to move around on because part of it is roped off for the VIP section. But if you can afford bottle service, come particularly early, or wait through the line, you'll find a sexy bar with a great terrace and Strip view. And if you want to tell your friends—Céline Dion, Shaquille O'Neal, and tennis stars Andre Agassi and Steffi Graf are owner-partners in this club. *Fri-Sun and Tue 10pm-4am.* Ⓒ▤ Caesars Palace, 702-731-7873, caesars.com

Pussycat Dolls Lounge • Center Strip • Nightclub/Lounge
Best Burlesque The Pussycat Dolls get their seduction on at their very own lounge next to the almighty nightclub PURE. Photographs of celebrity guest performers such as Paris Hilton, Christina Aguilera, and Charlize Theron adorn the red walls, and one wouldn't be surprised to see them flutter by. Performances from these sexy

ladies only last a few minutes, but come every half hour. Wipe your drool while they pop out of champagne glasses, and dance and sing while swinging from the ceiling. Note that between dances, it won't look like an MTV video, and depending on the night, it can be considerably quiet. *Tue-Sat 8pm-4am. First show at 10:30pm and every 30 minutes after.* ⊂☰ Caesars Palace, 702-731-7110, caesars.com

R Bar Café* • South Strip • Bar/Restaurant
This seafood restaurant and bar makes a great spot to rest and have a cocktail, a bite to eat, or both. It's the Vegas branch of celebrity chef Rick Moonen's growing empire. See *Cool Restaurants,* p.65, for details. *Sun-Wed 5-11pm, Thu-Sat 5pm-2am.* ☰ Mandalay Bay, 702-632-9300, rmseafood.com

Red Square* • South Strip • Nightclub
How can you not love a Communist-themed bar whose motto is "Come join the party"? Pairing capitalist excess with Bolshevik chic, Red Square, with its headless Lenin statue out front (the head's in the freezer inside), has 200 types of premium vodka and some of the priciest martinis in town. On weekends, it's not unusual for the 20- and 30-something, looking-for-fun crowd to be six deep at the solid ice bar. Of course you can always have your drinks brought to your table in the dining room (booths 3 and 4 are the most sought-after), which has a substantial menu that includes several caviars; light bites like blini, foie gras, and lobster salad; full plates like chicken Kiev and filet mignon; and a chocolate trilogy that truly says *decadence*. The only drawback: no bathroom. Management recently converted the facilities into a sequestered, and tastefully appointed, table for four—a curious move since, naturally, the whole point of supping on mounds of Beluga while tippling overpriced martinis is to have someone watch (preferably with a certain degree of envy) as you do it. *Sun-Thu 5pm-2am, Fri-Sat 5pm-3am.* ⊂☰ Mandalay Bay, 702-632-7407, mandalaybay.com

Scores • Southwest Las Vegas • Strip Club
One of the newer gentlemen's clubs to join the lot in Sin City, Scores is a national chain. With all the columns and ivory-colored staircases, you'd think you'd stepped into a private area of Caesars Palace. Not to worry; even though it's high class, it's still a comfortable club. Scores used to be Jaguars and is large at 50,000 square feet. It boasts a steakhouse, handmade cigars, and free admission, food, and drink for locals with business cards. Partly because the brand is well-known, you'll find a wide range of patrons here, both tourists and locals, with lots of groups of guys out to celebrate something or just have a wild time. *Nightly 5pm-8am.* ⊂☰ 3350 South Procyon (Desert Inn Rd.), 702-367-4000, scoreslasvegas.com

Seamless • East Las Vegas • Nightclub
Best After-Hours Clubs When it comes to nightclubs, the swank casinos usually have the market wrapped up. When it comes to naked women, zoning laws make it hard for places on the Strip to compete. But at Seamless, you'll find the best of both worlds, well, seamlessly melded together. Designed by former Light Group member Brandon Roque, the chic, modern space competes for flash and style with any of the on-Strip clubs like Jet or Tao. Before 4am, the club is a topless bar, with the ladies strutting their stuff on a glass catwalk that connects to the triangular-shaped bar. But when that magic hour hits, the stage is raised drawbridge style, the furniture is rearranged even as the strip club patrons continue to party, and a whole new crowd of under-35 hipsters hits, ready to dance to house and hip-hop. Big-name

DJs also come out late night, and the working girls put their tops back on, but stay on the floor (and inside the giant champagne glass at the entrance). *24/7.* C≡ 4740 S. Arville St. (W. Tropicana Ave.), 702-227-5200, seamlessclub.com

Shadow: A Bar • Center Strip • Ultra Lounge

This chic lounge with a frosted glass façade and the requisite comfy couches and plush chairs has bartenders who do everything from breathing fire to turning handsprings as they mix drinks. But the big draw is the sexy go-go dancers—called Shadow concierges—whose silhouettes gyrate on oversized screens that hide the actual women. In this flesh-peddling town, this tease seems a bit coy, but the small lounge is cool and unpretentious. Reserve one of the velvet VIP booths where you can even watch the dancers at your own closed-circuit table TV. Shadow: A Bar also features a decent and diverse menu with sushi, smoked salmon, oysters, crab cakes, a fruit-and-cheese platter, and Beluga caviar that's served until 10pm. *Daily noon-4am.* ≡ Caesars Palace, 702-369-6300, caesars.com

Spearmint Rhino • North Strip • Strip Club

Best Strip Clubs This is a high-energy, upscale gentleman's club that doubles as a hot nightspot for both sexes. It's a chain with clubs around the world and draws dancers from all nationalities and races, and many say the sexiest ladies in town can be found on these poles. In Vegas, Spearmint Rhino has the most customers and girls of any Sin City strip club. Don't be surprised to find it standing room only, especially on the weekends. This is a great spot for a bachelor party, and more than one celeb has been spotted in a VIP room. As in all strip clubs, Spearmint Rhino is hustle city—the girls are hustling, and the waitresses are hustling, but not in a pushy, turn-off way. It's located just off the Strip, on the north end. *24/7.* C≡ 3340 S. Highland Dr. (W. Desert Inn Rd.), 702-796-3600, spearmintrhino.com

Studio 54 • South Strip • Nightclub

Best Mega-Nightclubs Spinning such disco faves as "Ring My Bell," "Knock on Wood," and the anthem of jilted dancing queens everywhere, "I Will Survive," this reincarnation of Ian Schrager's paean to indulgence has shown that it, too, is stayin' alive. With its multiple dance floors, a funky lounge, disco Valkyries spinning on trapezes, and beautiful black-and-white photos of the glory days snapped by paparazzo Felice Quinto when the New York club was the ultimate celebrity playground, Studio 54 is the perfect blend of pop and techno music, industrial steel with luxe leather, catering to a 30- and 40-something crowd that still likes to have fun. But as the hour gets later, the crowd gets younger and the music gets harder. Tuesday is the hot night, and the line starts forming around 10pm. Keep your eyes peeled—pop gentry like Prince and the Go-Gos have stopped in unannounced for surprise performances. *Tue-Sat 10pm-dawn.* C≡ MGM Grand, 702-891-7254, mgmgrand.com

Tabú • South Strip • Ultra Lounge

Best Ultra Lounges MGM's new ultra lounge raises the bar so ultra high, others will need rocket boosters to catch it—it's that impressive. Meld Jeffrey Beers' architectural expertise with the special-effects artistry of Roger Parent, former art director for Cirque du Soleil, and the result is an interior that literally shifts and changes throughout the night. In the main cocktail area, provocative renderings of faces, eyes, lips, and stiletto-clad feet project onto the tables from above, and ripple and change when the table surface is touched. The Tantra Room, tucked off to one side, is an egg-shaped area with its own ice bar. And there's the VIP area, with its own bar, set off by a lattice wood wall. But really all of Tabù is VIP since every table is reservation and bottle service—with two-bottle minimums on busy nights. The bottle list is extensive and runs the gamut from Pernod to Herradura Seleccion Suprema to Hardy's Perfection. And surprisingly, from the door wranglers to the cocktail servers to the model-gorgeous bartenders clad in black bikini tops, all you'll get is splendidly courteous service. *Nightly 9pm-7am.* C≣ MGM Grand, 702-891-7129, mgmgrand.com

Tao Lounge* • Center Strip • Lounge
Get a taste of Tao without reserving a seat for dinner, or waiting in line late at night for the club. Tao everything is the hottest spot on the Strip, so you're just as likely to see the "it" crowd here getting drinks before the VIP lines open next door. The ambience is sultry Zen. It's open from early evening to late so there's really no excuse for not stopping by. If you want to soak up the scene without the crowds, come weekdays before 8pm. *Nightly 5pm-5am.* C≣ The Venetian, 702-388-8338, taolasvegas.com

Tao Nightclub • Center Strip • Nightclub
Best Nightclubs Tao Nightclub is worth the wait, and if you can wrangle a free VIP pass from a promoter in the lounge, you won't want to go anywhere else for the night. The dance floor is small, but there is plenty of plush seating for non-VIPs. Keep your eyes out for the bathing beauties: There are cement tubs filled with flowers and girls beneath the water fingering the flowers and looking at guests with suggestive glances. There are lots of rooms within Tao, and it's easy to get lost. But that could be a good thing. The bathrooms are see-through, until you're inside, and then they frost over. It's a decadent club—dress to impress. *Nightly 5pm-5am.* ≣ The Venetian, 702-388-8338, taolasvegas.com

Voodoo Lounge • West Flamingo • Bar/Lounge
Best Bars with a View Located high atop the Rio All-Suite Hotel and Casino—51 floors up to be exact—this dark arts–themed lounge, adorned with real voodoo talismans and fluorescent voodoo designs that glow in the blacklight, provides stellar views of Las Vegas from the Strip way out to the Valley. A sexy and wildly chic spot, Voodoo is at its best in the summer months when the party moves outside to the terrace. Expect a young, fun, mixed crowd here, drawing from the nearby Palms as well as locals and those looking for a break from the Strip. *Nightly 5pm-4am.* C≣ The Rio, 702-252-7777, harrahs.com

The Whiskey • Henderson • Bar/Lounge
Rande Gerber is behind this sleek, narrow lounge, designed by Michael Czysz, which features a dance floor at one end, a cozy VIP lounge area at the other, and an outdoor terrace opening to Whiskey Beach, where you'll find big mattress-covered daybeds. Since this is one of the few hip nightspots in Henderson, it's not unusual for locals to make the scene. Surprisingly, it's easy to get in. Better still, this is a great place to be a VIP, even if you're not a high roller or an A-lister. The relaxed VIP lounge has no bottle policy that requires you to purchase a $200-plus jug of booze before you can sit down. *Sun-Thu 5pm-2am, Fri-Sat 6pm-3am.* C≣ Green Valley Ranch Resort, 702-617-7777, midnightoilbars.com

Cool Las Vegas:
The Attractions

Agent Provocateur • Central Strip • Shop
The British design team behind Agent Provocateur's racy lingerie set out to break stuffy stereotypes about what proper English undergarments were. Today, its stores have grown to a global enterprise with a very loyal following. This is not lingerie for the Victoria's Secret masses. At AP you'll find gorgeous details like silk ribbons and fabric-covered buttons, along with a very knowledgeable staff that will fit you with the perfect purchase. *Sun-Thu 10am-11pm, Fri-Sat 10am-midnight.* Caesars Forum Shops, 702-696-7174, agentprovocateur.com

Art of Shaving • South Strip • Shop/Spa
Women aren't the only ones who like attention. Men like to get pampered, too. The Art of Shaving at Mandalay Place is one of the few salon spas on the Strip that caters specifically to men. In addition to buying high-end male grooming supplies, gentlemen can make reservations for barber service—the old-fashioned, straight-blade kind, from a beard trim to a "royal shave." And do make reservations—it can get crowded. Or head across the aisle to the Burger Bar for a brew and some sports while you wait. *Barber daily 9am-5:30pm; store 9am-11pm.* Mandalay Place, 702-632-9356, theartofshaving.com

Bear's Best • West Flamingo • Golf
Best Golf Courses Legendary golfer and course designer Jack Nicklaus (aka the Bear) made a lasting imprint on the game that goes far beyond his hall-of-fame career. The Bear's Best is simply that, an 18-hole compilation of his favorite holes from some of the most memorable golf courses in the world. Classic holes from Desert Mountain, Castle Pines, and Gleneagles in Scotland are re-created here down to a tee, including the 18th, which is patterned after the famously challenging 18th hole at PGA West. Mandatory caddies ensure your overall experience so that all you'll have to worry about is your swing. The clubhouse is a virtual museum of photos, plaques, and memorabilia from some of golf's greatest moments. The course is designed and operated to excel at hosting corporate tournaments, outings, and events of all sizes. The green fares range from $195 to $245. *Daily 6:30am-sunset.* $$$ 11111 W. Flamingo Rd. (Town Center), 702-804-8500, bearsbest.com

Caesars Palace Poker Room • Center Strip • Casino
Caesars Poker Room is one of the newest rooms on the Strip. Situated near the Sports Book in a ballroom, it has a large but private feel to it since it's away from the rest of the casino noise. It aims to be the home of daily tournament action, and has a separate tourney room adjoining the cash game tables. The players are a mix of poker fish with solid players of all ages woven in, and it has already held notable events like the NBC National Heads-Up event, a WSOP Circuit event, parties with Nicky Hilton, and poker bad boy Phil Helmuth's Fantasy Camp. *24/7.* Caesars Palace, 702-731-7110, caesars.com

Caesars Palace Sports Book • Center Strip • Casino

Best Sports Books This is the first choice among most sports fans looking to catch a game on the Strip. Its history makes it the granddaddy of sports books in Vegas, but its state-of-the-art entertainment system keeps it one of the cool kids on the block. Caesars has six 12-by-15-inch oversized screens, a 20-by-50-inch LED board, and 12 50-inch plasma screens throughout the Sports Book. There are 140 seats and a 12-inch flat screen at each of the tables. Build up your VIP status with Caesars well before the Super Bowl—it has the best party in town, but it's invite-only. *24/7.* Caesars Palace, 702-731-7110, caesars.com

Canyon Ranch SpaClub • Center Strip • Spa

Best Destination Spas Anyone with even a passing interest in spas has heard of at least one of the Canyon Ranch properties. They consistently rank high on best lists. This outpost at the Venetian will not disappoint those looking for the wellness icon's simple and straightforward take on relaxation. With its three-story rock-climbing wall just off the lobby and a lower-level fitness facility that can also be viewed from above, Canyon Ranch is also a destination for the active set. But it's the spa facilities in back that draw most of the savvy clients. Stone and wood elements combine in the wet rooms and treatment areas for a tranquil feel. Changing rooms in the women's area can be a bit cramped, but helpful attendants are on hand to provide all the necessities, from water to tea. *Daily 5:30am-10pm.* The Venetian, 702-414-3600, canyonranch.com

Fifty-Five Degrees Wine+Design • South Strip • Shop/Wine Tasting Bar

This sleek wine store, with its wood and stainless steel design, hails from the same team that did Aureole's wine tower. While it might not have as much impact as that endeavor, its 2,000-wine collection is sure to impress even the biggest wine snobs. If you're looking for a break while cruising the many boutiques of Mandalay Place, head to the back of the store, where there's an excellent wine bar with bottles all stored at that perfect 55 degrees. *Sun-Thu 10am-11pm, Fri-Sat 10am-midnight.* Mandalay Place, 702-632-9355, 55degreeslasvegas.com

The Forum Shops • Center Strip • Shops

This is the most dynamic collection of upscale shopping between Rodeo Drive and Madison Avenue, with more than 100 boutiques, including Louis Vuitton, Gucci, Versace, Escada, Bulgari, and Fred. Fanny-packing window-shoppers and fashionistas flood these high-fashion stores set in an ancient Roman atmosphere, which extends Caesars' theme with luxurious fountains, statues, and façades. Be anywhere but the Roman Great Hall at the top of the hour. That's when, starting at 10am and going strong until 11pm, the noisy (and hokey) production of the destruction of Atlantis plays out with animatronic action figures, fire, and smoke effects. *Sun-Thu 10am-11pm, Fri-Sat 10am-midnight.* Caesars Palace, 702-893-4800, forumshops.com

Guggenheim Hermitage Museum • Center Strip • Art Gallery

Made completely from specially aged Cor-Ten steel with rich maple floors and an undulating maple ceiling, this gallery looks exactly like a plain brown box wedged into the hotel's ornate Italianate façade. It was designed by Pritzker Prize–winning Dutch architect Rem Koolhaas to hold the Impressionist, Post-impressionist and Modernist gems by Cézanne, Picasso, Monet, Renoir—some rarely seen—from the Guggenheim, Hermitage, and Kunsthistorisches museums.

No doubt because of its steel walls, this gallery is one of the very few absolutely quiet places in the city—the perfect retreat when you need a break from the hum of the slot machines. Koolhaas developed some innovative architectural features for this space: Suspended walls make it seem as if the gallery is floating on air, and the interior walls rotate so the space can be reconfigured for different exhibits. An innovative system of heavy-duty magnets was designed to hang the masterworks on the steel walls. Take a look around the gift shop—it, like the gallery, was hewn from the hotel's former VIP lounge, and you can see the fancy Italianate moldings and chandeliers peeking through the gift shop's industrial corrugated plastic and steel décor. *Daily 9:30am-8:30pm.* $ The Venetian, 702-414-2440, venetian.com

Maverick Helicopter Tours • North Strip • Tour
The Maverick Company, well known in Las Vegas for its helicopter tours of the Las Vegas Strip, both in the day and at night, has kicked it up a notch. Now it does tours of the Grand Canyon combined with a Hummer rim tour. It also does tours of other canyons, like Bryce; golf tours that land you right on the greens; and a rafting tour that lets you get in a little white-water action. Those who have already ridden in a helicopter should ask about the new Eco Star. If you've been dying to travel like a VIP, this is the place to start. *Hours vary.* $$$ 6075 Las Vegas Blvd. (S. Russell Rd.), 702-261-0007, maverickhelicopter.com

MGM Grand Spa • South Strip • Spa
Best Destination Spas Vegas is hectic, but the MGM has gone to great lengths to make its spa a truly peaceful retreat. From its location in the back of the building, down a long hallway near the pools, to its Asian-inspired décor, MGM Grand Spa understands what its sophisticated clientele is after. While you'll find all the usual facilities, from a workout room to sauna and steam, it's the specialty treatments that have helped to build its reputation as one of the best spas in Vegas. The aboriginal-based Dreaming Ritual is such a popular treatment that the facility has introduced other location-themed rituals, including an Amazon one that starts with a scrub of plantain and cocoa powder, and also includes a body wrap using the South American herb una de gato, said to boost the immune system. Of course, there's also a massage in there. Note that this spa is only open to MGM Grand guests on the weekends. *Daily 6am-8pm.* MGM Grand, 702-891-3077, mgmgrand.com

Moorea Beach Club • South Strip • Pool
Set above the pool area at Mandalay Bay is the secluded Moorea Beach Club. It boasts a South Beach vibe and is best known as the luxurious spot where sunbathers can go topless. Guests lounge behind a frosted glass wall where beach patrons can't see in, but where the topless bathers can see out over the tropical 11-acre beach. It is available to all Mandalay Bay guests as well as those staying at the Four Seasons and THEhotel. Price of admission into Moorea Beach Club is $10 for females any day of the week, and $40 midweek and $50 weekends for males. Those looking for even more pampering can rent a Moorea Daybed or Opium Bed that has space for two or four lounge lizards ($200 to $300, call 702-632-9095). Note that this club is more a place to work on your tan than it is to play in the pool. $ *Mid-April–mid-Sept 8am-7pm; mid-Sept–late-Oct 9am-7pm; Nov 9am-5pm (closes Nov 19).* Mandalay Bay, 702-632-7777, mandalaybay.com

Richard Petty Driving Experience • North Las Vegas • Sport
Your hands are on the wheel, your foot is on the gas, and you're in the driver's seat around the track. At Richard Petty you can learn to drive like a NASCAR pro. You'll receive instruction on refining your driving line, building speed, and side-by-side driving at the Las Vegas Motor Speedway, located northeast of the city out near Nellis Air Force Base. Then they set you loose on the track. The Rookie Experience ($379) will buy you eight laps, and the King's package ($799) gives you 16 laps over a five-hour period. If you don't want to leave the driving to yourself, try a ride-along. $$$$ 6975 Speedway Blvd. Unit D-106 (Hwy. 15), 702-643-4343, 1800bepetty.com

Royal Links Golf Club • East Las Vegas • Golf
A tribute to the rich history and traditions of the game, the Royal Links, a par-72 course, reflects the spirit of play invented in the British Isles. Each of the holes on Royal Links was inspired by a different famous golf hole on a course where the British Open Championship was played. *Daily sunrise-sunset.* $$$ 5995 E. Vegas Valley Rd. (S. Sloan Ln.), 702-450-8123, waltersgolf.com

Shark Reef • South Strip • Aquarium
The coolest part about Shark Reef, the 90,560-square-foot aquarium with 1.6 million gallons of water and about 2,500 kinds of aquatic life (including 12 types of sharks), is the acrylic tunnel where you can watch schools of fish, sharks, rays and sea turtles swim right at you. Toward the end of this "walk-through" aquarium with a sunken temple and sunken ship theme is another gem—the jellyfish exhibit, where the tanks are backlit in brilliant colors so the jellyfish appear to glow. Especially popular with kids (and curious adults) are the supervised touch tanks, where they can pet hermit crabs, starfish, and even some small sharks. *Daily 10am-11pm.* $ Mandalay Bay, 702-632-7800, mandalaybay.com

Spa Mandalay • South Strip • Spa
This is a world-class 30,000-square-foot spa located on the lower level near the pool area. There are light earthy colors with four tiled hot tubs of varying temperatures in the women's spa. Spa Mandalay is known for interesting twists on the standard treatments. Try getting pampered with a Volcanic Dust Mask or pineapple-infused Fijian Sugar Polish. The environment here is much warmer and more relaxing than that of its über-modern counterpart across the property at THEbathhouse, and draws a crowd that knows its spas. Indulge in Roman-style baths, eucalyptus steam rooms, and beautiful mosaic whirlpools. There is a large fitness room down the hall, and the attendants can schedule you for one of the early-morning yoga classes. Whisk yourself away to the South Seas without leaving the Strip. *Daily 6am-8pm.* Mandalay Bay, 702-632-7220, mandalaybay.com

Taryn Rose • Central Strip • Shop
An orthopedic surgeon–turned–shoe guru, Taryn Rose began her personal reinvention with a Beverly Hills boutique in 1998. Her goal was to create fabulous shoes that were also easy on the feet. She succeeded. Year after year, Rose comes out with a chic, stylish collection that's as glamorous as it is comfortable. That has won her a strong Hollywood following, with many a leading lady heading down the red carpet in Rose creations. *Sun-Thu 10am-11pm, Fri-Sat 10am-midnight.* Caesars Forum Shops, 702-732-2712, tarynrose.com

Bachelor(ette) Las Vegas

Maybe you've heard—what happens in Vegas, stays in Vegas, except for certain STDs. But don't let that stop you from going wild. Whether you're a Glitter Gulch virgin or a dirty old regular, this is the town of fantasies. Always dreamed of being an international playboy? Rent a suite and pretend! Want to be a high roller? Max out the credit card and have a seat at baccarat. Whether it's ODing on flesh, booze, and questionable behavior, or a weekend of romance and maybe even a wedding, Vegas wants to please you, for a price. And it won't kiss and tell.

Note: Venues in bold are described in detail in the listings that follow the itinerary. Venues followed by an asterisk (*) are those we recommend as both a restaurant and a destination bar.

Bachelor(ette) Las Vegas:
The Perfect Plan (3 Nights and Days)

Perfect Plan Highlights

Friday
Afternoon	**Palms pool**
Cocktails	**Garduño's*, Little Buddha***, *Sirens*
Dinner	**Garduño's*, Little Buddha*, STACK**
Nighttime	*Chippendales, Thunder From Down Under*, **Olympic Gardens**, *Mystère*, **Jet**
Late-Night	**Rain, California Pizza Kitchen, Empire**

Saturday
Morning	**Valley of Fire, Reflection Bay, Desert Passage, Grand Canal Shoppes**
Lunch	**Pink Taco, Grand Lux Café**
Afternoon	**Spa, gambling**
Cocktails	**Manhattan Express, Diego*, Centrifuge Bar**
Dinner	**Diego*, Fiamma**
Nighttime	**Diego*, KRAVE, Coyote**
Late-Night	**Palomino Club, Risqué Alesium after-hours**

Sunday
Brunch	**House of Blues***
Morning	**King Tut, Obelisk, Flyaway Skydiving, Gun Store**
Afternoon	**Rehab at Hard Rock**
Cocktails	**Center Bar**
Dinner	**Simon, AJ's Steakhouse*, Shanghai Lilly's**
Nighttime	**The Joint, Hard Rock Casino, rumjungle**
Late-Night	**Body English, Drai's*, Mr. Lucky's 24/7**

Hotel: Palms (Fantasy Tower)

Friday

3pm Put on your suit, grab a cocktail, and swim up to the blackjack tables at the **Palms Casino Resort pool**. This very happening two-acre complex draws in some of Sin City's hottest bodies for long afternoons of summer fun, with private cabanas, massages, and lots of people-watching.

7:30pm **Garduño's/Blue Agave Cafe*** is a great spot to warm up for the night with a margarita or two. Or go to nearby **Little Buddha*** for a sleek cocktail with a stylish crowd. If you're looking for a bit of campy fun to help wash down your drinks, head to the *Sirens of TI* show at Treasure Island (at 7 or 8:30pm), where you can watch the pirate drama unfold from the comfort of the **Battle Bar.**

8:30pm **Garduño's/Blue Agave Cafe*** has more than great tequila. This is also a fun spot for tasty Mexican food. The same holds true for **Little Buddha***, where the scene gets more stylish with every passing hour, and the Asian fusion food will delight. But if you're looking to bring home brag-worthy stories of hot new restaurants, **STACK**, the hip carnivore's haven at the Mirage, and the sleek Chinese **Fin** under the same roof are immensely popular—and fun.

10:30pm If you're looking for Mr. Right Now, *Chippendales* is about to start, as is *Thunder From Down Under*—two of Vegas' steamiest male revues. Since we don't want to discriminate, men can watch the ladies take it off at **Olympic Gardens**. For a less risqué adventure, head to Cirque du Soleil's *Mystère* to be wowed by the troupe's amazing acrobatics. If you've been sitting too long, hit the dance floor at **Jet**, the hip nightclub at The Mirage.

12:30am Just can't get enough of the club scene? **Rain** is another "place to be." These doors don't close until well into the dawn.

3:30am Refuel with a bite to eat at **California Pizza Kitchen**, where you'll be in the company of California kids who know and love the pies and salads from this popular chain. If you've still got plenty of energy to burn, then **Empire Ballroom** is the ultimate Vegas after-hours scene. This stand-alone venue is one of the few non-casino hot spots, but it's definitely worth the cab ride for the sexy, teasing crowd.

Saturday

8am Time to get dirty. You're heading out to the Valley of Fire with **Adventure Las Vegas**. The dramatic red stone formations of the desert will make you feel like you've landed on Mars. But this is no see-it-from-a-bus-window affair. No—you're in command of your own ATV, racing through the back roads of this amazing wilderness. Not up to driving your own three-wheeler? You can also go by Jeep. You could also get your tee time at **Reflection Bay Golf Club**, the premier public course in town. Or, if fashion is more interesting than a 4-iron, wander the **Desert Passage** shops, where you'll find unusual jewelry made of antique coins at Ancient Creations, and luxurious skin-care products at Yves Chantre. If your bags aren't full, head down the block to the **Grand Canal Shoppes**, where gondoliers will serenade you as you stroll by the waterways.

1pm Lunch Make your way back to town and into **Pink Taco** at the Hard Rock for some creative Mexican food and maybe a margarita or two. Or check out the **Grand Lux Café** for big plates of classic favorites, buzzing crowds, and casino people-watching.

2:30pm Get beautiful for a night out on the town at the **Spa at the Palms**, where you can indulge in a Party Prep Facial. For the ultimate spa experience, though, head to **Paris Spa by Mandara**, where the Asian-inspired treatments will melt your muscles. Of course, this is Vegas, so if you'd rather get your adrenaline pumping, hit the tables at Palms and see if Lady Luck is with you.

6pm Make your way father down the Strip, check out The Bellagio Fountains, then ride the **Manhattan Express** roller coaster for a quick thrill.

7pm For fun over formality, you can't beat **Diego***. Tequila master Julio Bermejo serves only 100 percent blue agave and mescals in his creative margaritas. Or catch some sports and a drink at the **Centrifuge Bar**, also in MGM, where the male and female bartenders hop up and dance on the bar every half hour.

8pm Dinner Stick around at **Diego*** for delicious, creative Mexican dishes. For something a little more formal—and very romantic—head to **Fiamma Trattoria**, a low-key gem with unforgettable Italian food.

10:30pm You could just stay at **Diego***, where a DJ takes over after dinner and spins Latin beats for a fun crowd. But there's also **KRAVE**, a gay club on the Strip that draws a rowdy, mixed group to its giant dance floor. For a wild time, stop by the **Bar at Times Square** to help the dueling piano players, or head into **Coyote Ugly**. Yes, it's just like the movie, with bras on the walls and ladies welcome to join the female staff dancing on the bar. Somewhat surprisingly, there are as many women here as men.

12:30am Check out **Palomino Club**, where a grandfather clause in the local law allows for full nudity and a full bar. Call the club and it will send a car to pick you up. **Risqué** at Paris lives up to its name with its dance and lounge scene.

3am The party is just starting at **Alesium after-hours**. This late-late-night venue has a packed dance floor until well into the breakfast hours.

Sunday

11am Need sustenance? Head over to the **House of Blues*** for its Gospel Sunday Brunch. It's divine, for both your soul and your stomach.

12:30pm Keep heading south down the Strip to The Luxor, where you'll find a surprisingly good replica of **King Tut's Tomb and Museum**. Take a peek at the boy king's treasures, then get your blood pumping with a spin on **In Search of the Obelisk**, a not-too-terrifying thrill ride.

2pm Are you ready to kick things up a notch? Get yourself over to **Flyaway Indoor Skydiving** and get up to speeds of 120 mph. Training only takes 20 minutes, and then you can launch yourself over a jet propeller blade that has you weaving and bouncing in the air. Or play out your *Godfather* fantasies with a rented machine gun at the **Gun Store**.

No joke—this is one of the only spots in the United States where you can try out heavy-duty weapons on a firing range, no experience required.

3pm You've earned a little R&R. The Hard Rock serves up sultry, relaxing fun in the sun at the **Rehab pool party**, a Sundays-only, don't-miss event.

7pm Head down to the heart of Hard Rock's action at the **Center Bar**, literally smack in the middle of the casino. While you get your sip on, check out the scene as it begins to simmer—from the leather-clad cocktail waitresses to the crowds at the tables.

8:30pm Dinner **Simon Kitchen and Bar** is a fun, casual spot for dinner in The Hard Rock—and a favorite of the bands playing at The Joint. For an old-school, martini-and-steak time, check out **AJ's Steakhouse***. On the south end of the Strip at Mandalay Bay, you'll also find **Shanghai Lilly's**, where Chinese seafood is served in an elegant, dramatic setting.

10:30pm If live music is your style, see who is playing at the **Joint**, The Hard Rock's very rocking venue, which draws bands from Korn to Cheap Trick. Shows can start earlier here, so rock first, then eat if that's your choice. Trying your luck at the tables of the **Hard Rock Casino** is another

great option, and you're sure to find all sorts of action. For dancing, get yourself to **rumjungle**, where there's always a sexy young crowd grooving on the dance floor.

12:30am You can't call it a Vegas vacation without a night at **Body English**. Head through the nondescript door, down the staircase, and into Sin City's reigning nightclub. This is one of the best parties in Vegas, with some of the steamiest action in town.

3:30am **Drai's*** is your after-hours spot—though it's hard to believe it's in the Barbary Coast. Never mind the locale. We promise the crowd inside is hot.

5:30am Late-night (or early morning) dining is best done at **Mr. Lucky's 24/7**, where the clientele is as sleek as the food is good. Slide into a tiger-print booth and let the miniskirted waitresses bring you breakfast.

Bachelor(ette) Las Vegas: The Key Neighborhoods

Center Strip The area between Harmon and Spring Mountain Roads is the center of the action in Vegas, and you'll find lively crowds at all hours of the day and night. The Four Corners, where Las Vegas Boulevard intersects with Flamingo Road, is home to The Bellagio, Caesars Palace, Paris/Bally's, Flamingo, and Barbary Coast. Just south is The Aladdin/Planet Hollywood.

East Flamingo East of the Strip is where you'll find The Hard Rock, one of the epicenters of cool in Vegas.

North Strip Wynn holds court here, with The Stratosphere a bit farther down near older hotels like the Stardust and the New Frontier, making it a quieter stretch than the central or south end of the boulevard.

South Strip Mandalay Bay is the soul of the south Strip, but you'll also find Excalibur, the emerald-green MGM, The Luxor, the Four Seasons, THEhotel at Mandalay Bay, New York-New York, and Monte Carlo—and fun crowds wandering among them.

Summerlin This "master" planned community, 12 miles west of the Strip, is home to the Red Rock Casino, and is a wealthy, somewhat quiet residential suburb.

West Flamingo Head west of the Strip and there's probably only one place you're going: Palms, the epicenter of Bachelor(ette) Vegas. The area outside the casino doesn't hold too much for tourists, so cabbing it to the Strip happens often.

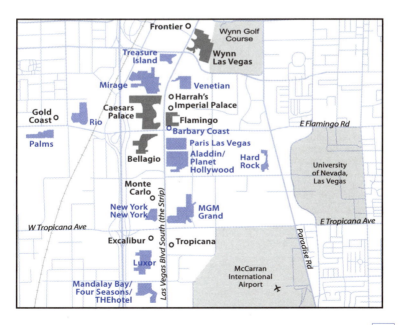

Bachelor(ette) Las Vegas:
The Shopping Blocks

Desert Passage

Spanning four areas with names like Moroccan Gate and the Lost City, and boasting an indoor thunderstorm, Desert Passage is as much spectacle as shopping. *Sun-Thu 10am-11pm, Fri-Sat 10am-midnight.* 3667 S. Las Vegas Blvd., 702-866-0710, desertpassage.com

Ancient Creations Interesting jewelry and accessories made from old Greek and Roman coins, among other items. 702-938-6755, ancientcreations.com

Houdini's Magic Shop Pens that shock, fake cigarette burns, tips on how to make coins disappear. Everything you need to become the next Copperfield. 702-314-4674, houdini.com

Showcase Slots Can't get enough of that *I Dream of Jeannie* slot machine? Take one home. 702-733-6464, showcaseslots.com

TeNo Titanium watches, steel jewelry, avant-garde sensibility. 702-735-8366, teno.com

Yves Chantre French line of skin-care products and perfumes, known for its hibiscus and ginger scents. Très chic. 702-732-8138, yveschantre.com

Las Vegas Premium Outlets

Outlet malls are notoriously careless with our feelings, one day offering up half-price treasures, and the next leaving us picking fruitlessly through mounds of rejects. Las Vegas Premium Outlets is no different from the rest, but still, we can't resist this downtown spot with some unusual offerings. *Mon-Sat 10am-9pm, Sun 10am-8pm.* 875 S. Grand Central Pkwy., 702-474-7500, premiumoutlets.com

Bose You'll find stereos, speakers, and high-quality electronics from a brand not often found in outlets. 702-384-4067, bose.com

L'Occitane Stock up on scrumptious lotions, candles, and beauty products with divine scents. 702-384-3842, loccitane.com

Puma This is the place to go to pick up the sneakers of choice for hipsters. 702-366-9921, puma.com

Theory You'll find tailored women's clothing, from stovepipe pants to straight skirts. 702-386-5022, theory.com

Wolford This boutique specializes in undergarments and hosiery from one of the best. 702-387-9626, wolford.com

Bachelor(ette) Las Vegas:
The Hotels

The Hard Rock Hotel & Casino • East Flamingo • Modern (644 rms)
Best Celebrity-Spotting Hotels Feel like you've wandered onto the set of *Swingers*? You're definitely at The Hard Rock. Owner Peter Morton loves his rock-'n'-roll, and his passion is reflected throughout the hotel. Lighting fixtures are Zildjian cymbals; elevators are inscribed with snarky musicians' quotes; chandeliers are fashioned from saxophones; gaming tables have faux piano keyboards on the ends; the pools have an underwater sound system so you don't miss a beat; and the rooms and hallways are hung with fabulous photos of rock artists. It's a mecca for cool that, even a few blocks removed from the Strip, manages to be the heart and soul of the Las Vegas party scene, especially for L.A. hipsters. Guys here (and oddly there does seem to be a disproportionate number of guys) sport perfectly gelled hair and tinted glasses; gals strut around in backless halters and enticing low riders. Ask for a Strip-view room to keep your eye on the action. The Hard Rock runs two shuttles to various locales on the Strip (and back) on the hour and half hour until 9:30pm. $$$ 4455 Paradise Rd. (Harmon Ave.), 702-693-5000 / 800-693-7625, hardrockhotel.com

Luxor • South Strip • Theme (4,473 rms)
The Luxor's Sphinx-guarded, towering black pyramid is one of the city's most recognizable icons. But like Caesars, Luxor, part of the Mandalay Bay Resort Group, has toned down its kitschier elements in recent years. During its last renovation, management hired Egyptologists to ensure accuracy in its reconstruction of the artifacts, hieroglyphics, carvings, and murals that adorn the hotel and the King Tut's Tomb and Museum. The result is a classy hotel that's a history lesson as well as a playground. Guests enter through a dramatic porte cochere carved into the Sphinx's belly, and the lobby is a re-creation of the temple of Abu Simbel, built by Ramses II. While the tower rooms are bigger, without question the pyramid rooms are far cooler (though they only have showers—no baths, except for Jacuzzi suites). To get to them, you take "inclinators," which glide up and down the pyramid at a 39-degree angle. At 30 stories high with a nine-acre footprint, the pyramid is a quarter-scale reproduction of the great pyramid at Giza, albeit one covered in ebony glass with flashing lights illuminating its edges, and that famous space beam shooting up from the top. $$ 3900 S. Las Vegas Blvd. (Tropicana Ave.), 702-262-4000 / 888-777-0188, luxor.com

The Mirage • Center Strip • Contemporary (3,039 rms)
This resort marks the end of one Vegas era and the beginning of modern days. The brainchild of visionary hotelier Steve Wynn, Mirage, built in 1989, has the now ubiquitous Y-shape hotel design, animal attractions, and splashy effects that put Vegas on the map as a destination for more than just gambling and cheap buffets. Twelve years later, the Polynesian rain forest–themed Mirage (a grand old dame by Las Vegas standards) can still hold its own. All the grandeur remains, including the volcano, which blasts smoke and flames into the sky every 15 minutes starting at dusk. Mirage renovated its standard and deluxe rooms in 2002, but they are still fairly ordinary. All have a cupola over the bed and slats on the doors, nicely

extending the island theme. There's no cable, although there are movies on demand. Great views from your room can be guaranteed for an additional $20 a day. Opt for "volcano view," which will give you a good shot of the Strip and the eruptions. The pool area is one of the nicest—an island oasis of meandering lagoons, waterfalls, towering palm trees, Asian statuary, and private cabanas. Set back from the action is Siegfried & Roy's Secret Garden and the Dolphin Habitat, home to nine Atlantic bottlenose dolphins, including a few babies born on the property. The casino has a legendary smoke-free poker room, which draws pros and semi-pros alike. Sunday through Thursday there are Poker Zone Tournaments starting at 7pm, which feature a wide variety of games. $$ 3400 S. Las Vegas Blvd. (Buccaneer Blvd.), 702-791-7111 / 800-374-9000, mirage.com

Palms Casino Resort • West Flamingo • Trendy (606 rms)

Best Celebrity-Spotting Hotels Redefining hip, Palms attracts celebrities from Tara Reid and Lara Flynn Boyle to Jamie Foxx and the 'N Sync boys. All of them come for its MTV-cool cachet and ultra-modern hangouts. The rooms are not large, but all have views of either the north or south strip and are furnished with the same beds found at the Four Seasons (made up with Frette linens to boot—something you don't often find in Vegas, and certainly not for this price). And considering that management is targeting a youthful demographic (at least in spirit if not always in age), stocking the room with Neutrogena bath products is very thoughtful. If you're taller than the average tourist, several suites come with beds and showers fit (literally) for an NBA basketball player. That's because the Maloof brothers, who own Palms, also own the Sacramento Kings basketball team. It also means that you can't bet on any NBA games in the race and sports book. But that's a small price to pay for beds that are 7 1/2 feet long and showers that are 6 1/2 feet high. The real draw, though, is the hipster vibe with hot clubs, popular weekly pool parties, and buzzing restaurants. Make sure you book a superior guest room in the new Tower—it rewards with a sleeker look, better amenities (such as Bose sound systems and Jacuzzi tubs), and high-rolling neighbors inhabiting the suites. $$$ 4321 W. Flamingo Rd. (Arville St.), 702-942-7777 / 866-942-7777, palms.com

Paris Las Vegas • Central Strip • Theme (2,916 rms)

The most Epcot-like of all the theme hotels, Paris Las Vegas is also the one that best carries through on the fantasy, with gorgeous reproductions of famous Paris landmarks like the Arc de Triomphe and Place de la Concorde fountain, façades of the Louvre, L'Hotel de Ville, and Paris Opera, and the giant balloon commemorating the Montgolfier brothers' first hot-air balloon flight. There are even street performers along the Boulevard, where you can get authentic French pastries and chocolates from Lenotre, Paris' top patisserie. The Paris theme never slips—even upstairs. Modeled after the famous 800-year-old L'Hotel de Ville, rooms are très magnifique, decorated in pseudo–French Regency style with crown moldings and wainscoting, stately armoires in place of closets, marble vanities and European fixtures in the bathrooms, as well as separate soaking tubs. But be warned, some are starting to say they are looking a little worn around the edges. However, ask for a room with a view of the Bellagio lake, and you may not even notice. Or inquire about upgrading to the elegant Lyons suite, which has a great canopied sleigh bed, an expansive living room with period furniture, a wet bar, and an extra half-bath. If it's available, it's possible to upgrade for a reasonable amount. $$ 3655 S. Las Vegas Blvd. (Flamingo Rd.), 702-946-7000 / 888-796-2096, parislasvegas.com

Bachelor(ette) Las Vegas:
The Restaurants

Ah Sin! • Center Strip • Asian Fusion
There are few al fresco dining spots right on the Strip and this is one of them. Located at Paris nearly beneath the Eiffel Tower and looking across the street at the Bellagio Fountains, Ah Sin! is a casual place to meet for dinner. It serves a wide variety of Pan-Asian cuisine, including Korean barbecue, Chinese noodles, Japanese sushi, dim sum, satay, and sashimi. And as you'd expect from Vegas, there's even a unique hand-washing ceremony before your meal with jasmine-scented water. If you're looking for the view, but aren't in the mood for the heavy French food that you'd get next door at Mon Ami Gabi, Ah Sin! is right for you. Make sure you hold out for a patio table. *Daily 11am-midnight.* $$$ B≡ Paris Las Vegas, 702-946-4593, parislasvegas.com

AJ's Steakhouse* • East Flamingo • Steakhouse
This '50s-style steakhouse, hung with super-realist paintings of the legendary Algiers, Sahara, and Flamingo motels, pays homage to Hard Rock owner Peter Morton's father, Arnie—creator of the original Morton's steakhouse—and evokes a time when men ate thick meat, smoked cigars, and drank whiskey without giving a prosciutto-wrapped fig about their arteries. In a town of excellent steakhouses, AJ's offers up all the classics, from iceberg lettuce topped with blue cheese, shrimp cocktail, and Caesar salad, to traditional bone-in rib eye, New York strip and porterhouse steaks, and even Maine lobster. Being at the Hard Rock, the crowd is young and hip. If nothing else, stop in for a drink at the clubby martini bar, complete with baby grand piano. *Tue-Thu 6-10pm, Fri-Sat 6-11pm.* $$$$ B≡ Hard Rock, 702-693-5500, hardrockhotel.com

California Pizza Kitchen • Center Strip • American
Best All-Night Eats This famed thin-crust pizza and chopped-salad joint has become comfort food for many West Coasters, and is a great place to nosh at all hours of the night. Its signature dish is the Original BBQ Chicken pizza, but you can have "normal" pizza toppings as well as duck, Jamaican jerk chicken, carne asada, or the kind of fixings you'd use to make a club sandwich. What sets this restaurant apart from other CPKs is that it's all Vegas, baby. This branch is near the front of The Mirage right next to the Race and Sports Book and close to the poker room. Stop by before or after you win big. *Sun-Thu 11am-midnight, Fri-Sat 11am-2am.* $ B≡ Mirage, 702-791-7357, cpk.com

Chinois • Center Strip • Chinese
This Wolfgang Puck outpost serves traditional Cantonese-inspired dishes like barbecued pork ribs, duck, and wok-fried lobster to a mixed crowd shopping and wandering Caesars Forum Shops. The bi-level restaurant is decorated in a yin and yang motif with rare artifacts from around the world restaurant as well as a Zen-like rock garden and water fountain. There's also a sushi bar, a private dining room, and banquet facilities. It attracts a mainstream, mostly casual crowd looking for an easy meal. *Sun-Thu 11am-10pm, Fri-Sat 11am-11pm.* $$$ B≡ Caesars Palace, 702-737-9700, wolfgangpuck.com

Diego* • South Strip • Mexican
Best Mexican Restaurants If you're craving a good mole, but don't want to lose the hip, fun vibe of Vegas, Diego is your spot. From the moment you walk into the vibrant red and pink room with its long bar and friendly servers, you'll know this isn't your typical taco stand. Diego chef Christopher Palmeri has created a menu of south-of-the-border tapas made for sharing—with guacamole mashed right at your table a constant favorite. Of course, there are dozens of tequilas, and even more variations on margaritas, which bring in a lively crowd looking for a casual bite to eat. On Friday and Saturday after the restaurant closes, Diego brings in a DJ to spin Latin beats for a dance party called Vida. *Nightly 5:30-10pm.* $$ ▣ MGM Grand, 702-891-3200, mgmgrand.com

Fadó Irish Pub and Restaurant* • Henderson • Irish
Made to spec in Ireland by the Irish Pub Company, then shipped to Green Valley Ranch, this Victorian-style pub, with its stained glass, dark cherry wood, and bric-a-brac culled from estate sales in Ireland, is one of ten Fadó pubs that have sprung up across the United States since 1997. Fun fact: The Frank J. Kenny & Co. Distillery mirrored sign is not really an antique, but an inside joke—it was made specifically for one of the pub's corporate owners. Take a table in one of the cozy alcoves, known as snugs, which were originally created at the turn of the last century so that women, children, and priests could enjoy the pub's convivial atmosphere while being shielded from its rowdier aspects. Order up a few pints of Guinness or some Midleton Irish whiskey and tuck into one of the signature boxtys, a traditional dish common to rural Ireland that consists of a potato pancake rolled and stuffed with a filling of grilled vegetables, chicken, and andouille sausage or seafood. There's live music five days a week (traditional Irish, punk, Celtic rock, and Irish punk). *Daily 11am-2am.* $$ ▣ Green Valley Ranch, 702-407-8691, fadoirishpub.com

Fiamma Trattoria • South Strip • Italian
Fiamma is a dimly lit, sleek, and sexy Italian trattoria in the middle of restaurant row at MGM Grand that's a hidden gem for those in the know—including locals and Vegas regulars who don't need to see and be seen. Most foodies rush to the MGM to try celebrity chefs Joël Robuchon, Michael Mina, Emeril Lagasse, and Tom Colicchio, but they'll miss one of the best meals in town if they walk past Fiamma. Celebrities who want to be seen will enjoy a table that opens up to the studio walk. Chef Carlos Buscaglia has created some unforgettable dishes, including the Polipo, a citrus-grilled octopus; the raviolini; and a braised short rib–filled ravioli. If truffles are in season, you're in for a treat. Impressive sommelier Elias Notus has a story behind his favorite bottles of wine. The atmosphere is romantic and the acoustics in the dining room allow for an evening of intimacy even if the room is full. There is a full-service bar and a modern fireplace lounge in the back for those who don't want to stay for a full meal. This is a terrific place to take a date. *Sun-Thu 5:30-10pm, Fri-Sat 5:30-11pm.* $$$$ ⃞⃝⃠ MGM Grand, 702-891-7600, mgmgrand.com

Fin • Center Strip • Asian Fusion
Fin, an awaited addition to the evolving Mirage, is a refined spot in an intimate glass setting with gold and jade accents—not at all your typical Chinese restaurant. The sleek décor is done in muted colors with touches like strands of hanging crystal bulbs and fine china on the tables. Chef Chi Choi is known to be a

master with a Hong Kong–style wok and features fresh seafood prepared steamed, baked, or wok-fried. Step into the chrysanthemum-shaped dining room and try one of his signature dishes such as imperial Peking duck, wok-fried beef tenderloin, lobster tail with XO sauce, and pork belly Taiwanese-style. High rollers will be pleased to find braised whole Japanese abalone on the menu. Fin is open for both lunch and dinner, and dim sum is available Friday, Saturday, and Sunday. Dress is casual, but the elegant surrounds will make you feel grubby if you don't upgrade from the flip-flops. *Daily 11am-2:30pm, 5-11pm.* $$ ▣ The Mirage, 702-791-7353, mirage.com

Gallagher's Steakhouse • Center Strip • Steakhouse

A New York original (since 1927), this sports-themed spot is famous for dry-aged steaks. Outside there's a massive meat locker, inside there's a dark polished wood bar, brass accents, and loads of vintage horse racing and baseball photos on the walls—making it a great spot for groups of guys looking to get ready for a Vegas night out. Its location in New York-New York, however, means it's off the trend radar, and draws guests mostly from inside the hotel. Menu highlights include the surf and turf, a Brazilian lobster tail (slightly spicier than Maine lobster) with a petite filet, along with some garlic mashed potatoes. *Sun-Thu 4-11pm, Fri-Sat 4pm-midnight.* $$$$ B▣ New York-New York, 702-740-6450, gallaghersnysteakhouse.com

Garduño's/Blue Agave Oyster and Chili Bar* • West Flamingo • Mexican

This cantina with its gorgeous poolside patio is known for cooking only with chilies from Hatch, New Mexico. It's snared best Mexican honors many times over from *Las Vegas Life* and the *Review-Journal*. Being at the Palms, its scene is almost as hot as its peppers, with hipsters in search of tequila covering every space, especially on warm summer days when the patio is the prime place for a taco or two. Start with margaritas and some raw or pan-fried oysters at the Blue Agave and be sure to leave room for Garduño's warm, fried pillowy sweetbreads liberally dunked in honey. *Sun-Thu 10:30am-10pm, Fri-Sat 10:30am-11pm.* $$ ▣ Palms, 702-942-7777, palms.com

Grand Lux Café • Center Strip • Continental

Best All-Night Eats There's nothing Denny's about this round-the-clock coffee shop that absolutely lives up to its name in every way—totally luxe and adorned in very grand style with gorgeous backlit glass, tiled floors, and big roomy booths that overlook the casino. "This is a coffee shop?" you'll find yourself musing. Why, yes it is, because it's owned by the Cheesecake Factory, so expect classic American fare served up in monster portions. But be warned—its location right off the casino means it gets a mix of every type of tourist in Vegas. This is a place for a good, easy bite to eat, not the place to come for the scene. *24/7.* $ B▣ Venetian, 702-414-3888, grandluxcafe.com

House of Blues* • South Strip • Cajun

Upstairs from the popular concert venue–cum-nightclub is a down-on-the-bayou eatery known for its authentic Creole and Cajun dishes like Tennessee baby back ribs, jambalaya, andouille sausage po' boys, étouffée, catfish filets, and lip-smacking sides like cornbread, mashed sweet potatoes, and turnip greens. After eating dinner at the restaurant, head downstairs to continue the fun, or if you can score a pass, upstairs to the exclusive members-only Foundation Room. Note: The public can crash this club on Mondays after 11pm. Don't miss the raise-the-roof Sunday Gospel Brunch with live music and endless buffet. *Sun-Thu 7:30am-midnight, Fri-Sat 7:30am-1am; gospel brunch: Sun 10am and 1pm; live music: Wed-Sun 9pm-3am.* $$$ ≣ Mandalay Bay, 702-632-7600, hob.com

Kokomo's • Center Strip • Continental

It's all tropical romance in this seafood and steakhouse tucked inside The Mirage. The large space is designed to look like a rain forest, complete with running waterfalls. Columns are decorated with blinking lights meant to resemble fireflies, and little silver fish swim across the ceiling. The food here, by chef Russ Hurry, is as tempting as the atmosphere. Huge, juicy steaks are served up with down-home sides like mashed sweet potatoes and spinach au gratin, and seafood dishes—mainly lobster and crab—are fresh and done to perfection. The lobster bisque is considered one of the best in the city. It's a mixed-ages crowd here of those attending shows at the Mirage, hotel guests, and couples seeking an intimate meal. The best tables are those along the rail by the waterfalls, for the full experience—although the running water can be a bit loud. *Nightly 5-10:30pm.* $$$ B≣ The Mirage, 702-791-7350, mirage.com

La Creperie • Center Strip • French

For breakfast, lunch, or a late-night snack, a crepe on the cobblestoned Le Boulevard at Paris Las Vegas is a magnificent treat. When the pomp and circumstance of the large cafes, all-you-can-eat buffets, and overpriced room service has gotten to you, step into Vegas' mini City of Light. Several standouts are the classic Suzette; peanut butter and banana crepe; and a seafood crepe with Gruyère cheese, baby shrimp, and scallops. You can grab a cup of joe here, too. Avoid late-breakfast and prime lunch hours to get away from long lines. *Mon-Thu 7am-11pm, Fri-Sat 7am-midnight.* $⊡ Paris Las Vegas, 702-946-7147, parislasvegas.com

Le Village Buffet • Center Strip • Buffet

Helmed by chef Christophe Doumergue, the buffet, a favorite with locals, features made-to-order dishes from the Brittany, Alsace, Burgundy, and Normandy regions, such as crepes, tilapia filet, veal stew, chicken mushroom vol-au-vent, grilled Alsatian sausage, and assorted French cheeses and pastries. On warm days, the outdoor patio is the place to be, but on cold desert mornings, the indoor fireplace draws the biggest crowd. On Sundays, there's a champagne brunch. *Daily 7am-10pm.* $$≣ Paris Las Vegas, 702-946-7000, parislasvegas.com

Little Buddha* • West Flamingo • Asian Fusion

Chinese meets Pacific Rim meets French in this spacious nouveau Asian restaurant with three dining rooms, a sushi bar, and what has to be the only cocktail bar in town with a river running through it. Under the benevolent gaze of two enormous Buddhas, diners, tucked into deep, cozy booths, sup on sushi and sashimi or other classic dishes, like Mongolian beef, spicy Szechuan shrimp, and orange chicken. Expect a crowd as chic as the food. *Sun-Thu 5:30-11pm, Fri-Sat 5:30pm-midnight.* $$$≣ Palms, 702-942-7778, littlebuddhalasvegas.com

Mr. Lucky's 24/7 • East Flamingo • American

Best All-Night Eats This is where hipsters come to end the night. One of the coolest coffee shops in town and a favorite of both locals and visiting celebs, Mr. Lucky's is like your favorite all-night diner, only sexier, and is adorned with concert posters and the occasional piece of real-life Vegas history, like the weathered sign for the old Ali Baba Motel. The hottie waitresses in the short black skirts will happily show you to a tiger-print booth where you can tuck into hearty plates of eggs, burgers, pastas, and salads. For events like the National Rodeo Finals, Mr. Lucky's adds specials like Western-style chicken and ribs. However, the one constant that's never on the menu is the surf-and-turf special. Ask, and the steak and shrimp combo, with potato, salad, and a roll, is all yours. *24/7*. $ ▤ The Hard Rock, 702-693-5000, hardrockhotel.com

Pharaoh's Pheast Buffet • South Strip • Buffet

Pharaoh's Pheast is your typical buffet in a not-so-typical atmosphere—it's done up like an archaeological dig, complete with sand, shovels, ropes and pulleys, and wood beams to hold it up. Even the servers are decked out in khaki dig garb. Don't stumble over the artifacts as you make your rounds of the Mexican, Italian, and Asian food stations. *Mon-Fri 7am-2:30pm, 4-10pm, Sat-Sun 7am-10pm*. $$ ▤ Luxor, 702-262-4000, luxor.com

Pink Taco* • East Flamingo • Mexican

Pink Taco is one of the more casual eateries at The Hard Rock. It is a hip taqueria with a tequila and margarita bar in the center. The atmosphere is festive, and it's open late for those catching a rock show at the Joint. The actual "Pink Taco," also called a Panucho, is a corn tortilla stuffed with beans and topped with grilled chicken, salsa roja, pickled onions, and avocado. This hot spot also serves traditional Mexican fare with a bit of a California spin. In fact, the menu is so creative that you'll find baby-back ribs on the same page as a carnitas platter. *Sun-Thu 11:30am-10pm, Fri-Sat 11:30am-midnight*. $ ▤ The Hard Rock, 702-693-5525, pinktaco.com

Samba Brazilian Steakhouse • Center Strip • Brazilian

This is a meat-lover's nirvana. Located right in the heart of The Mirage casino, this wildly colorful Brazilian rodizio joint features all manner of grilled meats, vegetables, poultry, and seafood, from bacon-wrapped turkey to slow-roasted pork. Sample a bit of everything with the Rodizio Experience, an all-you-can-eat parade of skewered, flame-cooked delicacies that are brought your table as they come off the grill. The servers will keep bringing the barbecued sausage, Hawaiian chicken, sirloin, salmon, ribs, flank steak, and pork until you say uncle (or turn up the red card on your table). *Nightly 5-10pm*. $$$ ▤ The Mirage, 702-791-7337, mirage.com

Shanghai Lilly's • South Strip • Asian

Marlene Dietrich immortalized Shanghai Lilly when she starred as a notorious prostitute by that name in the 1932 *Shanghai Express*. This Mandalay Bay spot seems to channel the sultry star's sense of style with an entrance marked by a giant water wall and a flaming neon sign. Inside, spicy Cantonese and Szechuan dishes are served on Limoges china under a ceiling draped with soft fabrics. Some of the best tables are cordoned off by cloth columns, giving a bit of privacy and adding even more romance to the room. The restaurant is popular with folks heading to the nearby *Mama Mia!*, as well as those seeking a casually elegant touch of romance. It's dressier than some Vegas spots, so no T-shirts, gentlemen. Shanghai Lilly's specializes in seafood, so expect dishes such as abalone with sea cucumber and Maine lobster sashimi. *Nightly 5:30-11pm.* $$$$ ≡ Mandalay Bay, 702-632-7409, mandalaybay.com.

Simon Kitchen and Bar • East Flamingo • Continental
When the Rolling Stones played The Joint, both the pre- and post-concert parties were held at this hip and casual American hot spot, opened by the "rock 'n' roll" chef Kerry Simon, late of Prime at Bellagio and New York City's Mercer Kitchen, and an *Iron Chef* favorite. The interior is chic and simple, and the upscale food takes on down-home classics (meat loaf with garlic mashed potatoes, roasted chicken, lamb chops, and pizza). Desserts also offer heaping servings of nostalgia, like fine-spun cotton candy or chocolate chunk cookies with milk. *Sun-Thu 6-11pm, Fri-Sat 6-11:30pm.* $$$$ B≡ Hard Rock, 702-693-4440, simonkitchen.com

Spice Market Buffet • Center Strip • Buffet
Featured on the Travel Channel's *Battle of the Buffets* and named the city's best by the *New York Post*, Aladdin's Spice Market Buffet is a cut above your typical smorgasbord, offering sophisticated twists on expected Chinese, Italian, and Mexican fare, like lettuce wraps, baba ghanoush, stuffed grape leaves, and hummus. Bonus: Dishes are made to order at each station's very own kitchen. On Saturdays and Sundays, there's a champagne brunch. *Mon-Fri 8-10:30am, 11am-2:30pm, Sat-Sun 8:30am-2:30pm, daily 4-9:30pm.* $$ ≡ Aladdin/ Planet Hollywood, 702-785-9005, aladdincasino.com

STACK • Center Strip • Continental
Yet another "scene and cuisine" notch in the trendsetting Light Group's belt, STACK is sure to add some hipness to the Mirage. Why? The cool new restaurant that makes you feel like you're eating in the depths of the Grand Canyon is run by the super duo that brought you Fix at Bellagio. That's right: Oliver Wharton and Brian Massie are bringing some energy back into the aging tropical paradise. Expect glorified American comfort food in a fun and inviting environment. Some of the more interesting dishes on the menu are Mac and Kobe Balls homemade pasta, Hot Rocks sirloin steak appetizer, and a 24-ounce cowboy steak. And don't think that it doesn't have Adult Tater Tots—it does! *Sun-Thu 5-11pm, Fri-Sat 5pm-midnight.* $$ B≡ The Mirage, 702-792-7800, stacklasvegas.com

Bachelor(ette) Las Vegas:
The Nightlife

AJ's Steakhouse* • East Flamingo • Martini Bar
This '50s-style steakhouse has a clubby, masculine martini bar, complete with piano, making it a great quiet spot. See *Bachelor(ette) Restaurants,* p.87, for details. ≣ The Hard Rock, 702-693-5500, hardrockhotel.com

Aladdin Theater • Center Strip • Live Shows
This theater was the only thing left standing when the original Aladdin Hotel was demolished back in 1998 to make room for the new Aladdin. Completely renovated, it hosts everything from Broadway shows—*Fosse, Evita, Beauty and the Beast*—to rock concerts—Tom Petty, Don Henley, Elton John. Hours and prices vary by show. C≣ Aladdin/Planet Hollywood, 702-785-5000, aladdincasino.com

Alesium after-hours • Central Strip • Nightclub
After hours—way after hours—the restaurant, sushi bar, and nightclub Seven turns into a hot spot. This is one of the few stand-alone nighttime destinations in town, but you won't have any trouble finding it. Just follow the pounding bass—the house, trance, and hip-hop music blaring from its red-curtained patio is louder on the street than inside the club. *Seven door opens at 10:30pm Fri-Sat, but the line for Alesium's after-hours party starts at 3am; Thu-Sun 2am-9am.* C≣ 3724 S. Las Vegas Blvd. (Flamingo Rd.), 702-739-7744, sevenlasvegas.com

Bar at Times Square • Central Strip • Bar
Know all the words to Don McLean's "American Pie"? This casual pub is the place for you. Bring plenty of cash—the piano players always start a friendly competition, pitting country fans against rock 'n' rollers over whose song will get played. The side that tips most hears its song while the others hit the bar for more drinks. *Daily 10am-3am; piano starts at 8pm.* B≣ New York-New York, 702-740-6969, nynyhotelcasino.com

Battle Bar • Central Strip • Bar
Adjacent to The Race & Sports Book, the Battle Bar has an outdoor patio overlooking Buccaneer Bay, which serves as the ideal spot for viewing the pirate battle. *24/7.* B≣ Treasure Island, 702-894-7330, treasureisland.com

Big Apple Bar • Central Strip • Bar
This sophisticated Art Deco casino lounge, reminiscent of the supper clubs of the '30s and '40s with a curvy bar, floor-to-ceiling velvet drapes, Bordeaux satin walls, and a big red apple hanging above, features nightly entertainment (8pm-3am). Join the casual crowd, mostly hotel guests, and try the Central Park Breeze, a citrus drink made with citron and mandarin vodka, sweet and sour, and lemon-lime soda. Or try the Red Apple, a mix of vodka, sour apple, sloe gin, and cranberry juice served straight up in a classic martini glass. *24/7.* B− New York-New York, 702-740-6969, nynyhotelcasino.com

Blue Man Group • Central Strip • Show

Best Shows Much expanded from the original New York, Chicago, and Boston productions, this show involves lots of drumming, splashing paint, Twinkies, Cap'n Crunch, marshmallows, a thrashing band, black light, and miles and miles of crepe paper that covers the theater and buries the audience. But it's a long-running success that draws diverse crowds, and the popularity of the electric-tone players is undeniable. *Nightly 7:30pm and Sat 10:30pm.* C▤ The Venetian, 720-414-1000, blueman.com

Body English • East Flamingo • Nightclub

Best Nightclubs Often the site for radio station Mix 94's Underground Lounge (intimate "unplugged" concerts broadcast from undisclosed locations), this tiny basement nightclub remains hot, hot, hot. Yes, there's a velvet rope, but even those not on the VIP list seem to have no trouble getting past the door crew if they sport the right look, though lines can get quite long after midnight, particularly on the weekends. To guarantee a ringside VIP booth, make reservations; on weekends, count on shelling out a $200 bottle fee on top of the booth fee, usually $200 to $300. Body English attracts some of the top DJ talent around, but if you don't love house and hip-hop music, this probably isn't the club for you. If you do, slip on your dancing shoes and join the melee. *Fri-Sun 10:30pm-4am.* C▤ The Hard Rock, 702-794-3623, bodyenglish.com

Center Bar • East Flamingo • Bar/Lounge

Best Meet Markets As its name suggests, this is the bar in the center of The Hard Rock. It's a meeting point in the casino and a destination in and of itself, with people coming here and staying here, skipping The Hard Rock's glitzy clubs. It attracts a hip L.A. crowd, definitely on the younger side. Look closely to see which are the cocktail waitresses and which are the beautiful people ordering the drinks. On weekends, you're likely to see A-listers. J. Lo, Gwen Stefani, Kid Rock, Ben Affleck, and the members of Mötley Crüe are just some who have partied here. Blackjack tables ring the bar at night, so you can play without missing any of the eye candy. *24/7.* C▤ The Hard Rock, 702-693-5000, hardrockhotel.com

Centrifuge Bar • South Strip • Bar

Best Meet Markets The Centrifuge is a popular pre-party, post-poker spot for a drink on the casino level of the MGM Grand. Truth be told, you don't have to have a reason to get a drink here, but it gives you a few. Every half hour the staff hop up on top of the circular bar and give you a little choreographed dance. If you're not getting a rise out of it, you're sure to get a giggle. It also serves specialty drinks from the MGM Grand's signature restaurants and displays them in Louis Treize Baccarat crystal bottles. Try the chai martini. *Sun-Fri 4pm-4am, Sat noon-4am.* C▤ MGM Grand, 702-891-1111, mgmgrand.com

Chippendales, The Show • West Flamingo • Show

It's described as the classiest of the male revues—maybe it's the bow ties worn by the dozen gentlemen who strut their stuff. Of course, they're not clad in much else as they gyrate through a number of steamy (or silly, depending on your mood) dance routines meant to whip the audience into a frenzy. The crowd here, mostly groups of women, doesn't need much encouragement—everyone wants a wild time. For an even more up-close encounter, book seats in the Sky Lounge. *Sun-Wed 8:30pm, Fri-Sat 8:30pm and 10:30pm.* C▤ The Rio, 702-777-7776, chippendales.com

Coyote Ugly • Center Strip • Bar

Like the movie come to life, this raucous upscale dive bar, with its weathered floor and flea market treasure decorations, features saucy, scantily clad bartender-dancers—called Coyotes—who breathe fire, pour booze, do body shots, and are known to douse you with water if you order a sissy drink (only beer and manly liquor served here—get your cosmo elsewhere, boys). They'll also cut off your tie if you're foolish enough to wear one in. It's gals-only up on the bar and women are invited to shimmy out of their Miracle Bras and donate them to the décor—look up and see the vast collection already adorning the rafters. *Nightly 6pm-4am.* C≣ New York-New York, 702-740-6330, coyoteuglysaloon.com/vegas

Diego* • South Strip • Nightclub

This hip Mexican joint turns into a spicy nightclub on Friday and Saturday nights after the restaurant closes doors. With DJs and dance tunes (lots of Latin beats), it's a fun place to down some margaritas and bust some tequila-induced moves. See *Bachelor(ette) Restaurants,* p.88, for details. *Restaurant 5:30-10pm, bar 5pm-late.* C≣ MGM Grand, 702-891-3200, mgmgrand.com

Drai's* • Center Strip • Nightclub

Best After-Hours Clubs Ignore that the Barbary Coast casino is an absolute dive. If you're into the party-beyond-dawn scene, make your way past the aging cocktail waitresses and the smarmy players with too many gold chains and really bad comb-overs. When you spot the crowd of 20-somethings decked out in D&G and Alexander McQueen, you've found the elevator that will drop you into Drai's, truly one of the classiest joints in town—like the old Copacabana or El Morocco, complete with red walls, tiger prints, abstract art, and a candlelit library lounge area. By evening, Drai's, with its lush supper-club décor, is one of the city's top restaurants, serving gourmet French food to well-heeled Las Vegans and savvy tourists. But come midnight, it morphs into the sizzling after-hours club, a total rave scene (hint: you'll pay more for bottled water than for a martini) that's also rumored to be a premier spot for couples looking to hook up with a third. *Wed-Sun midnight-dawn.* C≣ Barbary Coast, 702-737-0555, draisafterhours.com

Empire Ballroom • South Strip • Nightclub

Best After-Hours Clubs A relative newcomer on the after-hours scene, Empire Ballroom has quickly staked its place as a premier early-morning spot for both locals and hipster tourists. Designed by the backers of L.A.'s popular Viper Room, the club has a retro speakeasy feel with a giant crystal chandelier dominating the main dance floor, a coat check girl, and a rich color palette of brown and reds. Upstairs, VIPs can sequester themselves in one of eight private booths, or get a breath of air on the upper balcony (there's also a Strip-side patio for regular patrons, with its own sound system). Rockers like Prince and Macy Gray have already christened the place with performances (during regular club hours), but it's the 20-something crowd that shows up after 3am that really makes Empire the king of the late-night pack. *Club Fri-Sat 10pm-2am; after-hours 3am-close.* C≣ 3765 Las Vegas Blvd. S. (S. Las Vegas Blvd.), 702-415-5283, empireballroom.com

Fadó Irish Pub and Restaurant* • Henderson • Bar

This authentic Irish pub is a great spot for a rowdy whiskey or beer, with live music (think Irish punk rock). The food is good, too. See *Bachelor(ette) Restaurants,* p.88, for details. ≣ Green Valley Ranch, 702-407-8691, fadoirishpub.com

Freezone • Airport • Gay Club

Best Gay Bars and Clubs Home to the longest-running drag show in Vegas, Freezone is a palace for more than just the "Queens of Las Vegas." Thursday night is Boys' Night, Tuesday is Ladies' Night, and every night is a party with Sin City's premier alternative club and restaurant. It has constant events, so visit the website and check out its gallery for a peek at what's coming. *24/7.* ≣ 601 E. Naples (Paradise Rd.), 702-794-2300, freezonelv.com

Garduño's/Blue Agave Oyster and Chili Bar* • West Flamingo • Bar

This place makes a mean margarita, complemented by great, spicy Mexican food. See *Bachelor(ette) Restaurants,* p.89, for details. *Sun-Thu 10:30am-10pm, Fri-Sat 10:30am-11pm.* ≣ Palms, 702-942-7777, palms.com

Gipsy • Airport • Gay Club

Best Gay Bars and Clubs This nightclub is a favorite among regular alternative clubbers who love to dance. Even though it's a small place, it's known as one of the best gay dance clubs in the city. There is a strong locals scene and the DJs are well-respected. Make sure to also support their two new gay clubs in the "Froot Loop," 8 1/2 Ultra Lounge and Piranha nightclub. *Wed-Mon 9pm-3am.* C≣ 4605 S. Paradise Rd. (Tropicana Ave.), 702-731-1919, gipsylv.com

The Improv • Center Strip • Comedy

This world-renowned comedy franchise continues to launch the careers of some of the freshest funnymen around. The Harrah's Improv branch opened in 1995, and although it is often overshadowed by the big-name acts on the Strip, it's been voted the best comedy show four years running. Many big-name comics (Jerry Seinfeld, Jay Mohr, David Spade, and Drew Carey) cut their teeth on the infamous Improv's brick backdrop stage, as evidenced by the photos and hand-written jokes scribbled on the wall. There are two nightly shows showcasing at least three new comics weekly. *Tue-Sun 8:30pm and 10:30pm.* C≣ Harrah's, 702-369-5000, harrahs.com

Jet • Center Strip • Nightclub

Best Mega-Nightclubs PURE, Light, Tao, Tryst—and now Jet—how will you decide where to get your party on? The addition of Jet confirms that The Mirage is once again a true "destination resort," a concept it introduced to Vegas in 1989 when it opened. This sleek nightclub beckons you with its mysterious candlelit entrance, and then leads you into three different music rooms, each with its own theme. The main room jams with rock, hip-hop, and popular dance music, while a second room has house music spun by guest and international DJs. The third room jives to an eclectic mix of music ranging from '80s to rock. It's easy to get a drink at Jet, and VIPs and celebs have their own private drive-up entrance. Monday nights are locals' nights, when ladies with a Nevada ID get in free, drawing a different crowd. Be warned: The lines can be long and the bouncers less than friendly, but once inside you're guaranteed a good time. *Fri-Sat and Mon 10:30pm-4am.* C≣ The Mirage, 702-792-7900, jetlv.com

The Joint • East Flamingo • Live Music

Best Live Music This is where rock lives in Las Vegas. The Joint has hosted the Rolling Stones, the Eagles, Bob Dylan, Red Hot Chili Peppers, Korn, Matchbox Twenty, and Blink-182, among many, many others. Word to the wise: Given the marquee bands that perform, concerts are often oversold, which can lead to bone-crushing crowds and hit-or-miss drink service. Spring for the high-priced tickets that'll get you access to the VIP balcony, which is (somewhat) less crowded and at least has its own bar and restrooms. *Prices and showtimes vary.* C≣ The Hard Rock, 702-693-5066, hardrockhotel.com

KRAVE • Center Strip • Gay Club

Best Gay Bars and Clubs This is a friendly club that gets awards right and left including *2005 Las Vegas Weekly* Readers' Choice for Best Gay/Lesbian Club. Not only is it the only gay nightclub on the Strip, but it is always recognized as the most easygoing, where both gays and straights can have a good time. It is both a theater and dance floor and is home to the erotic *John Stagliano's Fashionistas* show, as well as the *Men of Vegas* male revue. There are plenty of themed nights, including Girlbar every Saturday and Planeta Macho for Latin lovers every Tuesday. *Nightly 11pm-dawn.* C≣ Aladdin/Planet Hollywood, 702-836-0830, kravelasvegas.com

Little Buddha* • West Flamingo • Bar/Lounge

Its Paris-based big brother, Buddha Bar, has a worldwide nightlife reputation. This Vegas branch is better known as a restaurant, but has a sophisticated lounge for a drink and a nibble. See *Bachelor(ette) Restaurants,* p.90, for details. *Sun-Thu 5:30-11pm, Fri-Sat 5:30pm-midnight.* ≣ Palms, 702-942-7778, littlebuddhalasvegas.com

Mamma Mia! • South Strip • Show

A guilty pleasure for Abba fans, this campy disco romp, featuring 22 songs from the '70s Swedish pop group, has spawned nine productions worldwide, the latest of which just moved into the 1,600-seat Mandalay Bay Theater. Conceived by Abba's Benny Andersson and Björn Ulvaeus with a book by British playwright Catherine Johnson, the plot of the show, which snared a 2002 Tony nomination for Best Musical, is pretty flimsy: About to be married, a young woman culls through her mom's diary, looking for clues about her heretofore-absent dad, then invites the three most likely candidates to her wedding, and all sorts of mayhem ensues. Really, it's just a fun excuse to hopscotch from one bouncy Abba favorite to another, like "Take a Chance on Me," "Dancing Queen," "SOS" and "Gimme! Gimme! Gimme!" *Sun-Thu 7:30pm, Sat 6 and 10pm.* C≣ Mandalay Bay, 877-632-4700, mandalaybay.com

Mist • Center Strip • Lounge

The best indicator that Treasure Island is trying to glam up its image is Mist, created by the team behind Bellagio's Caramel and the nightclub Light. It has class and style without attitude. Right off the casino, with its sleek glass façade, unobtrusive plasma screens, polished dark wood floors, and roomy maroon leather sofas, Mist has a decidedly upscale den-like feel. The best part—you don't need a reservation to settle into one of the clubby couches, nor do you need to purchase a $300 bottle for the privilege. *Nightly 5pm-4am.* C≣ Treasure Island, 702-894-7330, mistbar.com

Mystère • Center Strip • Show

Far less dark and macabre than the haunting productions Cirque du Soleil usually produces, *Mystère* is clearly courting a lighter audience with a playful show that's heavy on the humor and physical comedy and easy on the disembodied, often disturbing images that usually populate the Cirque mise-en-scène. The framing story (if this show can be said to have an actual story) is of two precocious babies wandering the world and encountering a bizarre but engaging assortment of characters, like the rowdy clown with Einstein hair who tosses popcorn at the audience. *Wed-Sat 7:30 and 10:30pm, Sun 4:30 and 7:30pm.* C≡ Treasure Island, 702-894-7111, cirquedusoleil.com

Olympic Gardens • South Strip • Strip Club
The oldest strip club in town is also the only one on the Strip. A parade of beautiful women in G-strings offer lap dances, but the occasional shower show, where the girls get playful with sudsy water, adds novelty. *24/7.* C≡ 1531 S. Las Vegas Blvd. (Oakey St.), 702-385-8987, ogvegas.com

Palapa Lounge • West Flamingo • Bar/Lounge
It's hip. Tuesday nights is the alt-music showcase, Acoustic Asylum. Wednesdays, it's Rock Star Karaoke, where anyone who's downed enough liquid courage can sing it loud and sing it proud with a real live band backing him or her up. Thursday through Saturday, Palms house band, Groove Kitty, plays a mix of pop hits and dance tunes that'll make any stray cat strut. *24/7.* ≡ Palms, 702-942-7777, palms.com

Palomino Club • North Las Vegas • Strip Club
Best Strip Clubs A convenient loophole in the North Las Vegas zoning codes allows this old-school club to have both a full bar and full nudity—making it the only one of its kind. A change in ownership hasn't affected the Palomino's vintage '70s feel. The red bordello-style main room still has a runway stage where exotic dancers put on a teasing and pleasing burlesque show to a three- or four-song set. The upstairs Lipstick Lounge has a more traditional setting with private dances. The surrounding area is shady, so don't hesitate to use the club's free shuttle transportation to and from the Strip. Limousines are also available, but you have to pony up for that. *Nightly 5pm-5am.* C≡ 1848 Las Vegas Blvd. N. (E. Owens St.), 702-642-2984

Pink Taco* • East Flamingo • Bar
One of The Hard Rock's hottest places for a Mexican bite also has a happening margarita and tequila bar in the center. It's a great place for a taco, a cold drink, or both. See *Bachelor(ette) Restaurants,* p.91, for details. *Sun-Thu 11:30am-10pm, Fri-Sat 11:30am-midnight.* ≡ The Hard Rock, 702-693-5525, pinktaco.com

Rain • West Flamingo • Nightclub
With its winding tunnel entrance, a dance floor surrounded by a moat and shrouded in fog, arcing fountains, and a metal contraption that descends from the ceiling and belches fire, the multilevel Rain has a sexy pop industrial vibe. DJs spin deep house and techno, and occasionally there are concerts with the likes of Macy Gray—who inaugurated the club—as well as Little Feat, Sugar Ray, Santana, No Doubt, and Ozzy Osbourne. It's plenty comfortable on the ground, but catch the scene from the cabanas on the second floor ($600 to $750) for an even more private party area, or reserve one of the six skyboxes ($1,000). Drink more and the club waives the reservation fee. You can also reserve VIP tables for $300 to $400. *Thu-Sat 11pm-5am.* C≡ Palms, 702-938-9999, palms.com

Risqué • Center Strip • Ultra Lounge

Upstairs from Paris Las Vegas' Ah Sin! is Risqué, a sexy ultra lounge with a sultry mix of traditional French and contemporary Asian décor and all sorts of decadent pleasures. Take your drinks and retire to a private nook with a lounging bed intriguingly sized for three and a private balcony overlooking the Strip. Then sample the Asian-influenced French pastries, like orange blossom crème brûlée and tropical fruit tempura, at the city's only dessert bar, helmed by executive pastry chef Jean-Claude Canestrier (winner of the 2002 World Pastry Championships). Dance on the intimate dance floor to house music, and check out the VIP Salon Privé with its own giant red velvet lounging bed and separate bar. Definitely take a peek at the bathrooms—men's and women's rooms are separated by a translucent partial wall. *Fri-Sun 10:30pm-4am.* C≡ Paris Las Vegas, 702-946-4589, parislasvegas.com

Rita Rudner • Center Strip • Comedy Show

The Rita Rudner show moved to Harrah's in the fall of 2006. Her stand-up act, at New York-New York in early 2006, was extremely popular and earned her recognition as Best Comedian from the *Las Vegas Review-Journal*'s Best of Las Vegas. The theater at Harrah's will offer her a much larger space, and we can expect great things from this funny lady. She has written several books, including the best-selling *Naked Beneath My Clothes. Call for show times.* C≡ Harrah's, 702-369-5000, ritafunny.com

rumjungle • South Strip • Nightclub

Best Meet Markets This restaurant and nightclub wins our vote for the coolest entrance—a dancing wall of fire that morphs into a cascading wall of water as you step into the club. More water walls are suspended throughout the place, as are those ubiquitous cages holding bikini-clad go-go dancers gyrating to the house, Caribbean, African, and Latin beats, stirring up a tourist crowd of mixed ages. During daylight hours, rumjungle serves Brazilian-style barbecue. At night, it more than lives up to its name, with its animal-print décor, open fire pit, dueling conga drums, and drink menu featuring more than 100 rums, stacked high above the bar like a petite Aureole wine tower. Try the volcano—its version of a mai tai, made with five rums—or the Havana Cubana, like a piña colada on the rocks. *Sun-Thu 11pm-2am, Fri-Sat 11pm-4am.* C≡ Mandalay Bay, 702-632-7408, mandalaybay.com

Tangerine • Center Strip • Lounge/Nightclub

Best Burlesque If you never thought the color orange was sexy, you will after going to Tangerine. It was voted "Best Cocktails" by the *Las Vegas Weekly*'s 2006 Readers' Choice for its drinks, and is always packed, with dancing being the main attraction. The dance floor takes over the center room, with some seating on the perimeter. Outside is a great deck that looks out onto the Strip and offers an up-close view of the *Sirens of TI* show. Fifteen-minute burlesque shows with a live band are on inside Tue-Sat starting at 10:45pm. The clientele is mostly on the younger side. Call the club to see when it's hosting the next model search or recruiting for upcoming TV shows. *Tue-Sat 6pm-4am; patio 5:30pm-midnight.* C≡ Treasure Island, 702-894-7580, treasureisland.com

Thunder From Down Under • Center Strip • Show

If there's one characteristic that seems to unite Aussie men, it's their love of a good time. In this show, which features a buff group of Down Under dancers, that fun-loving spirit is front and center. While the boys definitely deliver the goods, they do it with a bit of tease and a lot of over-the-top attitude. For 75 minutes, the all-female audience is given a taste of virtually every romance novel fantasy ever imagined—from pirates to firemen to men in uniform (and of course, since it's at Excalibur, a knight in shining armor). Be warned—this is an interactive show. Ladies are often welcomed onstage for everything from a walk down the pirate's plank to a fake orgasm contest. *Sun-Thu 8:30 and 10:30pm, Fri-Sat 9 and 11pm.* C≡ Excalibur, 702-597-7600, thunderfromdownunder.com

V Bar • Center Strip • Lounge

From David Rabin and Will Regan, owners of New York's Union Bar and Lotus, and Brad Johnson, of the Sunset Room in Los Angeles, comes V Bar. With its black and red décor, low leather banquettes, Eames chairs, rice paper lighting, and pumping club music, V Bar has a ultra-contemporary Asian vibe. Resident mixologists whip together a fabulous watermelon martini—using real muddled fruit. *Nightly 5pm-2:30am.* C≡ The Venetian, 702-414-3200, venetian.com

Bachelor(ette) Las Vegas:
The Attractions

Adventure Las Vegas • Various • Tour

From ATV tours through the Valley of Fire, to horseback riding deep in Red Rock Canyon, and helicopter tours to the Grand Canyon, this reliable tour operator has an adventure for every taste. It even offers mountain biking and Hummer tours of haunted gold mines. *Hours vary.* $$$ Various locations, 702-869-9992, adventurelasvegas.com

The Big Shot • North Strip • Ride

Best Thrill Rides This is the ride that you can see at the very top of The Stratosphere—the one where thrill-seekers get strapped into their seats before being shot straight up into sky. It only takes 2.5 seconds at 45 mph to launch 160 feet up. Does your adrenaline know what 4Gs of force feel like? But like all things that go up, this too must come down. Riders fall back toward the base and bounce three times until settled. If you can handle that, then you're probably ready for Insanity, The Stratosphere's newest ride, which flings its passengers 64 feet over the side of the tower. *Sun-Thu 10am-1am, Fri-Sat and holidays noon-2am.* $ The Stratosphere, 702-380-7777, stratospherehotel.com

Desert Passage • Center Strip • Shops

Aladdin's shopping theme park, Desert Passage, is a tricked-out bazaar that ambles in a mile-long circle through a North African marketplace mall. While you're browsing through Sephora, Hervé Léger, or Ann Taylor Loft, you'll assuredly encounter the mall's resident tumblers, belly dancers, fire-eaters, jugglers, stilt-walkers, acrobats, and guys who walk on glass. And of course, you don't want to miss the mall's indoor thunderstorm, which erupts hourly during the week and every 30 minutes on weekends. Aladdin/Planet Hollywood, 702-866-0710, desertpassage.com

Flyaway Indoor Skydiving • North Strip • Ride

Best Thrill Rides Ever wanted to skydive, but don't quite have the courage? Flyaway might be the perfect compromise. Located in a not-very-pretty warehouse just off the Strip, Flyaway is basically a giant vertical wind tunnel built over an airplane jet, and designed to blow patrons up into the air. After a quick orientation, you'll don a somewhat clean jumpsuit and helmet, and head into the tunnel one person at a time for about a 15-minute session. You'll bounce off the padded walls, hit face-first on the net below, generally look undignified, and hopefully get some really fun air-time. Be warned: It's loud, and takes more skill than you would think. And you will be tested to make sure you're not drunk before you start. *Daily 10am-7pm.* $$$$ ($70 per person) 200 Convention Center Dr. (Las Vegas Blvd. S.), 702-731-4768, flyawayindoorskydiving.com

Gambler's Book Shop • Downtown • Shop

Warning: Buying a book in this store can change your life. Maybe you'll become a winning sports gambler, a craps table commando, a new Las Vegas historian, or even a poker writer. This is a one-of-a-kind indie bookstore a short ride from downtown. Owner Howard Schwartz, the "librarian for gamblers," is a meat loaf–loving

Vegas legend who has helped authors and FBI agents decipher Sin City locals for decades. His story about the shop is as noteworthy as the gaming books inside; his files should be put in a museum. If you're looking for a "system," how-to book, or any book at all that has to do with gambling, it's right here. *Mon-Sat 9am-5pm.* 630 S. Eleventh St. (Charleston St.), 702-382-7555, gamblersbook.com

Grand Canal Shoppes • Center Strip • Shops

With its archways, bridges, and twisty cobbled streets that eventually spill out onto a replica of Venice's St. Mark's Square, the Grand Canal Shoppes is one of the city's unique malls. Along with great shopping at the high-end and mid-range stores (Ann Taylor, Banana Republic, the Canyon Ranch Living Essentials store), the Grand Canal Shoppes includes a quarter-mile canal where you can catch a gondola piloted by a singing gondolier (Sun-Thu 10am-10:30pm, Fri-Sat 10am-11:30pm) on either the inner canal or the outside canal. Each morning at 9:45 the boatmen march to the square from the mall's food court, singing as they go. If you miss the morning march, you can catch the afternoon shift change at 4:15pm. Along with the boatmen, the mall is filled with other entertainers, like "living statues" that resemble marble sculptures "performing" in the square, opera singers belting out Puccini, and actors costumed as Renaissance Venetian citizens who wander the walkways interacting with visitors. Stroll the shops or have a bite at one of the restaurants that ring the square, such as Wolfgang Puck's Postrio. *Sun-Thu 10am-11pm, Fri-Sat 10am-midnight.* The Venetian, 702-414-4500, venetian.com

The Gun Store • East Las Vegas • Shop/Sport

You could go for the security officer and firearm training, but it's a sure bet that you'll have more fun renting a machine gun and acting out a *Pulp Fiction* scene in the indoor shooting range. We're not kidding. This is one of the few places in the country where you can walk in, pay a very nominal fee (as low as $25 for an M16) and blast away on the firing range. It's got a gun for every taste, from an AK-47 assault rifle to an Uzi SMG. For those who just want to get some shooting practice with a regular pistol, it also has over 50 models of the little guys for rent. And gals, Tuesdays are Ladies' Day, with free use of the range. *Daily 9am-6:30pm.* 2900 E. Tropicana Ave. (McCloud St.), 702-454-1110, thegunstorelasvegas.com

IMAX Theater • South Strip • Theater

See first-run Hollywood films and 3-D flicks on a seven-story screen—one of two IMAX screens in town (the other's at Palms)—with an amazing sound system. *Daily 9am-11pm.* $ The Luxor, 702-262-4400, luxor.com

In Search of the Obelisk • South Strip • Ride

A motion simulator takes you on an Indiana Jones–type adventure through an archaeological dig, with lots of twists and turns. It's not the best ride on the Strip, but it's fun. *Daily 9am-11pm.* $ The Luxor, 702-262-4400, luxor.com

King Tut's Tomb and Museum • South Strip • Museum

Egyptian artist and sculptor Dr. Mahmoud Mabrouk, who restored the original Sphinx, painstakingly re-created the boy king's burial chamber and all of its lustrous artifacts (such as Tut's throne, sarcophagus, statuary, clay pots, and urns) just as it was when Howard Carter and Lord Carnarvon discovered it in 1922 in the Valley of the Kings at Luxor. The self-guided audio tour takes you

through the antechamber, burial chamber, annex, and treasury. A fine substitute if you don't plan to see the original anytime soon. *Daily 9am-11pm.* $
The Luxor, 702-262-4400, luxor.com

Madame Tussaud's Wax Museum • Center Strip • Museum

This waxworks collection, located on the second and third floors of Venetian's replica of the St. Mark's Library building, is the tenth in the family of Tussaud wax museums, which originally opened in London in 1835, and the only Tussaud outpost west of the Mississippi. The two-story museum cost $20 million to assemble and features 100 wax statues, each of which took six months and up to $40,000 to create. Along with featuring popular entertainment and sports figures, like Liz Taylor and Brad Pitt, this branch gives a nod to its surroundings, featuring some decidedly Las Vegas personalities, including gangster and hotelier Bugsy Siegel, Frank Sinatra, Wayne Newton, Tom Jones, and Liberace. All are freestanding, so you're free to wander up and pose for a picture. There's also a cool behind-the-scenes look at how the wax figures are crafted. An excellent way to spend a half-hour. *Daily 10am-10pm.* $$ The Venetian, 702-862-7820, mtvegas.com

Mandalay Beach • South Strip • Pool

Best Pool Scenes The 11-acre beach is open April to November and recently was renovated to provide an even bigger wave-pool area. There are three pools and a lazy river. The hotel operates strict entry procedures so you can be assured the only sunbathers here are hotel guests (of Mandalay, THEhotel, or The Four Seasons). There are nine private bungalows, 20 cabanas, and a half-mile jogging track (call 702-632-7997 to reserve a cabana). Snack shops are on-site with the Border Grill's upscale Mexican cuisine just on the other side of the enclosure. In the summer, the Beach boasts a Friday-night concert series that has hosted bands including Hall and Oates, the Beach Boys, and REO Speedwagon. This is a great Friday-night pool party. *Mid-April–mid-Sept 8am-7pm, mid-Sept–late-Oct 9am-7pm, Nov 9am-5pm (closes Nov 19); showtimes vary.* $$ Mandalay Bay, 702-632-7777, mandalaybay.com

Manhattan Express • Center Strip • Ride

Best Thrill Rides Hands-down the best roller coaster on the Strip, the Manhattan Express twists and turns around the hotel's simulated New York skyline, careening through a 144-foot drop, a stomach-churning loop, and a 540-degree spiral that mimics the tuck and roll a pilot experiences in a jet fighter. *Daily 10:30am-midnight.* $ New York-New York, 702-740-6969, nynyhotelcasino.com

Mirage Poker Room • Center Strip • Casino

Best Texas Hold 'Em Poker Rooms Once the hub of the poker world, this stalwart still offers great action. Daily tournaments offer good value and get good-sized fields. You'll find all the typical games here, but call ahead, as the waiting lists can get quite long. Many of poker's top players still take a seat at these tables, and some never left for the newer Bellagio experience. The average caliber of talent may surprise you, since the old guard of players remain loyal patrons. The Mirage hosts a very cool "Heads Up" tournament series, which is a great way to have fun while working on your heads-up game. Call the room for info. *24/7.* The Mirage, 702-791-7291, mirage.com

Palms Casino Resort Pool • West Flamingo • Pool
Best Pool Scenes It's young hard bodies here at the Palms pool, the kind that are a decade away from liposuction or Botox. That might make it a tough scene for those who prefer low lighting to offset their swimsuits, but it would be a shame to miss this great spot on a warm summer day. With three bars (including the Glass Bar, located under a glass-bottomed pool for very unique people-watching) and a brand-new two-acre pool area, this is one of the city's best spots to work on a tan and a cocktail or three. There are also poolside massages, swim-up blackjack, and 27 private cabanas, many with TVs and stereos, among other amenities. *Mar–Oct daily 9am-6pm.* $$ Palms, 702-942-7777, palms.com

Paris Spa by Mandara • Center Strip • Spa
Best Destination Spas Tucked away on the second floor of Paris Las Vegas and accessed by elevators from the Le Boulevard shopping area, Paris Spa by Mandara is considered one of the best on the Strip. As in other Mandara spas around the world, the theme here is Euro-Balinese. Dark wicker furniture is surrounded by an earth-toned palette that's broken up with rich silk fabrics and vibrant wall murals in areas like the wet rooms. The 26,000-square-foot space has 24 treatment rooms, including six suites designed for couples, with privacy in mind. Staying true to its Indonesian origins, the spa's treatments have a delicious exotic flair— with ingredients like frangipani and caviar in the facials. Of course, there is also a workout room—free to spa guests—for those looking to break a sweat. *Sun–Thu 7am-7pm, Fri-Sat 7am-9pm.* Paris Las Vegas, 702-946-4366, mandaraspa.com

Playboy Store • West Flamingo • Shop
Hugh Hefner and Playboy Enterprises are finally putting their mark on Sin City. While they won't be opening up their own resort on the Strip, they have joined up with George Maloof's Palms Casino & Resort to open not only a new Playboy Club, complete with cocktail waitress bunnies, but also a retail shop where fans can get the latest in Playboy-branded gear, from lingerie to toys. Check it out on the casino floor near the new Fantasy Tower. *Sun-Wed 10am-10pm, Thu 10am-midnight, Fri-Sat 10am-2am.* Palms, 702-942-7777, palms.com

Reflection Bay Golf Club • Lake Las Vegas Resort • Golf
Best Golf Courses There are lots of fantastic golf courses in Vegas, but unfortunately, there are a lot of rules about getting on the greens at most of them, not to mention the cost. That's what makes Reflection Bay a favorite for golf-lovers, both local and visiting. This is the first public course in Nevada designed by Jack Nicklaus, and the 7,261-yard, par-72 adventure includes three waterfalls and plays around arroyos and water—five holes are located along one and a half miles of Lake Las Vegas. *Daily 6:30am-sunset.* $$ Lake Las Vegas Resort, 702-740-4653, lakelasvegas.com/golf_reflection.asp

Rehab at Hard Rock • East Flamingo • Pool
Best Pool Scenes This is far and away the best way to spend a Sunday afternoon in Vegas. After three successful years of poolside partying, The Hard Rock added a new bridge, more cabanas, a new stage, and season passes. For $1,200, pass holders can get into every Rehab without a wait, and bring two guests with them. Mere mortals can pay a cover. Once inside, you'll have to make the decision on where to mark your territory. These days, it's not as much about how much sun you're getting as it is about positioning for optimum viewing. L.A. beautiful people and con-

nected locals put on their best bikinis, whether they have a hangover or not. The lagoon quickly fills up with revelers who refuse to leave Vegas without bringing home a story to brag about. This party makes all your trips to the gym worthwhile. *Sun noon-8pm.* $$ The Hard Rock, 702-693-5000, hardrockhotel.com

Rock Spa at Hard Rock • East Flamingo • Spa
The Hard Rock is a favorite haunt of Hollywood's hot young things, so it's no wonder that its spa caters to the pursuit of beauty with an L.A. edge—such as the organic veggie wrap, where clients are slathered in a mix of tomatoes, artichokes, and pumpkin to draw out the excesses of the night before. Of course, it's also possible to get a regular massage in this sleek space, designed with rock walls and hardwood floors. The facility also encompasses a workout room that overlooks the pools, as well as a sauna, steam, and whirlpools. Patrons tend to be young and body-proud, and often as much in pursuit of fun as calm. *Daily 6am-10pm.* The Hard Rock, 702-693-5554, hardrockhotel.com

Sirens of TI • Center Strip • Show/Site
Best Free Attractions The *Sirens of TI* show is Vegas camp at its best, and a spectacle you won't want to miss—even if you don't stay for the whole affair. Staged in a faux lagoon in front of Treasure Island, the pseudo-mythical tale centers on a group of barely clad sirens who sing out to a ship of passing—and also barely clad—pirates, hoping to lure them over for a visit. But it's no untimely death that awaits the swashbuckling renegades. No, this is Vegas. After a tough battle, the pirates finally succumb to a party with the sirens, and all is well again, at least until the next show. *Nightly 7, 8:30, 10 and 11:30pm.* Treasure Island, 702-894-7111, treasureisland.com

Spa at the Palms • West Flamingo • Spa
Whether you want to center your chi with a candlelight yoga class or loosen sore muscles with a soak and a massage, the Spa at the Palms has you covered. Spanning three stories and 20,000 square feet, it has plenty of room to spread out, with separate floors for men's and women's treatment rooms. A well-outfitted co-ed cardio room on the men's floor overlooks the pool area, offering great people-watching. The Shea Butter Body Buff and Stone Massage are two favorites, but we love the Party Prep Facial, too. *Daily 6am-8pm, last treatment appointment 7pm.* Palms, 702-942-6937, palms.com

Stratosphere Observation Deck • North Strip • Site
For now, The Stratosphere's 1,149-foot tower is still the tallest structure on the Las Vegas Strip. Elevators zip you up to the Observation Deck in less than a minute for a 360-degree view of the Vegas Valley. The windows extend out, so you're not looking straight down through a typical wall of glass. Your eye is naturally drawn outward. *Sun-Thu 10am-1am, Fri-Sat 10am-2am.* $ The Stratosphere, 702-380-7791, stratospherehotel.com

The Volcano • Center Strip • Site
From its three-acre lagoon—which took eight months and cost a cool $30 million to build—this faux volcano erupts 100 feet in the air in a massive Technicolor display of fire, smoke, and 3,000 lights that are meant to simulate lava flow. While The Bellagio's fountains have overshadowed its spectacle value, you'll still be hard-pressed to avoid stopping and staring when you see it. *Every 15 minutes, nightly 7pm-midnight.* The Mirage, 702-791-7111, mirage.com

Luxe Las Vegas

You'll notice that there is no apostrophe in Caesars Palace. Confused? Don't be—it's plural. When Jay Sarno designed it, he decided everyone would be a Caesar at this grand hotel. That regal ideal has spread all over the Strip. In Vegas, money buys a kind of over-the-top pampering you can't find anywhere else, a grandiose extravagance intrinsic to the town's personality. Sometimes it borders on vulgar, it's so decadent, and oh, how we love it. There's a reason they call it Sin City—at this intersection of indulgence and revelry, seven vices hardly seem enough.

Note: Venues in bold are described in detail in the listings that follow the itinerary. Venues followed by an asterisk (*) are those we recommend as both a restaurant and a destination bar.

Luxe Las Vegas:
The Perfect Plan (3 Nights and Days)

Perfect Plan Highlights

Thursday

Lunch	**Delmonico*, Bouchon**
Afternoon	**Venetian lobby, Eiffel Tower, Bellagio Fountains**
Cocktails	**Fontana Bar, Petrossian**
Dinner	**Joël Robuchon at The Mansion, Michael Mina, Prime Steakhouse**
Nighttime	**O, La Femme**
Late-Night	**Caramel, Light**

Friday

Morning	**Exotic Car Rental, Red Rock Canyon, Mt. Charleston**
Lunch	**Sensi, Olives**
Afternoon	**Bellagio Gallery, Bellagio Sports Book and Poker**
Sunset	**Sundance Helicopter**
Dinner	**Aureole, Fleur de Lys, Charlie Palmer Steak***
Nighttime	**Charlie Palmer Steak*, Fremont St. Experience, Neon Museum**
Late-Night	**Club Paradise**

Saturday

Morning	**Shadow Creek, Wynn Golf, Wynn Esplanade, Via Bellagio**
Lunch	**Bartolotta, Spago**
Afternoon	**Spa, swim**
Show	**Céline Dion, Elton John**
Dinner	**Guy Savoy, Alex at Wynn, Daniel Boulud**
Nighttime	**Cleopatra's, Tryst, Lure**

The Morning After

Brunch	**Wynn or Bellagio Buffet**

Hotel: **The Bellagio**

1pm Lunch **Delmonico Steakhouse*** at The Venetian has mouthwatering food in a refined yet friendly environment. This sophisticated Emeril Lagasse restaurant is a big favorite among steak lovers, and wins lots of awards. For a less formal vibe with just as many accolades, there's **Bouchon**. This delightful brasserie by celebrity chef Thomas Keller delivers a meal to remember.

3pm Stroll through the **Venetian**, gawking at the ceiling as you go—it's elaborately painted with replicas of famous Italian murals, surrounded by 24-karat gold frames. Be sure to bring your eyes down to earth to check out the canals and the intricate marble patterns on the floor.

4pm Continue your European tour with a jaunt up to the top of the **Eiffel Tower**, where you'll be treated to stellar views of the Strip and the Las Vegas Valley.

5pm Last stop: Lake Como. Check out the **Bellagio Fountains**, which throw more water into the air during the finale than it takes to fill a swimming pool.

LUXE

6pm If you're entranced by those fountains, get yourself inside **Fontana Bar** for a cocktail and a great view over the lake. The **Petrossian** at Bellagio, a refined spot with a piano player, also delivers chic cocktails.

8pm Dinner One of the hottest tables in Vegas is **Joël Robuchon at The Mansion** at MGM Grand. There are only 64 seats here, and you can be certain every one will be filled. If these reservations are just too hard to land, visit the lux **Michael Mina**, where you'll find elegant California cuisine from the world-renowned chef. **Prime Steakhouse** is one of the best for a stylish steak in an equally chic setting.

10:30pm *O*, the Cirque du Soleil show that has been a hit since the day it opened, is starting soon. For something a bit sexier, catch the very talented ladies in the topless revue *La Femme*.

12:30am Head down to The Bellagio and check out **Caramel** for a lively scene and a cool drink. For some dancing, try **Light**, another hot spot at The Bellagio that draws the young and beautiful.

Friday

9:30am There's more to Nevada than the Strip. OK, not much more, but still, it's time to hit the road. At **Exotic Car Rental**, pick up (or have it delivered) your Ferrari 360 Spider or Porsche Boxster Roadster and head for the hills. A mere half hour away is **Red Rock Canyon** (see p.174) at the edge of the Spring Mountains. Cruise the 13-mile scenic drive, or head a little further out to **Mt. Charleston** (see p.173). In winter, skiers and snowboarders take to Lee Canyon, and in the summer there are plenty of hikes. Snow in the desert? Yes, Mt. Charleston's peak is snow-capped well into spring.

1pm Lunch If you're entertaining a group of six or eight, try a chef's table at Bellagio's **Sensi**. The transparent kitchen gives an exciting view. Or have a leisurely, refined lunch at **Olives**, where chef Todd English's Mediterranean food is as inspiring as the view from the patio.

3pm It's time for culture. Take a few minutes to wander through the **Bellagio Gallery of Fine Art**, then meander to the lobby and stroll the Bellagio Conservatory, where the botanical displays change with the seasons.

4:30pm If you're itching to gamble, try the **Bellagio Sports Book**, where you can bet on any game under the sun. Or decide for yourself who has the best poker room. If you've been caught up in the Texas Hold 'Em craze on TV, you're sure to bump into some famous faces at both Caesars Poker Room and **Bellagio Poker Room**. The Caesars Poker Room is the new kid on the block, having opened over the 2005 holidays. The Bellagio is still home to the Big Game. As the name suggests, it's the biggest game in town; it starts when most people are coming home from work, and takes place in the glass room at the center of all the poker action.

7pm Sunset Now get ready for something you'll never forget—a **Sundance Helicopter** ride over the Strip at sunset or just after dark. What a way to watch the lights of the city turn on!

8pm Dinner The tasting menu at Charlie Palmer's **Aureole** will surprise and delight you, almost as much as the wine angels flying in the see-through wine cellar to retrieve your bottle. Next door is the award-winning **Fleur de Lys**. The atmosphere is one of refined sophistication with a creative twist. If you're reservation-less, head upstairs to **Charlie Palmer Steak***. Its Kansas City rib eye has fans coming back, and the atmosphere is both relaxed and comfortable. Request a table in the back of the room if you're looking for more privacy.

10:30pm For a very polished and quiet experience, check out **Charlie Palmer Steak***—the bar here is a secret Vegas gem. Or for a taste of vintage Vegas, hop a cab downtown and visit the **Fremont Street Experience**, home to the original casinos. Try your luck at the tables of classic places like **Binion's** and walk through the **Neon Museum**, an outdoor display of bright vintage signs that date back to the Sinatra days.

12:30am The upscale **Club Paradise** is a sexy spot for both single gentlemen and couples to experience a little bit of Vegas naughtiness.

Saturday

8am Grab some coffee from room service and head out to the links. If you're staying at an MGM property, **Shadow Creek** is your spot—it's reserved solely for guests, and on weekends you need an "invitation" from the hotel to hit these greens ... think big tip to the concierge. Another great option—right on the Strip—is **Wynn Golf**. If you'd prefer to exercise your credit cards, wander the **Wynn Esplanade** to check out some of Vegas' most chichi shopping and compare it to **Via Bellagio**. While you're there, marvel at the Lake of Dreams show over a cappuccino at Sugar & Ice. It's Vegas spectacle at its stunning best.

1pm Lunch **Bartolotta, Risorante Di Mare** showcases chef Paul Bartolotta's menu of fresh fish flown in daily from Italy, and it's not unusual to find celebrities dining in the bi-level space. You could also try **Spago**, the granddaddy of the celebrity chef movement. There are many Wolfgang Puck restaurants in town, but this

LUXE

classic remains the best, with modern takes on comfort food. But save room for dessert: Grab a pain au chocolat and espresso at **Jean-Philippe Pâtisserie** and admire the chocolate fountain. If you golfed at Wynn, though, stick around and lunch at the exclusive **Country Club.**

3pm Time for a bit of R & R. Why not book a massage at the decadent **Spa Bellagio**? If you're feeling energetic, you could even combine it with a private kickboxing class. There's also the **Four Seasons Spa**, with all the low-key luxury and class you'd expect. If the sun beckons you outdoors, The Bellagio's pool is a fun, relaxed scene where you can be the star of your own show in a private cabana. Have a drink or two and relax: Tonight's a big one.

7:30pm Cirque du Soleil might be tops when it comes to number of shows in Vegas, but two other acts win out for sheer draw: *Céline Dion: A New Day* and *Elton John: The Red Piano.* Do what you must to get tickets.

9:30pm Dinner Pull all strings necessary to get a table at **Restaurant Guy Savoy** at Caesars Palace. Savoy is bringing his three-Michelin-star talent to Glitter Gulch—it's the restaurant of the moment, located on the second floor of the Augustus Tower. Alternatively, you won't be disappointed by a trip to **Alex at Wynn**, where the room is dra-matic and the food extraordinary. For something more low-key but no less delicious, **Daniel Boulud** at Wynn has heavenly French-inspired food. Get a patio or window-front table for front-row seats to the Lake show.

Midnight Back to Caesars and onto **Cleopatra's Barge**. This kitschy classic has made a comeback in recent years, and is now a happening spot for a 30- to 40-something dance crowd.

1am Tryst at Wynn awaits you. This hot club has an intimate vibe and a classy clientele.

2:30am Close out the night in ultra-lush style at Wynn's very elegant lounge, **Lure**. Whether you're reclining inside on the leather banquettes or hanging outside at the firepit, you'll find stylish, fun company partying well into the dawn.

The Morning After

Bellagio Buffet or **The Buffet**: It's not luxe Vegas without a buffet—Wynn's can't be beat, but The Bellagio does its best to try. Either one is sure to satisfy.

Luxe Las Vegas:
The Key Neighborhoods

Center Strip Here's where you'll find the Four Corners, marked by The Bellagio, Caesars Palace, Paris/Bally's, Flamingo, and Barbary Coast. Just south is The Aladdin/Planet Hollywood. This is the heart of Las Vegas and the Strip.

Downtown Once a poor and dangerous area, downtown has been revitalized with the pedestrian-friendly Fremont Street Experience. Although Vegas was founded here and old casinos still reign, the outskirts are still somewhat seedy.

North Strip Wynn is the main attraction here, with older and less flashy spots like the Stardust farther down. This area is less vibrant—and crowded—than the lower part of the Strip.

South Strip Mandalay Bay is the destination of choice on the south Strip, but you'll also find Excalibur, MGM, The Luxor, The Four Seasons, THEhotel at Mandalay Bay, New York-New York, and Monte Carlo, making it a buzzing area.

Summerlin A "master" planned community 12 miles west of the Strip, it's home to the Red Rock Casino, and it's one of the area's wealthiest residential enclaves.

West Flamingo Head west of the Strip and there's probably only one place you're going: Palms, a hipster hot spot.

LUXE

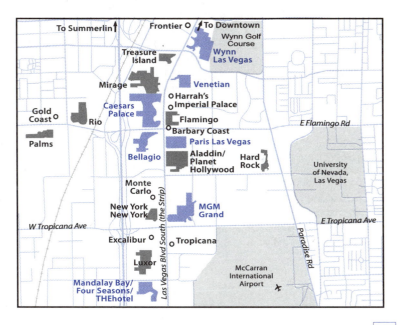

Luxe Las Vegas:
The Shopping Blocks

Via Bellagio

With high glass ceilings and lots of polished marble, Via Bellagio is one of Vegas' most elegant shopping spots, and offers a great view of the Bellagio Lake as an extra. *Daily 10am-midnight.* 3600 S. Las Vegas Blvd., 702-693-7111, bellagio.com

Fred Leighton If nearby Tiffany's is just too bland, Fred Leighton is your oyster. Famous for draping the silhouettes of Hollywood's leading ladies, this jeweler has everything from Art Deco designs to exotic replicas of the Maharaja's treasures. 702-693-7050, fredleighton.com

Hermès Grab a classic scarf, handbag, or even tableware at this temple of understated class. Whatever you purchase, it's sure to be worth passing on to future generations. 702-893-8900, hermes.com

Prada Do shoes get any better than this? The clothes aren't bad, either. Pick out the perfect outfit for a night on the town. 702-866-6886, prada.com

Wynn Esplanade

A hushed corridor connecting the street to the hotel proper, this stretch of shopping is Steve Wynn's one-better response to Via Bellagio, another of his creations. If you and your credit line are both exhausted, stop by Sugar & Ice for a lovely strawberry cupcake, a Rice Krispies treat, or a liquor-spiked hot chocolate, with patio seating close enough to the lake to feel the waterfall mist. *Sun-Thu 10am-11pm, Fri-Sat 10am-midnight.* 3131 S. Las Vegas Blvd., 702-770-7000, wynnlasvegas.com

Brioni There are some men who radiate confidence and civility at the same time, a savoir vivre that's irresistible. Those men wear Brioni. 702-770-3440, brioni.com

Chocolat Enormous milk chocolate–covered strawberries, cute dark chocolate lolipops, and oh, the éclairs! All from master French patissier Frédéric Robert. 702-770-3475

Jo Malone Simple and spare, yet so decadent, this perfume and skin care line from its British namesake offers choices from sophisticated to flirty, all in her trademark clear glass bottles. They are meant to be layered one on top of another, so don't be surprised if you leave here with a collection. 702-770-3485, jomalone.com

Manolo Blahnik If we have to explain why, you don't need to bother going. The Shoe God's first retail store outside Manhattan. 702-770-3477

Oscar de la Renta *Sex and the City* revitalized this fashion legend with a new, young following. Find out why at his only U.S. store. 702-770-3487

Luxe Las Vegas:
The Hotels

The Bellagio • Center Strip • Timeless (4,348 rms)
Named for the Lake Como village in northern Italy, Bellagio is the epitome of new Las Vegas—luxury without tackiness. Originally built by Steve Wynn and now part of MGM/Mirage Resorts, it's one of the city's few AAA five-diamond hotels, and it's a well-deserved designation. The Tuscan villa ambience runs like a subtle bass line through the resort. The lobby alone makes an indelible impression with a courtyard garden behind the registration desk, Sri Lankan marble floors, a chandelier bouquet of 3,000 brilliantly colored glass flowers (crafted by renowned glass sculptor Dale Chihuly), and a dazzling Italianate conservatory. Five of its concierges hold Les Clefs d'Or, the highest professional award given to a concierge (there are only 1,200 Les Clefs d'Or holders in the country). And the hotel also has some of the finest attractions and amenities under its roof: an opulent pool and spa; a fine art gallery; a small but stellar collection of shops like Tiffany & Co., Chanel, and Hermès; many of the city's haute cuisine restaurants; access to the best golf course in the world; the most awe-inspiring Cirque du Soleil production; and an equally mesmerizing fountain show that has become the symbol of new Las Vegas. All standard rooms (510 square feet) are luxurious, but for an extra $30 a night, you can guarantee one of the best views of the Strip, from the Eiffel Tower directly across the street at Paris Las Vegas to the fountain show below. An in-house TV channel pipes the synchronized music into your room so you get a private performance. $$$ 3600 S. Las Vegas Blvd. (Flamingo Rd.), 702-693-7111 / 888-987-7111, bellagio.com

Four Seasons • South Strip • Contemporary (424 rms)
Tucked away on the top four floors of Mandalay Bay, the Four Seasons upholds the chain's commitment to understated, impeccable luxury. Unlike almost every other fine hotel on the Strip, the Four Seasons has no casino, which means no constant jingling as you walk through the public spaces. It also means that this is the ideal retreat if you're looking to visit Sin City without the typical Vegas experience. Rooms are all about comfort and low-key style. You won't find flash here, but you will have L'Occitane bath amenities and even a dog walker if you decide to bring Fido along—personalized service is a point of pride. The facility also has a private entrance and valet, terrific restaurants including The Verandah (see p.124) and Charlie Palmer Steak (see p.117), and one of the best spas in the city (see p.130). Of course, patrons also have complete access to all that Mandalay Bay has to offer. Guests tend to be on the mature side, or in town on high-end business. The best rooms overlook the Strip, giving a sweeping view from the hotel's southern location. $$$$ 3960 S. Las Vegas Blvd. (Mandalay Bay Rd.), 702-632-5000 / 877-632-5000, fourseasons.com/lasvegas

Skylofts at MGM • South Strip • Modern (51 rms)
Like most casinos on the Strip, MGM has jumped into the high-end boutique hotel game with the Skylofts, a set of two-story ultra-luxury spaces (prices start at $800 per night) located on the top floors of the MGM Grand. Skylofts are less like hotel rooms and closer to condos. The difference is apparent the second you land at the airport, where all Skyloft guests will find a Maybach 62 limo waiting

to whisk them to the hotel. Once there, a personal concierge is on hand to handle every need, and you'll even get preferred seating at MGM restaurants and access to the 24-hour Skyspa to keep you relaxed. Ranging from one to three bedrooms, these plush pads are expansive, with separate living and dining areas, and at least one-and-a-half baths. Sleek furnishings are minimalist and elegant, in soothing Zen colors mixed with bold patterns—all designed to showcase the views through the giant floor-to-ceiling windows. Some rooms face the Strip for those who want to tower over the action, while others face the mountains for a serene escape. All of the suites have the same layout, so the view is really the deciding factor when requesting a room. Bathrooms have plasma-screen TVs, deep soaking tubs with an infinity edge, steam showers, and double vanities. $$$$ MGM Grand, 3799 S. Las Vegas Blvd. (Tropicana Ave.), 702-891-3832 / 877-646-5638, skyloftsmgmgrand.com

The Venetian • Center Strip • Classic (4,027 rms)
The attention to detail is amazing—no doubt because of the two historians hired to ensure architectural integrity and the team of 250 artisans, painters, and sculptors who made it happen. Many of Venice's famous landmarks are re-created here, including the Rialto Bridge, the Doge's Palace, St. Mark's Square, the Bridge of Sighs—and of course, the Grand Canal. Venetian rooms are large—700 square feet. Decorated in cheery blues and yellows, standard rooms have rather regal furnishings with a spacious canopied bedchamber and step-down parlor. Each room also has two 27-inch TVs, three dual-line phones, and a fax-copier-printer. Oversize bathrooms (130 square feet) feature dual vanities, separate glass-walled shower, deep tubs, and private water closet, all beautifully decorated in Italian marble. More lavish suites also come with shaving kits and toothbrushes, but anyone can request them from housekeeping. If you're looking for a bit more peace and quiet, book a room in the newish Venezia Tower. $$$ 3355 S. Las Vegas Blvd. (Flamingo Rd.), 702-414-1000 / 877-883-6423, venetian.com

Wynn Las Vegas • North Strip • Contemporary (2,719 rms)
Best Celebrity-Spotting Hotels Wynn Las Vegas is the new signature resort of Steve Wynn, who has become an icon in the city and is considered a living legend in America's adult Disneyland. It's the most expensive casino resort on the Strip, with a price tag of $2.7 billion, and sits behind an artificial mountain. Its newness still attracts some looky-loos, but the rest of the crowd is more high rollers and those who aspire to be. Its restaurants are among the trendiest in town, especially SW (p.124), Alex (p.115), and Okada (p.121). If you're looking for a high-quality dining experience without the see-and-be-seen atmosphere, make your reservations at Daniel Boulud (p.118) or Bartolotta, Ristorante Di Mare (p.116). The golf course was thoughtfully built on the old Desert Inn course and has a stunning waterfall on the 18th hole. The Lake of Dreams show, a highlight of the hotel, can also be seen from the casino level near the lobby. The best rooms are on the 27th to 35th floors. Request a room with the private VIP entrance for only $60 more. You can also ask for a room facing the Strip if you want a view of the Lake of Dreams show from your room, or a room on the golf course side of Wynn for a sweeping green landscape that is ideal if you're spending more time in your room. $$$$ 3131 S. Las Vegas Blvd. (E. Desert Inn Rd.), 702-770-7000 / 877-320-7123, wynnlasvegas.com

Luxe Las Vegas:
The Restaurants

Alex at Wynn • North Strip • French (G)

Best High-Roller Dining This is one of the most elegant dining rooms on the Strip, and certainly the fanciest at Steve Wynn's signature casino. But luxury doesn't have to compromise with fun. There is an eccentric design element throughout the restaurant. Take special note of the chair legs. They were designed with unique anthropomorphic features. The "Paulo" chair is so named because the legs of the chair represent the legs of Mr. Wynn's German shepherd, Paulo. As for dinner, chef Alessandro (Alex) Stratta, who was previously known for his six-year tenure at Renoir, where he was named a "Best Hotel Chef" by the James Beard Foundation, brings us a tasting menu straight from the French Riviera. Less than a year from opening, Alex at Wynn had already received the esteemed AAA five-diamond award. His tasting menus are seasonal and made from only the freshest market ingredients. Try the buttered leeks and black truffles, tenderloin of veal with spinach cannelloni and chanterelles, and roasted foie gras with caramelized peaches and aged balsamic vinegar. Savor the meal slowly and make sure to save room for pastry chef Jenifer Witte's signature banana and chocolate beignets with white chocolate and macadamia. *Nightly 5:30-10:30pm.* $$$$ ▬ Wynn, 702-770-3300, wynnlasvegas.com

Alizé • West Flamingo • French

Commanding the top floor of this hipster hotel, and named for the winds that tousle the French Caribbean islands, Alizé is the third restaurant in Chef André Rochat's culinary family, which includes the original downtown André's and André's at the Monte Carlo. You'll find many of Rochat's signature dishes—rack of lamb, Dover sole Veronique, venison, sauteed prime rib of beef—but here they're served up with 14-foot floor-to-ceiling window views of the Strip to a room equally mixed between foodies and scenesters. Rochat is also known for his mind-blowing wine cellars, and here he has two: one in the center of the restaurant to accommodate the labels on the 65-page wine list; the other in the front hallway, stocked with 1,000 bottles of champagne, Armagnac, and port. Another perk: Dinner at Alizé automatically gains you entry into Ghostbar, one floor below. *Sun-Thu 5:30-10pm, Fri-Sat 5:30-10:30pm.* $$$$ ▬ Palms, 702-951-7000, alizelv.com

Andre's • Downtown • French

Andre's is truly one of Las Vegas' hidden gems—although for locals, its excellence is well established. Located in a residential neighborhood near downtown, Andre's is consistently ranked as one of the city's best restaurants. Chef Andre Rochat (also of the Palms' Alizé) creates exquisite, authentic French fare in a picture-perfect setting. André's is set in a house, and dining areas are divided between four main rooms and a terrace—in warm weather, this cozy area is the best place to sit. Each one has a slightly different décor (and some can be reserved for parties as small as six), but all have impeccable charm with absolutely none of the flash you will find on the Strip. That's what makes this a top spot for romance and fine dining. You'll find none of the getting-ready-to-party crowds here. It's all sophisticated diners looking for a special night out. *Mon-Sat 5:30-9:30pm* $$$$ ⊟ 401 S. 6th St. (Chef Andre Rochat Pl.), 702-385-5016, alizelv.com/original

Aureole • South Strip • Continental (G)

Best Fine Dining It's all about the wine at the Las Vegas offshoot of Charlie Palmer's hugely popular Aureole in New York, which picked up four diamonds from AAA. What's the tip-off? The $1.2 million, four-story steel and glass wine tower in the center of the restaurant, inspired by *Mission: Impossible* and designed by Adam Tihany. Stocked with more than 9,000 bottles, it's run by a cadre of "wine angels" in black catsuits strapped into special harnesses that let them fly into the upper reaches and pluck the bottles from the appropriate bins (securing them in their holsters). It's a wonder in a town of wonders. Aureole's entrance is about halfway up this 50-foot tower. To reach the dining room, you cross the catwalk, then go down the stairs that curve around the tower. And what of the food? Palmer imported some of his signature, progressive American dishes from New York, like sea scallop sandwiches, crab cakes, and wood-grilled filet mignon in cabernet sauce. Other standouts include the sauteed foie gras with peppered donuts, lamb chops, veal mignon, and roasted pork saltimbocca. The best tables are 104 to 106, through a glass arch waterfall in the Swan Court dining room—a smaller, more formal space with just 13 tables, captain service, and a patio with outdoor tables for smoking and a pond complete with swans. For those not in the mood for a full meal, the small bar serves à la carte, and has intimate couches and low lighting for a romantic feel. *Nightly 5:30-10pm.* $$$$ B⊟ Mandalay Bay, 702-632-7401, aureolelv.com

Bartolotta, Ristorante Di Mare • North Strip • Italian

By day, Bartolotta is a great place to take a lunch meeting or spend a few hours transporting yourself back to that Italian meal you had on the coast of Italy way back when. The décor is colorful and modern like the rest of Wynn Las Vegas, but Paul Bartolotta's fresh seafood menu is traditional and rustic. By night, Bartolotta transforms into an elegant summer party. Whether you're there to have a romantic dinner for two, or entertaining a small group of six, make your reservations for an al fresco cabana table by the pond, or if it's chilly, inside looking out onto the patio. The risotto is divine, but you'd be missing out if you didn't see the tray of fish flow in daily from Italy; it's cooked to order by weight. *Nightly 5:30-10pm.* $$$ B⊟ Wynn, 702-770-9966, wynnlasvegas.com

Bouchon • Center Strip • French

Best Brasseries Vegas is known for emulating regions of the world and making them accessible to middle America. But Thomas Keller gives you a genuine taste of France with a "bouchon," or bistro, in the Lyonnaise tradition. Most come to this restaurant because they've dined at, or heard of, Keller's famed French Laundry in Napa, California. But they come back because they feel civilized here. All meals are worthy sampling, but breakfast stands out because the Strip doesn't have a whole lot in between buffets and coffee stands. Of course it has great dinners including items like steak frites and moules, but try the trout aux amandes, croque madame, or boudin noir to get a true taste of what we're missing way over here on the other side of the Atlantic. Culinary connoisseurs should order off the blackboard menu for the changing seasonal dishes. Bouchon is located in the new Venezia towers on the 10th floor. On a nice day, ask for an outdoor table overlooking the pool. It's even fun to sit at the Pewter bar up front if you're solo. *Daily 7-10:30am, 5-10:45pm; lunch Sat-Sun noon-2:30pm.* $$ B≡ The Venetian, 702-414-6200, frenchlaundry.com

The Buffet • North Strip • Buffet
Best Gourmet Buffets Not all buffets are created equal. Like everything done by Steve Wynn, this one—simply named The Buffet—rises above the competition in terms of both setting and food. The space itself has a garden theme divided up between several small rooms, giving it a more intimate feel than some of the dining-hall environments of other buffets. The atrium room is especially pleasant, with a conservatory-like feel. The food—with offerings from carving and seafood stations to Chinese and sushi—changes daily, but is always of top quality. Even the desserts here are delicious, giving the meal a decadent finale with items like oversized crème brûlée and homemade ice cream. Lines here tend to not be as long as those at The Bellagio, especially if you come on the early side for breakfast. *Sun-Thu 8am-10pm, Fri-Sat 8am-10:30pm.* $$$ ≡ Wynn, 702-770-3340, wynnlasvegas.com

The Buffet at Bellagio • Center Strip • Buffet
Best Gourmet Buffets This buffet boasts mix-and-match international delicacies such as venison, Kobe beef, duck breast, steamed clams, mako shark, salmon sashimi, and apple-smoked sturgeon. Be warned: Lines can get long at prime hours. *Mon-Fri 8am-10pm, Fri-Sun 8am-11pm.* $$$ ≡ The Bellagio, 702-693-7111, bellagio.com

Charlie Palmer Steak* • South Strip • Steakhouse
Best Steakhouses This bastion of manly sophistication is a great place for a classic meat meal, but we also love the lounge for a quiet, intimate meeting of the business or social variety. *See Luxe Nightlife, p.125, for details. Nightly 5-10:30pm; lounge 5pm-12:30am.* $$$ ⊑ The Four Seasons, 702-632-5120, charliepalmersteaklv.com

Le Cirque • Center Strip • French (G)
If the city is a circus, then this tiny haute-cuisine French restaurant is one of the greatest (food) shows on earth. With just 65 seats, Le Cirque is by the Maccioni family, who established the original Le Cirque as one of New York's must-dine restaurants. The dining room, designed by Adam Tihany, is a sophisticated play on the Big Top—a fitting backdrop for the kitchen's astonishing feats of culinary greatness. It's decorated in reds and golds with a silk tented ceiling, striped furniture, and wall murals that give a nod to the original Le Cirque monkey murals. With a AAA four-diamond rating to go with its four stars from Mobil, it's no wonder that it's one of the most expensive meals in Las Vegas, although gourmands may grouse that, while excellent, it's not the best. But add in a window-side table overlooking the Bellagio fountains, and we're certain you will have a lovely memory of this meal. *Nightly 5:30-10:30pm.* $$$$ B⊑ The Bellagio, 702-693-8100, bellagio.com

The Country Club • North Strip • Continental
This exclusive-feeling spot at Wynn is a favorite of those hitting the links, but is also open to the public. It's a modern take on a classic club, with dark wood and plush chairs inside, and a lovely outdoor patio that overlooks the golf course

and the waterfall from white-linen tables. The food, courtesy of chef David Walzog, is updated steakhouse fare, with lots of continental options. You'll find a refined set dining at this spot, mostly couples or groups looking for good food in a serene setting. *Daily 8-10:30am (continental breakfast starting at 6am), 11:30am-3pm, (club menu 3-5:30pm), 5:30-10:30pm.* $$$ B☐ Wynn, 702-770-3315, wynnlasvegas.com

Daniel Boulud Brasserie • North Strip • French
Best Brasseries There are other Wynn restaurants that get more hype. That's fine with us—it makes it just a little easier to get a reservation at this underrated gem. Tucked on the lower level of Wynn next to the lake, Daniel Boulud is an oasis of calm sophistication. The food is fabulous, especially the burger the place is famous for, but don't miss out on more upscale items like the steak au poivre. Perhaps the best part of this place is the attitude, or lack of it. Servers are knowledgeable, but not pretentious. For the most part, you'll find a 30- and 40-something crowd that knows good food. In summer, the prime tables are outside overlooking the Lake of Dreams. In winter, try for a cozy booth. There is also a bar area great for a quick bite and a quiet drink. *Nightly 5:30-10:30pm.* $$$$ B☐ Wynn, 702-770-3300, wynnlasvegas.com

Delmonico Steakhouse • Center Strip • Steakhouse
Best Steakhouses Elegant and old-school, Delmonico is tucked down a quiet hallway of The Venetian. The dining room isn't visible from the casino, but a cozy and casually upscale bar makes a great place for a pre-dinner cocktail, or an anytime escape from the madness of the nearby gambling. Once you pass through the enormous oak doors into the sophisticated dining room, you'll be in the company of a mature crowd looking for a refined experience—the perfect setting for chef Emeril Lagasse's stellar spicy dishes like Creole boiled gulf shrimp and pepper-crusted dry-aged beef sirloin. *Sun-Thu 11:30am-2pm and 5:30-10:30pm, Fri-Sat 11:30am-2pm and 5:30-11pm.* $$$$ B☐ The Venetian, 702-414-3737, emerils.com

Drai's* • Center Strip • French
Early evening, it's a romantic fine French restaurant that constantly rates as one of the city's favorites, but come back a few hours later, and this is one of Vegas' hottest after-hours scenes. See *Bachelor(ette) Nightlife,* p.95, for details. *Nightly 5:30-10pm.* $$$ ☐ Barbary Coast, 702-737-0555, draisafterhours.com

Eiffel Tower Restaurant • Center Strip • French
Located a third of the way up the half-scale replica of the hotel's Eiffel Tower, the restaurant offers amazing panoramic views of the Strip and fountains of Bellagio from its floor-to-ceiling windows. The elegant dining room has crimson velvet booths, a piano bar, and tables for two that ring the windows, giving couples the most romantic vantage points—these are the ones to reserve. Start with some foie gras or caviar. Entrée specialties include roasted rack of lamb Provençal, lobster thermidor, and braised quail. *Sun-Thu 5:30-10pm, Fri-Sat 5:30-10:30pm.* $$$$ B☐☐ Paris Las Vegas, 702-948-6937, eiffeltowerrestaurant.com

FIX* • Center Strip • Continental
This was the first restaurant project from the illustrious Light Group. Knowing that, expect a place where eating is nearly secondary to being seen. Located in The Bellagio next to the upscale shopping row that connects with the Strip, FIX is as hot as its clientele. You'll find flashy diners that are catching a Kobe

slider between craps games, or sucking down mojitos from the bar while they scope out the crowd that's dining. There are no walls facing the casino, so if you do want to show off whomever you're with, ask for a table on the rail, but for privacy, ask for a table away from the casino floor. It's a great place to start off a late night, whether your agenda is a show, gambling, or clubbing. Don't leave without trying the fried mac and cheese. *Sun-Thu 5pm-midnight, Fri-Sat 5pm-2am.* $$$ ▤ The Bellagio, 702-693-8400, fixlasvegas.com

Fleur de Lys • South Strip • French

Those following Sin City's celebrity chef roster delight in making Herbert Keller's Fleur de Lys a must stop. Nestled next to Aureole and across from Red Square at Mandalay Bay, this reformist French cuisine is well suited for the sophisticated palate. The dining room has banquette and table seating beneath high ceilings. Those coming for special occasions may request one of the four secluded cabana rooms, or try the slightly chilly wine room upstairs that overlooks the restaurant. It prides itself on top service as well as Keller's mastery, and was named one of the nation's Hot 50 restaurants of 2005 by *Bon Appetit*. When you go, look at the flower sculpture in the shape of a leaf. It is made from 3,500 fresh roses, with 300 to 400 changed daily. Sitting under its soft scent is a treat. *Nightly 5:30-10:30pm.* $$$$ B▤ Mandalay Bay, 702-632-9400, fleurdelyssf.com

Jasmine • Center Strip • Chinese

Jasmine is a cut above and then some from your typical out-of-a-cardboard-box-with-splintery-chopsticks Chinese restaurant. Chef Philip Lo, who's known for his nouvelle Hong Kong cuisine, serves elegant Cantonese, Szechuan, and Hunan dishes. The setting is a beautiful Victorian dining room, adorned with authentic Chinese art pieces and a front-row view of the dancing fountains. *Nightly 5:30-10pm.* $$$$ ▤ The Bellagio, 702-693-7111, bellagio.com

Jean-Philippe Pâtisserie • Center Strip • Cafe/Dessert

Willy Wonka, eat your heart out. The chocolate fountain at this spot, located toward the back of the hotel past the conservatory, brings onlookers from all over Vegas. While some come to enjoy the handmade delicacies from master pastry chef Jean-Philippe, or walk away with a tasty gelato, it's the spewing, churning, swirling fountain that captivates. It is said to be the largest chocolate fountain in the world, a 27-foot-tall engineering marvel holding more than 2,000 pounds of gooey goodness. Six rivers pour from the ceiling, feeding dark, milk, and white chocolate down a series of suspended, handcrafted glass vessels and into the floor, where heated pumps recirculate the chocolate back to the top. It's completely enclosed in glass, and runs 24 hours a day. It took two years to engineer and design this one-of-a-kind treasure. *Mon-Thu 7am-11pm, Fri-Sun 7am-midnight.* $ ▤ The Bellagio, 702-693-7111, bellagio.com

Joël Robuchon at The Mansion • South Strip • French Fusion (G)

Best High-Roller Dining The Mansion is the newest addition to the MGM Grand's impressive collection of celebrity chef restaurants. Chef Jöel Robuchon has already received some of the most prestigious awards in his field, including being named Chef of the Century. This is his first restaurant outside France, and he's actually opened with two Jöel Robuchon dining rooms. L'Atelier de Jöel Robuchon is right next door and focuses on a more casual atmosphere, including counter service. As the name would suggest, The Mansion has both the elegance and grandeur of a fine private residence, but pleases connoisseurs with the intimacy of a dining room for only 64. There is seating for 12 in the "indoor garden," an exclusive enclave of villas that run the rate of $500 to $15,000 a night, and a private dining room for up to ten overlooking it. The preferred way to dine here is by choosing one of the two tasting menus, either 6 courses or 12, but dining à la carte is not forbidden. Make sure you save plenty of time to enjoy this meal, and book your reservations at least a week in advance. *Nightly 5:30-10:30pm.* $$$$ ⬛ MGM Grand, 702-891-7358, mgmgrand.com

L'Atelier de Joël Robuchon • Center Strip • French (G)
L'Atelier, whose name refers to an artist's studio, is one of the two hot new Joël Robuchon restaurants to come to the United States. Who? The celebrated Chef of the Century, he is one of France's favorite masters of the kitchen. The Mansion is the fancier of the two restaurants here, and located just next door. L'Atelier attracts those who are looking to see what the hype is all about without putting on fancy evening wear or paying through the nose. Not that the Mansion isn't worth it—it is—but L'Atelier reaches a larger audience of culinary connoisseurs. Here, diners can watch the creative process of the chef, and eat off an à la carte menu that features delicate roasted rack of lamb perfumed with thyme, and free-range quail stuffed with foie gras and served with truffle-mashed potatoes—all from seating at the bar or at one of the very few tables. The chef de cuisine is actually Steve Benjamin, who has been trained by Robuchon, but Robuchon does appear at the MGM five times a month to do the cooking himself. Because of its bar seating overlooking the kitchen, this is a fantastic spot for a solo fine-dining experience. *Sun-Thu 5:30-10pm, Fri-Sat 5:30-10:30pm.* $$$$ Ⓑ⬛ MGM Grand, 702-891-7358, mgmgrand.com

Lutèce • Center Strip • French
This chic 90-seat space is the hip younger sibling to the older, more established New York original. It has a beautiful patio (our favorite place to sit) overlooking The Venetian's outdoor canal with its singing gondoliers, and Mirage's erupting volcano. The all-white décor is ultra cool, drawing celebrities like P. Diddy and Ozzy Osbourne. Chef David Feau, who divides his time between the two restaurants, pushes the boundaries of French cuisine with impressive dishes like the foie gras with chocolate and orange marmalade. Other highlights include the black bass with lobster sauce and herb noodles, or the applewood smoked codfish in white truffle oil. *Nightly 5:30-10pm.* $$$$ Ⓑ⬛ The Venetian, 702-414-2220, arkvegas.com/lutece

Luv-It Custard • South Strip • Ice Cream
On scorching days, locals and savvy tourists line up at this tiny shack to cool off with Luv-It's famous custard. There are no tables or chairs, only a walk-up window. But once you taste this creamy treat, you won't care that you're standing in a parking lot next to a Citgo station, steps from the Olympic Gardens strip club. Greg Tiedemann, who bought the business from his grandmother and now runs it with his wife, makes four or five flavors fresh every day. Purists savor it solo, but you can mix things up in one of his ever-popular sundaes, like the Western, made with hot fudge, caramel, and salted pecans, or the Scotch Jimmie, made with butterscotch, sliced bananas, Jimmies, and a cherry. *Tue-Thu 1-10pm, Fri-Sat 1-11pm.* $ ⬛ 505 E. Oakey Blvd. (S. Las Vegas Blvd.), 702-384-6452, luvitfrozencustard.com

Michael Mina • Center Strip • Seafood

Star chef Michael Mina's eponymous restaurant (formerly known as Aqua) offers succulent signature seafood in a sleek and elegant atmosphere. Mina is a San Francisco giant in the culinary world. He was named *Bon Appétit* Chef of the Year in 2005 for his innovative seafood menu, which presents fish in a way that has traditionally been reserved for meats. Mina's daring Mediterranean- and French-influenced cuisine aims to be surprising without being outrageous. Highlights include the seared foie gras in a thick pinot noir wine sauce, miso-glazed sea bass, and mussel soufflé. Adventurous epicureans might opt for the five-course tasting menu, featuring the AAA four-star diamond restaurant's signature dishes (tuna tartare, lobster pot pie), each paired with a carefully chosen accompanying wine. *Nightly 5:30-10pm.* $$$$ B= The Bellagio, 702-693-8100, michaelmina.net

Okada • North Strip • Japanese

This is modern sushi on the Strip that doesn't try to compete with Nobu—and why should it? It's all Wynn, which means it has enough style of its own without playing copycat. Tucked away off the casino floor, Okada has spacious seating, a curved sushi bar, and a teppanyaki room. Both rooms have high floor-to-ceiling windows that look out at the waterfalls and La Bete Lagoon. If you're dining as a couple and looking for privacy, sit in the main dining room, as the teppanyaki tables are shared. If you're coming to people-watch, get reservations for the weekend. There is even a private pagoda table outside for no less than $1,200. Adventurous eaters can take a caviar tasting tour. And remember, if you want Nobu, just go to Nobu. *Sun-Thu 5:30-10pm, Fri-Sat 5:30-11pm.* $$$ B= Wynn, 702-770-3320, wynnlasvegas.com

Olives • Center Strip • Mediterranean

Todd English, named *Bon Appétit's* 2001 Restaurateur of the Year, James Beard's Best Chef in the Northeast, and an Iron Chef, serves up his inventive spins on Mediterranean dishes in this delightful cafe, located along Via Bellagio's arcade of shops. The romantic dining room is festooned with brilliant mosaic tiles, brightly colored art glass—including a magnificent chandelier—and cafe-style seating. There's even patio seating with a view of the lake. Be sure to try the flatbread pizzas, wild boar pappardelle, or rabbit piccata with some falling cake for dessert. *Daily 11am-3pm, 5-10:30pm.* $$$$ B= The Bellagio, 702-693-8181, toddenglish.com

Osteria del Circo • Center Strip • Italian

This is the more casual restaurant in the Le Cirque family, but in fact, one kitchen serves both dining rooms. Osteria del Circo is even bolder and brighter than Le Cirque, with a more whimsical vibe. A brass monkey peddles a unicycle on the high wire stretching across the open front grill, sculptures fly above the diners, and multicolored balls spin. There's so much going on in the dining room it really feels like a circus, and that high energy flows onto the plates where northern Italian dishes are served with panache. Save room for the sweet stuff, like panna cotta or upside-down warm chocolate cake with acacia honey ice cream, and see why *Las Vegas Life* voted Osteria del Circo Best for Desserts. *Sun-Thu 5:30-10pm, Fri-Sat 5:30-10:30pm.* $$$$ B= The Bellagio, 702-693-8150, osteriadelcirco.com

Palm Restaurant • Center Strip • Steakhouse

When it comes to steakhouses, The Palm is a true classic. What started as a New York City chain in the '20s has since spread across the country from East Hampton to Los Angeles. Located just inside the Forum Shops, this white-linen eatery is a favorite with local celebrities like Mayor Oscar Goodman and tennis star Andre Agassi. Menu highlights include its classic three-pound-plus lobsters, filets, porterhouses, chops, and prime rib along with veal made five ways, including marsala, parmigiana, piccata, malfata, and martini. The Palm also features classic steakhouse fixings like hearts of palm or lettuce salads, clams casino, shrimp cocktail, and lobster bisque, along with sides like creamed spinach, gargantuan baked potatoes, and crispy onion rings. When you're done with dinner, check out its selection of fine cigars, including Macanudo, Hamilton, and Monte Cristo. *Sun-Thu 11:30am-10pm, Fri-Sat 11:30am-11pm.* $$$$ B≡ Caesars Palace, 702-732-7256, thepalm.com

Picasso • Center Strip • French-Mediterranean (G)

This rustic yet elegant restaurant is hung with nine original Picassos (with carpet and furniture designed by the master painter's son Claude) and has a beautiful lakeside view of the fountain show. Of course, there's the food. A James Beard Award winner who made his reputation at the four-star San Francisco French restaurant Masa's, chef Julian Serrano presents a four-course prix fixe menu or a five-course degustation that changes regularly. Serrano is clearly doing something right as he has captured AAA's five-diamond award twice and snared Mobil's five stars as well. This isn't a place for a casual meal—Picasso is about fine dining, and caters to a sophisticated, moneyed crowd looking for a culinary adventure to brag about. *Wed-Mon 6-9:30pm; closed Tue.* $$$$ ▭ The Bellagio, 702-693-8105, bellagio.com

Prime Steakhouse • Center Strip • Steakhouse

Best Steakhouses This Vegas addition to über-chef Jean-Georges Vongerichten's culinary empire is an elegant Wedgwood blue and brown '30s-style chophouse. It's a steak lover's steakhouse, featuring prime cuts with signature sauces that run the gamut from obvious to esoteric, and a wine list that's heavy on the bold French and American reds. The shellfish platter, served on sterling, makes a great opener. The New York strip, seasoned with six types of ground peppercorn, and the rich, cheesy gratin potatoes are favorites. The Valrhona chocolate dessert, perhaps with a snifter of Hardy's Perfection, makes a decadent finish. On nice nights, the best seats are out on the patio or by the window, where the Bellagio fountain show takes place. *Nightly 5:30-10pm.* $$$$ B≡ The Bellagio, 702-693-8484, bellagio.com

Restaurant Guy Savoy • Center Strip • French (G)

Best High-Roller Dining French art can sometimes be hard to swallow. Not so at world-renowned, Michelin three-star chef Guy Savoy's namesake restaurant. The elegant, upscale eatery, located on the second floor of the Augustus Tower, replicates Savoy's critically acclaimed flagship restaurant in Paris. High ceilings give the intimate 75-seat dining room a toned-down cathedral look and feel, enhanced by the gray walls and dark wood paneling. Unlike some Vegas restaurants that are more about the scene than the cuisine, here the understated, ethereal setting plays a perfect complement to Savoy's gastronomic masterpieces, which resemble fine art as well as fine dining. Specialty dishes include the artichoke black truffle soup, crispy sea bass, butter-roasted veal sweetbread, and chocolate ganache served with tonka beans. A cheese cart presents more than 20 varieties of the best French cheeses, while the impressive 1,500-bottle wine list ranges from old world vintages to affordable American boutique choices. *Wed-Sun 5-10:30pm.* $$$$ B☐ Caesars Palace, 702-731-7286, caesars.com

Sensi • Center Strip • Asian Fusion

Sensi is a sleek chef's kitchen in the back of Bellagio that, as its name suggests, caters to all the senses of the diner. The waterfall flowing over gray slate at the entrance is immediately soothing. Inside, the sight of chefs preparing food in the see-through kitchen and the buzz of people talking bring the dining experience to life. There are chef's tables next to the kitchen, but those sitting a row back can still see all the action. You'll mostly find Bellagio hotel guests dining here. The braised beef short rib with horseradish mashed potatoes, spinach, and black pepper jus, and the miso-glazed sea bass are recommended over the red chicken curry or crispy tai red snapper. The crisp fried shrimp will have you wanting a second plate. *Daily 11am-2pm and 5-10:30pm.* $$$$ B☰ The Bellagio, 702-693-8800, bellagio.com

Shintaro • Center Strip • Japanese (G)

Best Sushi Restaurants Shintaro is an elegant experience boasting a huge, gorgeous jellyfish tank where you can watch the creatures' languid ballet while munching on their relatives at the sushi bar, all backlit in brilliant colors—as the jellyfish float, they look like living lava lamps. But that's not the only entertainment. The main dining room features teppanyaki tables where chefs play with fire, performing tricks while they cook for a well-heeled clientele. There are non-teppanyaki tables as well, but really, why not? *Nightly 5:30-10:30pm.* $$$ B☐☰ The Bellagio, 702-693-8141, bellagio.com

Spago • Center Strip • Continental

There are about as many Wolfgang Puck eateries in Las Vegas as dice and blackjack tables. But Spago, the "it" restaurant of the '80s, is still one of the finest, serving California cuisine in a beautiful dining room designed by Adam Tihany, creator of Aureole's enormous wine tower, and adjoined by a more casual cafe. The food here is outstanding, featuring upscale twists on comfort favorites like smoked salmon, caviar, and crème fraîche pizza and pancetta-wrapped meat loaf with garlic-mashed potatoes served in the cafe. The menu also features sophisticated entrées like soft-shell crab with shrimp risotto, veal sweetbreads, roasted black bass, and teriyaki-glazed red snapper, served in the main dining room. Be sure to leave room for the decadent caramel fudge tart or the warm melting chocolate cake for dessert. You'll need a reservation for the dining room, but not the cafe. *Cafe: Sun-Thu 11am-11pm, Fri-Sat 11am-midnight. Dining room: nightly 6-9pm.* $$$$ B☰ Caesars Palace, 702-369-6300, wolfgangpuck.com

Sterling Brunch • Center Strip • Buffet

Best Gourmet Buffets Bally's is anything but grand, but you'd never guess from glancing at its visually impressive buffet, where there's a high-quality selection of contemporary, sophisticated dishes—broiled Maine lobster, sushi, rack of lamb, Japanese baby octopus, smoked salmon, duck, and veal. East to west, this haute buffet lures even the most discerning palates. *Sun 9:30am-2:30pm.* $$$ ☰ Bally's, 702-967-7999, caesars.com/Ballys/LasVegas

SW Steakhouse • North Strip • Steakhouse

You've heard of Steak and Syrah; well, this is Steak and a Show—if you sit outside. Inside Wynn Las Vegas, make your way to the big waterfall and SW will be on your left at the bottom of the escalator. The restaurant overlooks the lagoon and mountain setting. Seats on the patio get a front-row view of the *Lake of Dreams* light and water show, which runs every 45 minutes after 8pm. Chef Eric Klein serves up high-quality steak for even the pickiest of carnivores. He is known for his work at Spago and Maple Drive restaurants in Beverly Hills, and uses Alsatian influences to create a slightly different experience than the usual steakhouse fare. Expect a well-heeled, well-dressed crowd. *Nightly 5:30-10:15pm.* $$$$ B≡ Wynn Las Vegas, 702-770-9966, wynnlasvegas.com

The Verandah • South Strip • American

The Verandah is the breakfast, lunch, and dinner spot for The Four Seasons. Like all things associated with the hotel, it delivers impeccable service as well as excellent California cuisine in a very sophisticated setting. You'll mostly find hotel guests enjoying breakfast on the patio (some of the best seats) or having a quiet dinner inside—that's a shame. The Verandah is such a lovely experience that it's worth it for non-guests to make the trip. *Mon-Fri 6:30-10pm, Sat-Sun 7-11pm.* $$$ ☐ The Four Seasons, 702-632-5121, fourseasons.com

Zeffirino Ristorante • Center Strip • Italian

This two-story restaurant, named for chef-owner Paulo Belloni's father, evokes an old-time Genoa restaurant, particularly in the downstairs wine cellar and seafood bar where you can have a cold antipasto and watch the shoppers drift by just as if you were sitting in a little tavern. Upstairs, the dining's more formal, though not fussy. The menu is all about seafood Italian-style, and highlights include red snapper, lobster tail, filet of sole piccola, and swordfish steak. *Mon-Sat 11:30am-midnight, Sun 10am-midnight.* $$$ B≡ The Venetian, 702-414-3500, venetian.com

Luxe Las Vegas:
The Nightlife

Caramel • Center Strip • Lounge
Best Ultra Lounges It's hard to figure out why Light's lower-key sibling (and sister lounge to Mist at Treasure Island) is called Caramel when the entire décor is more claret and black. But Caramel has sexy corseted bartenders who make a mean martini that you can enjoy at the polished cherry wood bar, or better, reserve one of the black leather banquettes. This spot is Bellagio's answer to the hipster hot spots at places like Palm and Hard Rock, and you'll find a 20- and 30-something crowd lounging, scoping, and having fun. *Nightly 5pm-4am.* ▤
The Bellagio, 702-693-8300, lightgroup.com

Céline Dion: A New Day • Center Strip • Show
Caesars built a $95 million, 4,000-seat coliseum to house this production, one of the hottest tickets in town. Created by Franco Dragone, who's known for crafting Cirque du Soleil's *O* and *Mystère, New Day* blends theater, dance, song, and sophisticated stage technology as the company's 48 dancers swirl around the pop star. Go to see the stagecraft. Buy your tickets in advance—you may have trouble wrangling them once you get to Las Vegas. *Wed-Sun 8:30pm.* ▣▤
Caesars Palace, 702-731-7110, celinedion.com

Charlie Palmer Steak* • South Strip • Restaurant/Lounge
Best Quiet Bars This is the place where a man can eat steak in the bar, smoke a cigar, and savor a brandy. It is elegant, but not romantic, and located high up in the Four Seasons resort far away from the casino clatter. You will see some families, but the bar has a sitting area with comfy lounge chairs that entice you to sit and enjoy a mellow good time in comfort, whether solo or with companions. *Dinner nightly 5-10:30pm; lounge 5pm-12:30am* ▭ Four Seasons, 702-632-5120, charliepalmersteaklv.com

Cleopatra's Barge • Center Strip • Nightclub
A few years ago, this temple of classic Vegas kitsch had floated away into the land of passé. But a huge remodel has brought it back, mooring it firmly in the cool nightlife scene of modern-day Vegas. The crowd here tends to be a little bit older and more well-behaved than those at some of the Strip's trendiest nightspots, maybe because of the emphasis on R & B, led by Anita Sarawak and the Rhythm Nation at packed weekend dance parties. *Tue-Sun 10pm-4am.* ▤
Caesars Palace, 702-369-6300, caesars.com

Club Paradise • East Flamingo • Strip Club
Club Paradise is still the most upscale strip club in all of Las Vegas and regularly boasts girls that you've seen in *Playboy* and *Maxim*. It's also located close to The Hard Rock, which means it draws in a younger, hipper clientele. There is no other club in Las Vegas that comes close for sheer quality of eye candy. But in general, the lap dances are tame. If you want a place to bring your girl and introduce her to the world of strip clubs, this is it—she won't be the only non-working woman in the room. *Mon-Fri 5pm-8am, Sat-Sun 6pm-8am.* ▣▤
4416 Paradise Rd. (Flamingo Rd.), 702-734-7990, clubparadise.net

Elton John: The Red Piano • Center Strip • Show

Best Shows The legendary musician from London, England, who has rocked the charts over the course of 30 years came to Vegas and blew us away. Sir Elton John's show, *The Red Piano*, is an unforgettable performance that sails through the course of his career and continues to sell out shows in the $95 million, 4,100-seat Colosseum theater. In 2004, he racked up a handful of local awards including "Best All-Around Performer, "Best Performer Las Vegas 2004," "#1 Las Vegas Show of 2004," and "Most Exciting Show of 2004." What was originally supposed to be 75 shows over a three-year period has been extended to another 150 through 2008. *Nightly 7:30pm (except Mon and Thu), showtimes vary by season, call for schedule.* C≡ Caesars Palace, 702-866-1400, caesars.com

La Femme • Center Strip • Topless Revue

Best Shows With its intriguing play of light on skin, this artsy topless revue imported from Paris blends eroticism with classical and modern dance. Staged in the intimate *La Femme* cabaret-style theater, which re-creates the original Crazy Horse on Avenue George V, this production, featuring a brief behind-the-scenes film of life at the Crazy Horse and 13 classically trained ballet dancers from the original *La Femme* company, is tasteful enough for a date, but will probably disappoint men looking for stripper action. *Nightly 8:30pm and 10:30pm.* C≡ MGM Grand, 702-891-7777, mgmgrand.com

FIX* • Center Strip • Bar/Lounge

This sleek dining spot, with undulating wood ceilings and an open view out across the casino floor, has a great bar and lounge that's a hot spot for meeting singles and hanging out. Try a pineapple mojito. See *Luxe Restaurants,* p.118, for details. *Sun-Thu 5pm-midnight, Fri-Sat 5pm-2am.* ≡ The Bellagio, 702-693-8400, fixlasvegas.com

Folies Bergère • South Strip • Topless Revue

Las Vegas' longest-running feather-and-sequin show, this classic carries off Ziegfield-style production numbers with its parade of showgirls gliding down endless staircases wearing little more than towering headdresses and a string of rhinestones. The show offers a glimpse at some of the award-winning numbers from past *Folies* shows along with spectacular new production numbers. Comedian Wally Eastwood, who has a wonderfully wry, self-deprecating style of humor, does some truly astonishing things with a set of balls that will absolutely leave you rolling. *Mon-Sat 7:30pm and 10pm.* C≡ The Tropicana, 702-739-2222, tropicanalv.com

Fontana Bar • Center Strip • Lounge

Best Quiet Bars Bellagio has so many hip bars it can be easy to overlook this romantic, supper-clubby lounge off the main casino. Don't. It's the perfect getaway for a quiet cocktail and slow-dancing with your sweetie. The circular, sophisticated room is rarely crowded, and its patio offers one of the prettiest places to view Bellagio's lake and dancing fountains. Plus, there's a bar menu, with delicacies like Valrhona-dipped strawberries. *Mon-Thu 5:30pm-2am, Fri-Sat 1pm-2am.* ⊟ The Bellagio, 702-693-7989, bellagio.com

Le Rêve • North Strip • Show

Franco Dragone, the former Cirque du Soleil director who masterminded the hits *O* and *Mystère*, and later went freelance to aid Céline Dion with her Vegas spectacle, has merged his talents with Wynn's impressive pocketbook. The result is a very Cirque-esque show complete with water, lots of visually stunning feats, and a scrawny backbone of a story. The plot centers around a Lord of Dreams guiding a common man through a maze of adventures. Anyone familiar with other Cirques will get the idea. The specially built theater provides an intimate circular space, with virtually no bad seats in the house. *Thu-Mon 7:30pm and 10:30pm.* C☰ Wynn, 702-770-7110, wynnlasvegas.com

Light • Center Strip • Nightclub

Best Nightclubs Light is hands-down one of the best clubs in town. Unlike some spots that seem to exclusively draw 20-somethings, those a bit older (and more sophisticated) won't be out of place here. The interior reveals a small rectangular room with two bars, a spacious dance floor ringed with VIP booths and heavy draperies, and chain mail–clad go-go dancers for atmosphere. Reserving one of those VIP booths is just about the only way you'll get a seat, and they don't come cheap. There's no booth fee (just the $20 cover at the door), but expect to pay upwards of $300 per bottle for the privilege of sitting on those velvet cushions. Otherwise, you'll find yourself relegated to the other side of the shoulder-high walls that surround the dance floor; there's a smattering of bar stools on the outer edges, so if you're lucky enough to grab one, keep it. *Thu-Sun 10:30pm-4am.* C☰ The Bellagio, 702-693-7111, lightgroup.com

Lure • North Strip • Ultra Lounge

Best Ultra Lounges This sleek, sophisticated ultra lounge is an enticing, high-class, low-key alternative to club impresario Victor Drai and Steve Wynn's other nightlife venture—Tryst. An alluring purple hue illuminates the charmingly intimate, candlelit interior of this upscale casino bar. Cushy couches, wall-lined booths, and bottle service tables are separated by sweeping white curtains. The long, narrow mahogany bar opens up to a small outdoor patio with an inviting fire pit. Sexy waitresses and tempestuous dancers shimmering in gold-sequenced flapper dresses set a naughty and nice tone, while the seductive down-tempo grooves serve as a backdrop to the chill-out vibe. The stylishly coiffed and coutured crowd consists of well-heeled tourists and well-connected locals, engaging in cheap conversations and expensive cocktails. Hot tip: If you're coming with a group of four or more, your best bet would be to reserve a table and put the combined cover charges toward your first bottle. *Tue-Sat 9pm-close.* C☰ Ladies are always free. Wynn, 702-770-3375, wynnlasvegas.com

O • Center Strip • Show

Best Cirque Shows Taking its name from the phonetic sound of the French word for water, *eau*, *O* was without question the most ambitious of the Cirque du Soleil offerings before the new *Beatles: Love* hit the scene. Even though it's no longer the new kid on the trapeze, its synchronized swimmers, divers, aerialists, and clowns create an astonishing treat for the eye above, in, and below the water—along with the most dazzling curtain-raising you'll ever see. Don't be late, or you won't be allowed in until it's over. *Wed-Sun 7:30pm and 10:30pm.* C☰ The Bellagio, 702-693-7722, cirquedusoleil.com

Penn and Teller • East Flamingo • Show

Penn and Teller probably need little introduction. The comedy and magic duo has been a team for 30 years, racking up TV and stage appearances across the globe. Penn, the loud, talkative half of the act, takes great glee in his outspo-kenness—explaining to audiences exactly how the tricks are done, commenting on other magicians, and generally giving his views on the world at large. Teller, of course, doesn't make a peep. In this 90-minute Vegas staple, Penn and Teller stick to the classics. The theater is large, so to really get a good look, splurge for up-front tickets, and make sure you come early—guests are invited onstage before the act begins to examine the props for the first trick to see if they can figure out how it works. Don't worry if you're stumped—Penn will be happy to explain. *Wed-Mon 9pm; dark days change, call for schedule.* ᴄ≡ The Rio, 702-777-7776, pennandteller.com

Petrossian Bar • Center Strip • Bar
With its live piano, this elegant lobby bar makes a good stopping point for an afternoon or evening cocktail. It serves afternoon tea with fresh baked scones and clotted cream, preserves, sandwiches, and pastries as well as Petrossian caviar, smoked salmon, and champagne. *24/7; afternoon tea 2-5pm.* ≡ The Bellagio, 702-693-8100, bellagio.com

Phantom of the Opera • Center Strip • Show
Andrew Lloyd Webber's worldwide phenomenon is the latest Broadway musical to hit the Vegas strip. This all-new 95-minute version, which includes all the original songs, reunites Webber with 20-time Tony winner, director Harold Prince. *Phantom* tells the tragic love story of a disfigured musical genius, hid-den away in the Paris Opera House, who terrorizes the theater company for the unwitting benefit of a young protégé whom he trains and loves. The Venetian's specially built state-of-the-art theater will host the special effects–laden show, which includes an onstage lake and an exploding replica of the Paris Opera House chandelier. *Sun, Mon, Thu, Fri 7pm, Wed and Sat 7pm and 10pm.* ᴄ≡ The Venetian, 866-641-7469, phantomlasvegas.com

Sapphire Gentlemen's Club • North Strip • Strip Club
Best Strip Clubs A $26 million renovation turned the former Sporting House fit-ness club into a very different kind of hard-body showcase. The owners claim this brand-spanking-new 24-hour strip-o-rama is the largest in the world. Upwards of 300 gals take it off nightly. Black-gowned hostesses direct you through the mar-bled entrance to the giant main dance room for a prime view of hotties shaking it on the raised stages and at tables all around. A hundred dollars and a drink will get you three private dances in the less trafficked VIP lounge. Note: It's not right on the Strip, but one block behind the Stardust. *24/7.* ᴄ≡ 3025 Industrial Rd. (E. Desert Inn Rd.), 702-796-6000, sapphirelásvegas.com

Tryst • North Strip • Nightclub
In less than a year, Wynn Las Vegas changed its premier nightclub from La Bête to Tryst. It opened in time to ring in 2006 and is primed for big dance parties with room for 1,100 people. There is a big VIP section, and when the weather is nice, a big glass wall opens up to the outdoor lagoon area. The dance floor is both indoors and outdoors, with a 94-foot waterfall as the backdrop. It is located near Okada on the registration side of the casino, a short walk from the gaming floor. This club is packed with beautiful people on the weekends and is surely bound for success with Victor Drai and his team Jesse and Cy Waits behind the market-ing. *Thu-Sun 10pm-4am.* ᴄ≡ Wynn, 702-770-3375, wynnlasvegas.com

Luxe Las Vegas:
The Attractions

Bellagio Fountains • Center Strip • Site
Best Free Attractions Giving new meaning to water ballet, 1,000 fountains set in Bellagio's eight-acre lake (meant to resemble Lake Como) dance to the music of Frank Sinatra, Aaron Copland, Johann Strauss, Elton John, and Luciano Pavarotti (to name a few) in this astonishing water show, which sprays 240 feet high and leaves enough water suspended in the air during the finale to fill a home pool. Even jaded city dwellers can't help but stop and stare. *Every 30 minutes Mon-Fri 3-8pm, Sat-Sun and holidays noon-8pm. Every 15 minutes nightly 8pm-midnight.* The Bellagio, 702-946-7000, bellagio.com

Bellagio Gallery of Fine Art • Center Strip • Art Gallery
The gallery showcases traveling exhibits of museum-quality paintings, sculpture, works on paper, and costumes. Past exhibits include works by Calder, Fabergé, and Andy Warhol. Currently, an Ansel Adams exhibit fills the space until May 2007. Exhibitions in this small gallery typically run for about eight months, and each show has an audio guide, often recorded by celebrities—Liza Minnelli did the audio tour of the Andy Warhol exhibit. *Daily 9am-9pm.* $ The Bellagio, 702-693-7871, bellagio.com

Bellagio Poker Room • Center Strip • Casino
Best Texas Hold 'Em Poker Rooms Bellagio is where the pros play and home to the Big Game. As the name suggests, it's the biggest ongoing high-stakes poker game in Vegas, with a typical spread of $2,000 to $4,000. Legends like Doyle Brunson, Chip Reese, Phil Ivey, Howard Lederer, and Eli Elezra are some of the regular players. It's played in Bobby's Room, the new glass area that sits like a centerpiece for the rest of the room. It's named after the MGM Mirage's head cheese and was added when the poker room went through remodeling in April 2005. You can find games as low as $4 to $8 and $8 to $16 Hold 'Em in the main room, and attendants at the podium will put your name on the list. Middle limit games of $15 to $30, $30 to $60 Hold 'Em and $20 to $40 Omaha 8 or Better are also available. The room that's slightly elevated in the back plays even higher limits. The World Poker Tour was born out of the Bellagio Poker Room, and it holds three tournaments here throughout the year. If you plan on coming to play a lot of poker, ask for the poker rate. *24/7.* The Bellagio, 702-693-7290, bellagio.com

Bellagio Sports Book • Center Strip • Casino
Best Sports Books The Bellagio is as much an all-around meeting place as it is the book to place your bets. You'll find men taking meetings in hushed tones in the booths or at the bar. During game times for fights, football, and big basketball games, the place will be packed. Meanwhile, the bar by the Sports Book is a good place to look for some high-rent action—of the "companionship" kind, if you know what we mean. Just follow the signs to the poker room and you'll see the Sports Book right next to it in the back of the casino. *24/7.* The Bellagio, 702-693-7111, bellagio.com

Binion's Gambling Hall and Hotel • Downtown • Casino

Opened by legendary gambler Benny Binion, this is a classic downtown casino, where there's no lounge act, no dancing fountains, and no white tigers. Think you can bluff with the big boys? Sit yourself down at one of the 14 tables featuring Hold 'Em, Omaha Hi-Lo 1/2 Kill, or 7-Card Stud, and bask in the mystique. Binion's hosts the World Series of Poker (April) and Hall of Fame Poker Classic (August), attracting serious, top-notch players. *24/7.* 128 Fremont St. (S. First St.), 702-382-1600, binions.com

Eiffel Tower • Center Strip • Site

The half-scale Eiffel Tower is an authentic replica that mirrors the original down to the color of the paint, the lighting, and the steel rivets. The observation deck is at the top, with extraordinary 360-degree views. *Daily 9am-1am.* $ Paris Las Vegas, 702-946-7000, parislasvegas.com

Exotic Car Rental • Airport • Car Rental

Also called RAV, Exotic was started by people who were car lovers through and through. It is conveniently located two blocks from McCarran International Airport, and rents fancy sports cars to drivers over 21 years of age. If you feel like cruising the Strip in a Lamborghini Gallardo—go for it. Want to drive a BMW 645Ci sport convertible instead? Ferrari, Mercedes, Porsche, and Hummer H2 cars are also available. All car rentals are for 24 hours, and the folks at RAV are happy to pick you up from the airport or your hotel. Prices range from $129 to $3,000. And for the real car lovers, it has a Super Car Tour where you can sample driving five mighty sports cars. Note that it doesn't take debit cards or corporate credit cards unless the cardholder also owns the business. *Sun-Thu 10am-11pm, Fri-Sat 10am-midnight.* $$$ 5021 Swenson St. (Tropicana Ave.), 702-736-2592, exoticcarrentalslasvegas.com

Four Seasons Spa • South Strip • Spa

Compared with other spas on the Strip, this one is pretty cozy at 12,000. But because there is no casino on the property, the Four Seasons provides a much more relaxed atmosphere. The décor has an Indonesian influence and is reflective of its JAMU Asian rituals. These treatments incorporate Hindu, Chinese, and European elements. Upon entry, you are greeted by the image of the goddess of compassion, and you can even take your treatment outside with a Zen Garden massage. It made the 2006 Mobile Travel Guide's Best Spas list with a four-star rating. *Daily 6am-9pm.* Four Seasons, 702-632-5300, fourseasons.com/lasvegas

Fremont Street Experience • Downtown • Shop/Site

Best Vintage Vegas Covered by a nine-story steel canopy, this five-block pedestrian mall—often called Glitter Gulch for its narrow stretch of hotels dominated by blinking neon signs—encompasses the strip of nine old-time Las Vegas hotels (with six other historic hotels nearby), creating a time capsule of a bygone Vegas era. Fremont Street is anchored by the Plaza at the west end, the site of the former Union Pacific railroad depot, and Neonopolis to the east, a $100 million open-air mall that includes shops, restaurants, a movie theater, and a Jillian's bowling alley and arcade. Along with free concerts held on the center mainstage, the Sky Parade is the big draw, projected hourly from dusk until midnight on the overhead canopy. With 2 million lights and a high-tech sound system, this is one of the best free shows in town. *24/7.* Fremont St. (Main St.), (no phone), vegasexperience.com

Liberace Museum • North Las Vegas • Museum

Best Vintage Vegas The museum's reverential take on the man known as Mr. Showmanship is unflinchingly upbeat, luxuriating in his flamboyant extravagance, which amply demonstrated that money and good taste don't necessarily go hand in rhinestoned glove. Though the guides take things very seriously, it's the kitsch factor that makes it fun. Try to keep a straight face as you take in the hot pink cape of turkey feathers Liberace wore when he popped out of a Fabergé egg during an Easter special, or the 300-pound rhinestone suit worn with a white mink, also trimmed with rhinestones. Or the 115,000-carat (no, that's not a typo) crystal given to him by Swarovski to commemorate his return to Caesars Palace. The unbridled indulgence boggles. And yet perhaps the biggest surprise is not the couture fantasy costumes and other accoutrements Liberace favored, but his impressive collection of rare, antique pianos, including a Broadwood that dates from 1788 (believed to be one of the oldest in existence), and the grand piano George Gershwin used for many of his compositions—all with nary a rhinestone. *Mon-Sat 10am-5pm.* $ 1775 E. Tropicana Ave. (Spencer Ave.), 702-798-5595, liberace.com/museum.cfm

Neon Museum • Downtown • Site

The Fremont Street Experience is home to the fledgling Neon Museum (more an outdoor collection), which encompasses nine restored neon and blinking signs that once adorned long-gone Las Vegas hotels, restaurants, and other businesses, now clustered in two groups on Fremont Street. Four were installed in 1997 in the little plaza just outside The Saloon bar and restaurant, where Las Vegas Boulevard meets Fremont Street. The former Hacienda Hotel's huge rearing horse and rider is planted in the boulevard median, giving a friendly welcome as it waves visitors onto Fremont Street. Two blocks over on 3rd Street is the cul-de-sac with the remaining five signs. Like most things in Las Vegas, you'll enjoy this more at night when the signs are lit. *24/7.* Fremont St. (Main St.), 702-387-6366, neonmuseum.org

9/11 Memorial • Center Strip • Site

On September 11, 2001, New York-New York guests placed candles in front of the hotel in honor of the Trade Center's fallen heroes. The idea caught on, and before long a spontaneous memorial of T-shirts and sweatshirts from fire, police, and emergency services departments sprang up on the wrought-iron fence that surrounds the hotel. New York-New York's management has since created a shadow-box memorial exhibit to protect the objects. A more formal memorial is in the planning stages. New York-New York, 702-740-6969, nynyhotelcasino.com

Shadow Creek • North Las Vegas • Golf

Best Golf Courses Located out by Nellis Air Force Base and hidden behind an enormous fence, this Tom Fazio–designed course, rumored to cost $60 million, sits on 350 acres and features waterfalls, streams, lush tree-lined fairways, exotic birds, and a colonial-style clubhouse. You'll swear you're anywhere but Las Vegas. The course is open only to guests of MGM properties (Bellagio, MGM Grand, Mandalay Bay, Mirage, Luxor, Excalibur, Treasure Island, New York-New York, Monte Carlo, and, heaven help you, Circus Circus). Private cars are not allowed on site and are turned away, even if you show up in your rented Hummer. Transportation is provided by the hotel. Guests can make weekday reservations, but the hotel must "invite" you to play on weekends. Talk to the concierge, money in hand. (Be warned: Don't go on windy days—Steve Wynn built the course near a pig farm and on windy days, well, you can imagine the aroma.) *Daily 6:30am-sunset.* $$$$ 3 Shadow Creek Dr. (Loose St.), 702-791-7161, shadowcreek.com

Spa Bellagio • Center Strip • Spa

The Bellagio kicked off 2005 with a brand-new spa and salon. It was transformed from its Roman bath design into a sleek Zen-influenced 65,000-square-foot spa and salon. Now spa-goers can walk through the long quiet halls and pause by a reflection pool with fresh flowers, or sit in the meditation room while they wait for a treatment. One of the best spas on the Strip, Spa Bellagio maintains its throne by offering innovative treatments that guests can go home and brag about. At the top of the list are the Ashiatsu Massage, which is done with the technician's feet as she hangs from bars on the ceiling, and the Watsu Massage, also known as Water Shiatsu, which is performed in a special pool. If you're traveling with a group or celebrating a bachelorette party, look into renting some of the rooms for a catered party. Those that live a high-octane life can try practice their kickboxing in the Bamboo Studio, a 1,000-square-foot exercise room. No matter what treatment or practice you're looking for, Spa Bellagio is ready to serve. *Daily 6am-8pm, treatments 7am-7pm.* The Bellagio, 702-693-7472, bellagio.com

Sundance Helicopters • Airport • Tour

It's hard to really get a grasp of what an oasis Las Vegas is until you see its desert surrounds from above. With Sundance Helicopters, you have the option of taking in not only this spectacular vista, but also visiting the best sights of the Southwest in one afternoon. Sip champagne before boarding your helicopter—or jet copter—for a fascinating flight over Las Vegas, Lake Mead, or even the Grand Canyon. You can even land at the Canyon and take a Hummer tour around the rim, or indulge in a quick white-water rafting adventure. Or opt for the City Light flight, which lets you enjoy the sunset on the Las Vegas Strip as the lights of the city turn on. No matter what you choose, Sundance will pick you up at your hotel and return you when it's done. While many tours offer lunch, it's not a stellar option—better to come back and enjoy one of the great restaurants on the ground. *Hours vary.* $$$$ 5596 Haven St. (E. Sunset Rd.), 702-736-0606, helicoptour.com

21 Historic Markers • Downtown • Tour

Best Vintage Vegas If you really want to explore the Old Vegas, take a walk downtown and look for the 21 historic markers that pay tribute to the beginnings of Las Vegas. They were made to celebrate the Las Vegas Centennial in 2005, and were chosen by the Historical Marker Initiative. The historic markers are all over town. Some of our favorites are Block 16 at North 1st Street between Ogden and Stewart Avenues, which was notorious for prostitution until 1942; Gaming and Helldorado at 1st and Fremont streets; and the Railroad Cottages at 2nd (now Casino Center) to 4th and Garces to Clark. Main St. (Fremont St.), (no phone), lasvegas2005.org

Venetian Hotel • Center Strip • Site

Best Free Attractions The Venetian hired a duo of historians to ensure the architectural integrity of this splendid grand hotel, and sent them to Italy to research the details. More than 250 artists, from painters to sculptors, labored to make the final product perfect, replicating Venice icons including the Rialto Bridge, the Doge's Palace, St. Mark's Square, the Bridge of Sighs (named for the laments of 14th-century prisoners who had to cross it on their way to jail)—and of course, the Grand Canal. The lobby ceiling is hand-painted with elegant, gold-framed frescoes, copies of works by artists including Nicolò Bambini, Giambattista Tiepolo, and Paolo Veronese. 3355 S. Las Vegas Blvd. (Flamingo Rd.), 702-414-1000, venetian.com

Via Bellagio • Center Strip • Shops
This high-ceilinged arcade that runs alongside the lake and fountains has some of Vegas' most high-end shopping, including the only outlet of Tiffany & Co. in the city. This is not a mega-mall, but more of an exclusive enclave where you'll find nine über-luxury stores including Giorgio Armani, Prada, Chanel, Hermès, Moschino, Fred Leighton, Yves Saint Laurent, and Gucci. It's a great place to mingle with some of Sin City's most affluent visitors. *Daily 10am-midnight.* The Bellagio, 702-693-7722, bellagio.com

Wynn Esplanade • North Strip • Shops
This hushed corridor of shops with its high ceilings above and red and gold patterned carpet below oozes exclusivity. It's more than image. The stores here are very high end, from Brioni to Oscar de la Renta. Sprinkled in between are a few lovely boutiques and specialty shops, such as Jo Malone, England's goddess of luxury scents. Other standouts include Manolo Blahnik, Cartier, Christian Dior, Louis Vuitton, and a nearby Ferrari-Maserati dealership that opened with much fanfair. Also of note is Sugar & Ice, a cute cafe with excellent desserts, and even coffee and liquor drinks to revive your spirits. *Sun-Thu 10am-11pm, Fri-Sat 10am-midnight.* Wynn, 702-770-7000, wynnlasvegas.com

Wynn Golf Course • North Strip • Golf
Tom Fazio does it again. He has magically transformed the old Desert Inn Golf Course into an 18-hole oasis right on the Strip—making it the easiest place to play—if you're a Wynn guest, that is. This place is strictly off-limits to those who choose to stay elsewhere. Fazio even managed to keep 1,200 of the trees, some of which were more than 50 years old. Celebs and businesspeople come to experience this forgiving course because it is beautiful, exclusive, and not too tough. There's even a big waterfall at the 18th hole, which is stunning to look at from the country club. *Daily sunrise-sunset.* $$$ Wynn, 877-321-9666, wynnlasvegas.com

Wynn Las Vegas Poker Room • North Strip • Casino
Best Texas Hold 'Em Poker Rooms This is a popular poker room with 27 tables that are often filled to capacity. If you come on the weekend, expect to wait at least 15 minutes. This might be a drawback for some, but for those staying upstairs—no worries. Even the standard rooms offer guests the ability to log in to the poker room from their TV and watch their name move up the list in the comfort of their own bedroom. The daily poker room rate is $129 on weekdays and $199 on weekends. The players at the tables are a fairly even mix of regulars and tourists. The room has common low- and mid-limit Hold 'Em games, as well as $1 to $2, $2 to $5, and $5 to $10 NL Texas Hold 'Em games. In February 2006, Phil Ivey won $16 million from Texas banker Andy Beal in the Wynn Poker Room. *24/7.* Wynn, 702-770-7800, wynnlasvegas.com

Wynn Las Vegas Sports and Race Book • North Strip • Casino

Best Sports Books A travel writer once claimed, "If I had to die in a sports book, this would be the place." That might be a bit more enthusiastic a response than most fans will report, but the Wynn Las Vegas Sports and Race Book is definitely a cut above others. Just take a seat in the decadent yellow leather chairs and dare yourself to leave. It's on the main casino floor between Zoozacrackers and Corsa Cucina near the poker room. The three big screens grab your attention first, but you'll notice that racing is the favorite sport here. Clientele consists mostly of hotel guests and gamblers taking a break from the tables. *24/7*. Wynn, 702-770-7800, wynnlasvegas.com

PRIME TIME
LAS VEGAS

Everything in life is timing (with a dash of serendipity thrown in). Would you want to arrive in Pamplona, Spain, the day *after* the Running of the Bulls? Not if you have a choice and you relish being a part of life's peak experiences. With our month-by-month calendar of events, there's no excuse to miss out on any of Las Vegas' greatest moments. From the classic to the quirky, you'll find all you need to know about the city's best events right here.

Prime Time Basics

Eating and Drinking

When it comes to normal hours in Vegas, throw away your expectations. This is a 24/7 town, even on holidays. However, as in most major cities, you'll find restaurants and bars busy during the customary hours: breakfast around 9 to 10am, lunch from noon to 2pm, and dinner from 7:30 to 9pm. Sunday brunch kicks off around 11am. If you're having trouble scoring restaurant reservations, consider an early seating around 6:30pm, or late at 9:30pm, especially if you plan on seeing a show. For bars, you will find drinking company at any hour—even the morning—but trendy spots heat up about 10pm, with nightclub lines beginning as early as 11pm. And when it comes to partying late, know that after-hours in Vegas starts at about 3am and goes until sunup. As in most urban centers, the club circuit tends to hit different spots on different nights. This changes often, especially as new places open. For now, Sundays in Vegas are the night to visit Body English; Monday is Jet; Tuesday is PURE or Ghostbar; Wednesday is Tao or Tabú; Thursday is Tryst or Tao; and the weekends are busy everywhere. Bottle service—a great way to skip lines—costs around $400 plus tax and tip for three to four people. Note: While most casinos have a plethora of dining and nightlife options, Night+Day includes only those that meet our high standards, rather than listing everything available. And we only list 14 hotels—but that's over 35,000 rooms, more than you'll find in all of San Francisco.

Seasonal Changes

Month	Fahrenheit High	Fahrenheit Low	Celsius High	Celsius Low
Jan	60	37	16	3
Feb	69	44	20	6
Mar	72	47	22	8
Apr	88	60	31	16
May	90	65	32	18
June	101	73	40	22
July	106	80	41	27
Aug	105	73	40	22
Sept	92	69	33	20
Oct	79	54	26	12
Nov	67	46	19	8
Dec	57	39	13	4

Weather and Tourism

Dec–Mar: Winter in Vegas is mild, but it's the wet season. Temperatures range from the high 30s up to the high 60s. You won't notice because they have air conditioning running. What you will notice is that most of the pools are closed. Crowds are big around holidays, though, culminating at New Year's Eve, one of the most popular times to visit.

Apr–June: Temperatures warm up in the spring, but it's still possible to ski on Mt. Charleston in April. This is also the time when the pools open up and start their parties. May temperatures can get up into the high 80s, with June heading into the 90s and reaching 100 on the hottest days.

July–Aug: This is the hottest time of the year. Temperatures can soar to 105 or more. It's a dry heat, which means that you won't mind so much at 95, but when it gets to triple digits, you definitely will. Still, bring a sweater because the casinos keep their indoor temperatures on the cool side. Note that there will be periods with summer rain and electric storms. It's also a packed season for tourists, with more families than in other seasons.

Sept–Nov: Fall means that it's warm, but not too hot. Lows are in the 50s with highs in the low 90s and high 80s. There are lots of clear dry days during autumn, and this would be a good time to go for those that like mild climates. Although it might seem odd to some, Thanksgiving can be a busy time, and the weeks between this holiday and New Year's get increasingly crowded.

National Holidays

New Year's Day	January 1
Martin Luther King Day	Third Monday in January
Valentine's Day	February 14
Presidents' Day	Third Monday in February
Memorial Day	Last Monday in May
Independence Day	July 4
Labor Day	First Monday in September
Columbus Day	Second Monday in October
Halloween	October 31
Veterans' Day	Second Monday in November
Thanksgiving Day	Fourth Thursday in November
Christmas Day	December 25
New Year's Eve	December 31

Listings in blue are major celebrations but not official holidays.

PRIME TIME

The Best Events Calendar

January
- Adult Entertainment Expo
- Consumer Electronics Show (CES)

February
- Super Bowl Weekend
- Valentine's Day

March
- March Madness
- St. Patrick's Day
- UAW–DaimlerChrysler 400

April
- Baseball Season
- City of Lights Jazz Festival
- National Hot Rod Association
- UNLVino

May

June
- Cinevegas International Film Festival

July
- Red, White, and Boom
- Star Spangled Spectacular and Patriotic Parade
- World Series of Poker

August
- Las Vegas Music Festival
- Magic Marketplace

September
- Las Vegas Bike Fest

October
- AC Delco Las Vegas National Hot Rod Association Nationals
- Fetish and Fantasy Halloween Ball
- PGA Las Vegas Invitational

November
- All Harley Drag Racing Association (AHDRA)
- Professional Bull Riders Built Ford Tough World Championships

December
- Las Vegas International Marathon
- National Finals Rodeo
- New Year's Eve

Night+Day's Top Five Events are in blue.

The Best Events

January

Adult Entertainment Expo
Sands Expo and Convention Center, 866-486-3399, showadultentertainment.com

The Lowdown: This annual awards and trade show for the adult film industry is held in conjunction with CES to take advantage of the conventioneers in town. While the show is mounted for industry professionals, certain hours are reserved for attendance by the general public, when porn fans mix and mingle with the 400 adult film stars who turn out, happily sign autographs, and pose for pictures. The hottest event is the AVN Awards night, but these industry-only tickets are very hard to come by. *Second week in January, usually beginning on a Wednesday. Hours vary. Day ticket $45 in advance (web purchase), $50 at door, $135 for three-day pass.*

Consumer Electronics Show (CES)
Sands Expo and Convention Center, 703-907-7637, cesweb.org

The Lowdown: A tech geek's nirvana featuring the latest in consumer electronics technology, CES is one of the biggest trade shows to come to Las Vegas each year—it attracts more than 122,000 computer industry pros, along with a ton of media searching for the next latest thing. The high budgets here mean top-end restaurants get booked far in advance, and many clubs host private parties that are worth trying to score an invite to attend. *Second week in January. Online registration before December 29 is free, $200 after this date.*

February

Super Bowl Weekend
Various locations, 877-847-4858, visitlasvegas.com

The Lowdown: Why do more people go to Las Vegas on Super Bowl Weekend than to the game's host city? The sports books, where you can make a bet on virtually any proposition your imagination can concoct, in the company of hundred of fans. This weekend attracts the year's greatest concentration of high-end gamblers, creating an incredible buzz in the casinos (the biggest players will most likely be in the casinos at Bellagio, Caesars Palace, Mandalay Bay, MGM Grand, Mirage, and Venetian), and a fun-loving spirit in the restaurants and nightclubs. *Date varies, game on Sunday. Free.*

Valentine's Day
Various locations, 877-847-4858, visitlasvegas.com

The Lowdown: The weekend closest to Valentine's Day is one of the busiest and liveliest of the year. Couples book their reservations months in advance to secure a decent room. Even if you're not getting married in Vegas over V-Day, head downtown and watch the lines of brides and grooms in front of the wedding chapels. Ministers will be ordering them to say "I do" around the clock, in balloons, helicopters, broadcast on the internet, and any other way you can think of to do it. *Friday-Sunday closest to February 14. Free.*

March

March Madness
Various locations, 877-847-4858, visitlasvegas.com

The Lowdown: It's no secret that sports fans love coming to Las Vegas to make their bets. The Super Bowl is an obvious weekend to look out for, but don't be surprised to find the sports books flooded with testosterone in March, too. That's when NCAA men's basketball is in its high season, with the "Final Four" being the biggest games of all. This is also the biggest action of all, with legal wagers on the NCAA tournament often exceeding those placed on the Super Bowl. *The month of March. Free.*

St. Patrick's Day
Various locations, 877-847-4858, visitlasvegas.com

The Lowdown: It's O'Vegas as they turn The Venetian's canals green. This holiday, especially if it touches the weekend, draws a crowd. Casinos include festive scenery, Irish singers, green beer, shamrock playing chips, and, of course, a rowdy parade (this usually takes place on the weekend after if the holiday falls during the week, in a suburb like Henderson). If you haven't had enough, there are several pubs like Fadó's Irish Bar that will bring out your lucky charm. *March 17. Free.*

UAW-DaimlerChrysler 400
702-644-4444, lvms.com

The Lowdown: Get your motor running! The Las Vegas Motor Speedway hosts this NASCAR's Nextel Series race at the speedway's oval track, drawing in thousands of die-hard fans. The speedway is scheduled to be closed for repairs soon after the 2006 event, so check the website for updates. *Dates and ticket prices vary, though many casinos do room-ticket packages for this event.*

April

Baseball Season—Las Vegas 51s
Cashman Field, 702-386-7200, lv51.com

The Lowdown: Wear your blue and red and cheer on Sin City's own Las Vegas 51s. This is a minor league team for the Los Angeles Dodgers that plays downtown at Cashman Field. These intimate baseball viewing sessions are gaining in popularity, with an average of 4,600 attendees at each game. Great fun for baseball lovers of all ages, and anyone looking to take a break from the casinos. *Season runs April to September. Tickets about $12.*

City of Lights Jazz Festival
Hills Park at Summerlin, 800-969-83427, yourjazz.com

The Lowdown: One of American's newest jazz events, the City of Lights festival is already one of the best attended; aficionados of this audio art form flock from all over the country to enjoy the two-day outdoor concert. The locations change from year to year; best to check the website for current info. *Friday and Saturday in April, dates vary. General admission $65, VIP $100.*

National Hot Rod Association Summit Racing Car Nationals
Las Vegas Motor Speedway, 702-644-4444, nhra.com

The Lowdown: About 800 hot rods careen at 325 mph down the Las Vegas Motor Speedway's quarter-mile track, competing for $2 million in prize money. Cars race side by side in 22 categories, including four pro categories (Top Fuel, Funny Car, Pro Stock, and Pro Stock Bike) that bring out hot-shot stars like John Force and Larry Dixon. *Dates and ticket prices vary.*

UNLVino
Various locations, 702-876-4500, unlvino.com

The Lowdown: Raise your glass to higher education at this multi-day, multi-event wine-tasting fundraiser for University of Nevada Las Vegas scholarships. Sample 250 wines from 100 winemakers and check out the Southern Nevada Wine and Spirits auction of specialty wines. The main event is the Grand Tasting, usually held on a Saturday. *Dates vary. Tickets $50 in advance, $75 at the door.*

June

Cinevegas International Film Festival
Palms, 702-992-7979, cinevegas.com

The Lowdown: A nine-day festival screening high-profile Hollywood pictures, independent films looking for distribution, world premieres, documentaries, shorts, and cult flicks from around the world. Held at the Brenden Theaters inside Palms Casino Resort, the festival has drawn celebrities including Samantha Morton, Nicolas Cage, and Dennis Hopper in recent years. *Dates and ticket prices vary.*

July

Red, White, and Boom
Desert Breeze Park, 702-455-8200, redwhitenboom.com

The Lowdown Clark County's annual July 4 celebration offers a little something for everyone. The two-day event at Desert Breeze Park boasts contemporary and classic music acts (past participants include Social Distortion, Train, Hawthorne Heights, Ne-Yo), food, crafts, and a spectacular fireworks show. *Tickets are $17.50 in advance, $22 day of, $30 both days. A VIP package ($75) includes VIP parking, AC tent, and discounted food and beverages. July 4 weekend.*

Star Spangled Spectacular and Patriotic Parade
Various locations, 702-895-2787

The Lowdown: This family-style Independence Day event kicks off with a parade through the streets of Summerlin, showcasing dozens of community-sponsored floats, marching bands, dance groups, and performers. The Las Vegas Philharmonic plays patriotic tunes at Hills Park in the evening, capping the night off with a stirring and stunning fireworks finale choreographed to classical music. Be sure to come early to stake out a comfy spot on the green grass before the huge crowds arrive. *Tickets are $20 in advance and $25 at the gate. July 4.*

World Series of Poker
The Rio All-Suite Hotel, 323-330-9900, worldpokertour.com

The Lowdown: This is the big one: the battle royal that decides the world champion of poker, drawn from the pro and amateur ranks alike. Long held at Binion's, the WSP was picked up by the Bellagio, and now is at The Rio. The grand purse can reach into millions of bucks. For poker aficionados, this one is it. *Begins late June and extends for about six weeks. Free to watch, buy-ins vary by game.*

August

Las Vegas Music Festival
UNLV, 702-895-3949, lasvegasmusicfestival.org

The Lowdown: Classical music students and professional musicians from around the world gather at UNLV's Performing Arts Center for ten days of concerts and recitals, which culminate in a final concert featuring a renowned guest artist. *Dates vary, usually the first two weeks in August. Tickets about $10.*

Magic Marketplace
Las Vegas Convention Center, 877-554-4834, magiconline.com

The Lowdown: Also known as Magic, this fashion industry trade-only show attracts some 100,000 participants and is considered to be one of the most comprehensive marketplaces for the apparel and accessories industry. While the show itself is off-limits to non-fashionistas, the town goes wild with very high-profile parties that you may be lucky enough to crash. The show features more than 1,800 exhibitors in 7,000 booths. *Four days in the last week of August. Closed to public.*

September

Las Vegas Bike Fest
Cashman Center, 866-BIKE-FEST, lasvegasbikefest.com

The Lowdown: This three-day motorcycle event held downtown has loads of events and happenings, like the Charity Chili Cook-Off, a Bloody Mary Breakfast, a custom bike show, a wet T-shirt contest, a Miss/and Mr. Las Vegas Bike Fest, tattoos, and best bikes. *Four days in mid-September, usually Thu-Sat. Tickets $10, Sunday free.*

October

AC Delco Las Vegas National Hot Rod Association Nationals
Las Vegas Motor Speedway, 800-644-4444, nhra.com

The Lowdown: If you're a speed freak, this is the event for you. Hundreds of hot rods hit speeds of more than 300 mph around the quarter-mile track. Cars race side by side in 22 categories for millions in prize money. *Dates vary. Tickets $16-$130.*

Fetish and Fantasy Halloween Ball
Location to be determined, 702-284-7777, halloweenball.com

The Lowdown: Indulge your ultimate fantasy with 6,000 fellow fetishists, clad in leather, latex, and other delightfully naughty costumes. Anything goes at this sexy masquerade ball, a nonstop parade of self-styled exhibitionists and erotic performances. As of press time, a new venue had not been confirmed, though the Tropicana is an early contender. *Saturday closest to Halloween. Tickets $75 general admission, $195 VIP (only 300 sold).*

PGA Las Vegas Invitational
The Players Club, 702-242-3000, pgatour.com

The Lowdown: The professional golf scene kicks it into high gear when the PGA tour comes to Sin City. The 2007 dates are not yet announced. You can go for the day, or treat yourself to a VIP weekend package, where you'll be able to wander the tents in cool comfort. *Four days in mid-October, covering a weekend. Tickets range from $15 for a day pass to $350 for VIP packages.*

November

All Harley Drag Racing Association (AHDRA)
Las Vegas Motor Speedway, 702-644-4444, ahdra.com

The Lowdown: A Harley-Davidson fan's delight! Watch those hogs haul down the quarter-mile strip at the Las Vegas Motor Speedway. Then check out the crowds, who are almost as entertaining as the racers. *Second weekend in November, dates can vary. Saturday day pass $25, weekend pass $40.*

Professional Bull Riders Built Ford Tough World Championships
Mandalay Bay and Thomas & Mack Center (UNLV), 719-471-3008, pbrnow.com

The Lowdown: Cowboy enthusiasts throng Las Vegas to watch the top 45 riders from the Professional Bull Riders circuit compete for a $1 million purse at UNLV's Thomas & Mack Center. This event is the culmination of 31 regular-season competitions, so emotions are running as high as the bulls are bucking. Ride 'em, cowboy! *Two consecutive weekends in late October or early November. Tickets about $100 and up.*

PRIME TIME

December

Las Vegas International Marathon
Las Vegas Boulevard, 702-731-1052, lvmarathon.com

The Lowdown: Now in its 38th year, this three-race event takes place along the old Los Angeles Highway (now Las Vegas Boulevard) and attracts runners from around the world. A qualifier for the Boston Marathon, this run is held in conjunction with the Health and Fitness Expo at the Tropicana. The best viewing is along Las Vegas Boulevard from State Road 145 to the Belz Factory Outlet Mall. *December 10. Entry fee $85-$105. Free to watch.*

National Finals Rodeo
Thomas & Mack Center (UNLV), 888-464-2468, nfr-rodeo.com

The Lowdown: The world series of rodeos has a $4.5 million purse and brings in 170,000 attendees to watch the top 15 male contenders ride bulls and broncos, wrestle steer, and rope calves while the top 15 women riders barrel race. Held at the Thomas & Mack Center, the rodeo is one of the hottest tickets in town and sells out a year in advance. The best seats are rows 1 to 12 of the center plaza, but even if you don't get a ringside seat (or any seat), with all the cowboys and cowgals descending on the city, there are lots of other Western-themed entertainment and events to grab your attention, like the NFR Cowboy Gift Show, a Western-wear trade show at Cashman Field. And there's a lot of action that happens elsewhere as well. Country and Western stars headline at the clubs, restaurants bust out the cowboy-themed specials, and you'll be hard pressed to step on a dance floor without being two-stepped on by a pair of boots. *Ten days in December, dates vary. Tickets $70-$1,050.*

New Year's Eve
Various locations, 877-847-4858, visitlasvegas.com

The Lowdown: On one of the biggest nights in Las Vegas, the Strip turns into a veritable outdoor carnival packed with revelers for miles. In fact, the city shuts it down to traffic from Mandalay Bay to Circus Circus. Downtown also gets in on the action with an amazing coordinated fireworks display shot off in tandem by the downtown and Strip hotels. If you're looking to put Times Square to shame, this should do the trick. But book restaurants and hotels well, well in advance. *December 31. Free.*

HIT THE GROUND RUNNING

Enjoying a Vegas insider experience is easy—just keep these key tips in mind when you plan your trip. From the lowdown on local transportation to finding your favorite newspaper, from what to wear to how to get past the velvet rope, we give you the resources to help you plan a flawless visit. You'll also get advice on mixing business with pleasure and making the most of your time at the airport, as well as some interesting facts to impress the locals.

City Essentials

Getting to Las Vegas: By Air

Las Vegas McCarran International Airport
702-261-5211, lost and found: 702-261-5134, mccarran.com

Rated tops in the United States for customer service by a recent JD Power Global Airport Satisfaction Study, McCarran International Airport is served by most airlines with nonstop and direct flights and is conveniently located just minutes from the hotels and casinos on the Strip. The airport has two terminals. Domestic flights arrive and depart from gates A, B, C, or D (the latter two are connected by monorail), while international and charter flights arrive and depart from Terminal 2. There's also ample shopping for souvenirs and plenty of fast food and sit-down dining opportunities. The airport has a Wells Fargo Bank (plus numerous ATMs throughout the terminals), a post office (plus FedEx and UPS drop boxes), and a 14,000-square-foot 24-Hour Fitness, equipped with cardio and weight-training machines and exercise classes, that's open to all visitors. (Members of this national chain can use the facility for free; one-day passes are available for $10, including a towel.) Finally, since McCarran is well-equipped with slot machines, you can start gambling the very minute you deplane.

Flying Times to Las Vegas

Nonstop From	Airport Code	Time (hr.)
Chicago	ORD	4
London*	LHR	11
Los Angeles	LAX	1
Miami	MIA	5½
New York/ Newark	JFK/ EWR	5
San Francisco	SFO	1½
Seattle	SEA	2½
Washington, D.C.	IAD	5

* Not nonstop flights

Note: If you are a guest of the MGM Grand, New York-New York, Bally's, Paris, Caesars Palace, Flamingo, or Las Vegas Hilton, you can visit these properties' off-site lobbies (located in the baggage claim area) to check in, pick up room keys, and buy show tickets.

Airlines Serving McCarran International Airport

Airlines	Website	800 Number	Terminal
Alaska Airlines	alaskaair.com	800-426-0333	A
Allegiant Air	allegiant-air.com	877-202-6444	B
Aloha Airlines	alohaairlines.org	800-367-5250	C
America West Airlines	americawest.com	800-235-9292	B
American Airlines	aa.com	800-433-7300	D
American Trans Air (ATA)/Com	ata.com airfly-comair.com	800-435-9282	D2
Delta	delta.com	800-221-1212	D
Frontier	flyfrontier.com	800-432-1359	A
Hawaiian Airlines	hawaiianair.com	800-367-5320	2
Japan Airlines	jal.co.jp/en	800-525-3663	2
JetBlue Airways	jetblue.com	800-538-2583	A
Midwest Express Airlines	midwestexpress.com	800-452-2022	D
Northwest	nwa.com	800-225-2525	D2
Singapore Airlines	singaporeair.com	800-742-3333	2
Southwest	southwest.com	800-435-9792	C
Spirit Airlines	spiritair.com	800-772-7117	D
Sun Country	suncountryairlines.com	800-359-6786	D
United	ual.com	800-241-6522	D
US Airways	usairways.com	800-428-4322	A
Virgin Atlantic Airways	virgin-atlantic.com	800-862-8621	2

Into Town By Taxi: Fares run $9 to $13 to get to most hotels on and around the Strip and $15 to $18 to downtown hotels. Cabs that originate at the airport charge an additional $1.20. Cab fares start at $2.20 and charge $1.50 per mile. Complaints about cabs should be directed to the Nevada Taxicab Authority, 702-486-6532.

- Deluxe Taxicab Service 702-568-7700
  (drop-off service only at Strip hotels and airport)
- Desert Cab Company 702-386-9102
- Las Vegas Transportation 702-248-2631 / 800-621-1535
  (Town Car to Strip/downtown hotels, $40; limousine to Strip/downtown hotels, $50 to $70)
- Nellis Cab Company 702-248-1111
- Yellow/Checker/Star Transportation 702-873-2000
- Western Cab Company 702-736-8000
- Whittlesea 702-384-6111

HIT THE GROUND

The Three Best Ways to Get Out of the Airport

You are almost guaranteed to find an extraordinarily long taxi queue at the curb outside the airport baggage claim area. To bypass this problem:

1. If you stay often or are a high roller, have your hotel comp you a limo.
2. Reserve private limo service in advance of arrival, or use one of the limos at the airport.
3. Whether you have checked luggage or just a carry-on, use a porter who, when thanked with a $10 tip, will jump to the front of the queue.

Into Town By Airport Shuttle Service: Several shuttles circle between the airport and the hotels on the Strip, off the Strip, and downtown. Upon arriving, you'll find them outside the airport in designated areas near the taxis. When you leave, it's recommended to call 24 hours in advance for reservations, although many shuttle services offer regular service at the major hotels with no reservations required.

• Bell Trans 702-739-7990, 4:30am-1:30am
Serves Strip hotels ($5), downtown/off-Strip hotels ($6.50); sedan limo ($36/hour), stretch limo ($43/hour), minibus ($49/hour), and deluxe bus ($56/hour). Note: Fuel surcharge of $3 for all vehicles.

• Las Vegas Limousine 702-736-1419, 7am-2am
Serves Strip hotels ($50), downtown hotels ($60), off-Strip hotels ($11 average), Henderson hotels ($45 in sedan).

• Showtime 702-261-6101, 7am-11pm
Serves Strip hotels ($4.50 one-way/$8.75 round trip) and downtown hotels ($6 one-way/$11 round trip).

Getting to Las Vegas: By Land

Driving to Nevada isn't a popular option for East Coasters, but it's not a bad journey from the West Coast. Although much of Nevada is barren, or has only smaller towns, the flat roads make the drive easy. However, be warned: You will get a speeding ticket if you are not careful. The cops are well aware that you're in a hurry to get to the Strip. Also note that traffic from places like Los Angeles and San Francisco can be heavy at peak times, such as Friday afternoons getting into town, and Sundays getting out. Holidays are another difficult driving time, and you will need to add at least an hour to your expected arrival time.

From Los Angeles: Take I-15 North into Las Vegas. As soon as you cross the California-Nevada state line, there are three casinos on the Nevada side, in Primm, where you can gamble immediately. Whiskey Pete's Hotel/Casino (800-851-1703) makes a good rest stop since it's still another 45 minutes to the Strip from Primm.

Driving Times to Las Vegas

From	Distance (mi.)	Approx. Time (hr.)
Los Angeles	270	4
Phoenix	287	5½
Salt Lake City	420	6
San Diego	331	5
San Francisco	571	8½
Santa Fe	634	9¼

From San Francisco: Take I-80 East to U.S. 95 South to I-15 South.

From Seattle: Take I-90 East to I-82 East to I-84 East to U.S. 93 South to I-15 South. I-15 runs parallel to Las Vegas Boulevard, also called the Strip.

Lay of the Land

This may be the easiest city in the world for visitors to get to know. Unlike vast Berlin (which is a virtual city-state) or Tokyo (where street names and numbers may not even exist), this town's a snap to learn! The Strip (Las Vegas Boulevard) runs north-south from Mandalay Bay all the way downtown and serves as a dividing line for the city—everything on the Mandalay Bay, Bellagio, Mirage, Treasure Island side of the Strip is west; The Venetian, MGM Grand, Aladdin side is east.

Starting at the south end of the Strip, you'll find the Mandalay Bay and Four Seasons. Traveling north, you'll hit The Venetian and Harrah's. From there, the Strip veers to the northeast, past Fashion Show Mall and Circus Circus. As you travel northward, you'll hit the Gateway District, home to Las Vegas' more artistic residents, and then hit downtown when you cross Charleston Boulevard, a major east-west artery. Farther out, you'll find Vegas' many golf courses. One important note: The Strip might not look that long, but walking from one end to the other is much farther than it seems. Unless you're looking for a workout, you'll want transportation.

HIT THE GROUND

Getting Around Las Vegas

By Car: Lots of people drive to Vegas or rent cars, and most casinos have free parking, though it can be a hike from the garage. That said, traffic is bad on the Strip (and elsewhere, as the city's population continues to grow), especially at night and peak hours. Since cabs and public transport are everywhere, they are the preferred mode of travel.

The major freeway that runs parallel to the Strip is I-15, and it intersects with the main east-west thoroughfares, like Tropicana Avenue, Flamingo Road, Sahara Avenue (named for the casinos that sit where the streets meet Las Vegas Boulevard), and Spring Mountain Road. I-15 also intersects with I-215, the city's nearly completed beltway, which takes you out to the airport. Other routes that will get you up and down the Strip with less hassle include Paradise Road, which runs north-south on the east side of the Strip, and Industrial Road, which runs north-south on the west side of the Strip.

By Taxi: Taxis can be found outside most hotels and tourist attractions; restaurants and bars will call a cab if requested. While you're not allowed to hail a cab from the street, it's OK to approach an empty cab when it's sitting at a stoplight. See the list (p.147) for a full resource of local taxi companies.

By Shuttle: Many off-Strip hotels run shuttles to key points on the Strip and back again. Ask the concierge for the shuttle schedule for your hotel.

By Tram: There are four trams running from casino to casino in Las Vegas. There's a tram known as "the monorail," which runs from MGM Grand to Bally's. While convenient, it's also expensive: $3 every time you board, though there are frequent-passenger specials if you plan many trips in one day. One tram runs from Bellagio to the Monte Carlo. And there are also shuttles between Mirage and Treasure Island, and Excalibur and Mandalay Bay.

By Other Public Transportation: You can also hop the old-fashioned Las Vegas Strip Trolley (702-382-1404) that cruises the Strip, stopping at the major hotels and casinos as far north as the Sahara Hotel and Casino approximately every 15 minutes. The fare is $2.50 or $6.50 for an all day pass (exact change required). It runs 9:30am-1:30am.

"The Deuce" also makes a 17-mile round trip along the Strip starting at the south end and going all the way to the Transportation Center in downtown Las Vegas. A day pass will cost you $5 and a one-ride pass is $2. Look for street-side signs marking its stopping points.

Rental Cars: If you're just planning to walk the Strip and downtown casinos, there's no reason to rent a car since taxis are plentiful, public buses traverse the Strip regularly, and many of the off-Strip hotels run shuttles to the Strip and the outlet malls for shopping. However, if you are planning to make a day trip to Lake Mead, Hoover Dam, Valley of Fire, Mt. Charleston, Red Rock Canyon, or St. George, Utah, a rental car is in order. Car rental companies located at the McCarran International Airport baggage claim area include:

Agency	Website	800 Number	Local Number
Avis	avis.com	800-331-1212	702-261-5595
Budget	budget.com	800-527-0700	702-736-1212
Enterprise	enterprise.com	800-325-8007	702-261-4435
Hertz	hertz.com	800-654-3131	702-736-4900
National	nationalcar.com	800-227-7368	702-261-5391
Payless	paylesscarrental.com	800-729-5377	702-736-6147
Sav-mor	savmorrac.com	800-634-6779	702-736-1234
Thrifty	thrifty.com	800-367-2277	702-896-7600

Limos

- Las Vegas Transportation, lasvegastransportation.com 800-621-1535
- Starlight Limo, starlightlimoslasvegas.com 877-615-2666

Luxury Self-Driven Cars

- Exotic Car Rental, exoticcarrentalslasvegas.com 800-372-1981

Parking Garages and Lots: It surprises many visitors to learn that hotels do not charge for parking in their self-park areas, whether or not you are a hotel guest. Virtually all the major casinos have large attached garages, and these are your best bet on the Strip. Bellagio is a favorite among them because it is very easy to navigate, with many entrances and exits. Others, like Mandalay Bay, are vast and can leave you walking a ways to get to the hotel. And still others, such as The Venetian, reserve much of the parking for valet and employees. Despite all of these options, on busy weekends, it can still be hard to find a spot. Of course, you can very easily valet-park anywhere; just pull up and toss them the keys.

HIT THE GROUND

Other Practical Information

Money Matters (Currency, Taxes, Tipping, and Service Charges): Las Vegas takes hard, cold cash—100 cents to the dollar! We recommend using the ubiquitous ATM machines, rather than traveling with massive amounts of cash. Cirrus networks (800-424-7787) span the globe, and you'd be hard-pressed to travel more than a block in any direction without finding a cash machine.

Metric Conversion

From	To	Multiply by
Inches	Centimeters	2.54
Yards	Meters	0.91
Miles	Kilometers	1.60
Gallons	Liters	3.79
Ounces	Grams	28.35
Pounds	Kilograms	0.45

That said, many national banks have branches here—and if you use yours, you may save the typical $3 transaction fee with every withdrawal.

Hotels add 9 percent for taxes to all quoted price. Sales tax in Clark County is 7 percent. Tipping for taxis and restaurants is expected, and should be in the 15 to 20 percent range. Be kind, and leave $3 per day for the housekeeping staff. Karma is everything!

Safety: In general, areas of Las Vegas frequented by tourists are safe and police are everywhere. This said, we know you know that it's always better to err on the side of safety. Leave marks of conspicuous consumption in the hotel safe, unless you're being escorted by private transportation throughout. Purse-snatching is probably the most common crime, so keep pocketbooks in your sight and close to your body. Gentlemen should keep their wallets in their front coat pockets whenever possible for maximal safety. Most hotel doors lock automatically, but not always; be sure that yours does, or lock it from the inside to ensure the safety of your possessions. And chances are you will not be traveling in the northeast part of Las Vegas. If for whatever reason you do, know that the disadvantaged neighborhoods in this part of town have seen the increased presence of gangs, and are best avoided, especially after dark.

Gay and Lesbian Travel: Oddly, Las Vegas is not the gay mecca you'd think. There are reasons for this: a) for desert lovers, Palm Springs has long ruled the gay travel roost; b) other than service jobs, Las Vegas isn't exactly career central; and c) look at the map: You're in a red state, dear. This said, the gay and lesbian scene is changing as Las Vegas' population grows. For travel arrangements and information, we recommend the Gay & Lesbian Travel Association (800-448-8550, iglta.org).

Numbers to Know (Hotlines)

Emergency, police, fire department, ambulance, and paramedics	911
Clark County Poison Control	702-732-4989
Rape Crisis Line	702-366-1640
Suicide Prevention	702-731-2990
Problem Gambling Help Line	800-522-4700

Along the highways, you'll find call boxes for emergency use.
If you have a cell phone, dial *647 to reach the Nevada Highway Patrol.

Traveler's Aid Society McCarran International Airport, 8am-5pm	702-798-1742
The Dental Referral Service	800-422-8338

24-hour emergency rooms:

• University Medical Center 1800 W. Charleston Blvd.	702-383-2000
• Sunrise Hospital and Medical Center 3186 Maryland Pkwy.	702-731-8080

24-hour Walgreens pharmacy:

• The Strip, opposite Monte Carlo 3765 Las Vegas Blvd.	702-739-9645

Traveling with Disabilities: There's good news and bad. Happily, virtually every hotel and casino is well-equipped for disabled travelers, and since many of the best restaurants and shows are also on hotel grounds, you'll navigate easily. Unfortunately, getting around between hotels can be difficult: Unlike in urban centers, distances between hotels are not pedestrian- or wheelchair-friendly. The Nevada Commission on Tourism (800/638-2328, travelnevada.com) offers information for disabled travelers, and you may also want to contact private companies such as Wheelchair Getaways (800-642-2042, wheelchair-getaways.com) for more information.

HIT THE GROUND

Print Media: Las Vegas has two daily papers of note: *The Review-Journal* (lvrj.com, lasvegas.com) is published in the morning. *The Las Vegas Sun* (lasvegassun.com) is published in the afternoon. In addition, three free weeklies—*Las Vegas Weekly* (lasvegasweekly.com), *City Life* (lasvegascitylife.com), and *The Mercury* (lasvegasmercury.com)—are full of listings of cool things to do around town. In virtually every hotel room, you'll also find free copies of *Las Vegas Magazine* (lvshowbiz.com) and also buzzing issues of *What's On* (ilovevegas.com), essentially fluffy PR material about the Strip hotels' headliners.

The Las Vegas Advisor is an insider newsletter and website that provides tips on everything from gaming odds and tournaments to hotel deals, buffets, and drink and dinner specials (800-244-2224, lasvegasadvisor.com).

Las Vegas Convention and Visitors Authority (877-847-4858, 702-892-7575, visitlasvegas.com) offers a book of discount coupons for hotels, restaurants and casinos. Also, check out the Las Vegas Chamber of Commerce (702-735-1616, lvchamber.com).

Shopping Hours: Standard hours for the major malls are 10am to 9pm during the week, 10am to 8pm on Saturdays, and 11am to 6pm on Sundays. Shops in hotel arcades have varying hours, and may be open later than 8pm, on a case-by-case basis.

Radio Stations (a selection)

FM Stations

88.1	KCEP	Urban
89.5	KNPR	NPR/Classical
91.5	KUNV	Jazz/Alternative
92.3	KOMP	Rock
93.1	KBGO	Oldies Rock
94.1	KMXB	Top 40
95.5	KWNR	Country
96.3	KKLZ	Classic Rock
97.1	KXPT	Classic Rock
98.5	KLUC	Top 40
100.5	KMZQ	Soft Rock
101.9	KWLD	Hip-Hop, R&B
103.5	KISF	Spanish
104.3	KJUL	Nostalgia & Now
105.5	KSTJ	Contemporary Hits
106.5	KSNE	Adult Contemporary
107.5	KXTE	Alternative

AM Stations

720	KDWN	Talk, Sports, & News
840	KXNT	Talk
920	KBAD	Sports Talk
970	KNEWS	News

Size Conversion

Dress Sizes

US	6	8	10	12	14	16
UK	8	10	12	14	16	18
Europe	34	36	38	40	42	44
France	36	38	40	42	44	46
Italy	38	40	42	44	46	48

Women's Shoes

US	6	6½	7	7½	8	8½
UK	4½	5	5½	6	6½	7
Europe	38	38	39	39	40	41

Men's Suits

US	36	38	40	42	44	46
UK	36	38	40	42	44	46
Europe	46	48	50	52	54	56

Men's Shirts

US	14½	15	15½	16	16½	17
UK	14½	15	15½	16	16½	17
Europe	38	39	40	41	42	43

Men's Shoes

US	8	8½	9½	10½	11½	12
UK	7	7½	8½	9½	10½	11
Europe	41	42	43	44	45	46

Attire: Las Vegas is generally a casual town, and there are few places where you wouldn't be welcome in T-shirt and shorts, especially if your money's green. That said, the recent openings of deluxe restaurants and hip nightspots mean that the city is dressier these days—but it's less of a formal, stuffy affair than it is a West Coast hipster thing. That means you'll get more Hollywood fashion than New York little black dress action, although either will be acceptable. For men, it's designer casual, with very few places requiring a tie, except for the most formal restaurants. As well, if you plan to stay at the Four Seasons or another way-upmarket property, you'll want to look the part.

Finally, consider what you want to do while you're here; this is one of the few places where you can actually snow-ski in the morning atop Mt. Charleston and then water-ski in the afternoon out at Lake Mead, so consider packing a bathing suit and ski pants. And if you're dreaming about lounging at the pool, call your hotel to make sure it's open. Though some are open year-round, others close once the weather gets cool (September or October) and don't reopen until it starts to warm up again (April).

When Drinking Is Legal: You must be 21 or older to drink legally in Nevada; traveling with ID is de rigueur. It is legal to drink from open containers on the Strip (as opposed to most municipalities in the United States), but not in residential parts of town, so beware. Las Vegas cops show no mercy to those who drive under the influence (with good reason), so—as always—do not drink and drive.

Smoking: This may be the most lenient city in America when it comes to smoking. Casinos, bars, and other venues all allow smoking, probably much more so than where you live. Restaurants with more than 50 seats must offer a nonsmoking area, although this is sometimes loosely interpreted. Smoking is not allowed in government buildings or medical offices, on buses, or in elevators. Don't worry if you are a nonsmoker. The days of hazy casinos are long past. All of the newer establishments have high-tech ventilation systems that are constantly pulling the smoke out of the air. The place where you might notice it the most, however, is in the rooms. Make sure to get a nonsmoking room if that second-hand smoke smell is going to be a bother.

Drugs: As everywhere, controlled substances are illegal in Nevada. More to the point, as lax as authorities are with alcohol consumption, there's little tolerance for drug possession; even smoking a joint in public can get you hauled in. That doesn't mean you won't see it in clubs, but just be warned: Getting busted in Nevada is no fun.

Time Zone: Las Vegas operates on Pacific Standard Time (PST)—that is, the same time zone as San Francisco and Los Angeles and three hours earlier than New York. Nevada observes daylight saving time from 1am on the first Sunday in April through 1am on the last Sunday in October.

Additional Resources for Visitors

Las Vegas Convention and Visitors Authority Pick up brochures, maps, and tour information. *Daily 8am-5pm.* 3150 Paradise Rd.

Foreign Visitors

Foreign Embassies in the United States: state.gov/misc/10125.htm

Passport requirements: travel.state.gov/travel/tips/brochures/brochures_1229.html

Cell phones: North America operates on the 1,900MHZ frequency. Cell phones may be used while driving in Nevada. For buying or renting a phone go to telestial.com/instructions.htm

Toll-free numbers in the United States: 800, 866, 877, and 888.

Telephone directory assistance in the United States: 411

Electrical: U.S. standard is AC, 110 volts, 60 cycles, with a plug of two flat pins set parallel to one another.

The Latest-Info Websites

vistitlasvegas.com

And of course, **pulseguides.com**

Party Conversation—A Few Surprising Facts

- There are more than 25 poker rooms where Texas Hold 'Em is played. Professional players Doyle Brunson, Johnny Chan, Phil Ivey, Gus Hansen, and Chip Reese can often be found playing at the Bellagio. Look for "The Big Game" held in Bobby's Room, a single poker table surrounded by glass, in the center of all the poker action back near the sports book.

- About 120,000 weddings take place per year in Las Vegas. If you're planning on tying the knot in Sin City, note that there's no blood test required, the $55 marriage license fee must be paid in cash, and drive-through weddings and Elvis officiants do exist.

- Bugsy Siegel, inspired by the legal gambling in Nevada, went back East and convinced his "friends" to finance his dream: The Flamingo, named for his girlfriend Virginia Hill's nickname, opened New Year's Eve 1946. Even though The Flamingo was not an immediate success, it had an impact, and was the anchor for what the Strip would become.

- The entire Bellagio fountain show is choreographed to 30 different songs. Each performance lasts two to eight minutes with "super shooters" pumping water 460 feet into the air at its peak.

- In 1967 motorcycle daredevil Robert "Evel" Knievel attempted to jump the row of fountains at Caesars Palace. Evel cleared the fountains but got smashed on the landing. He was unconscious for 29 days. Thirty-two years later he married Crystal Kennedy at Caesars.

- The Rat Pack was the nickname for the popular group of 1950s entertainers that included Frank Sinatra, Dean Martin, Sammy Davis, Jr., Joey Bishop, and Peter Lawford. They made Vegas history with their swingin' shows at the Sands, and even starred in the original *Ocean's Eleven*.

- Las Vegas casinos follow a formula when coming up with destinations and attractions. Each one has its allotment of restaurants, nightclubs, gimmicky attractions, and shopping. The latest trend is the hotel-within-a-hotel concept, including MGM's high-end Skylofts and Mandalay Bay's stylish THEhotel.

The Cheat Sheet
(The Very Least You Ought to Know
About Las Vegas)

It's always a good idea to know a bit about the places you're going. Here's a countdown of everything you need to feel like a consummate Vegas insider.

Movies

Bugsy (1991) directed by Barry Levinson Levinson's sly dark dramedy is a classy character study of Bugsy Siegel and his obsessive dream to build a gambling mecca in the desert.

Casino (1995) directed by Martin Scorsese Sex, money, power, greed, deception, violence, and murder—*Casino* has it all. Scorsese's gangster epic is based on a real-life bookie who ran a Las Vegas casino for the mob.

Diamonds Are Forever (1971) directed by Guy Hamilton Sure, the familiar "save the world from a megalomaniac" plot is played out and it's more hokey than hip, but it's got girls, guns, and Sir Sean Connery.

Fear and Loathing in Las Vegas (1998) directed by Terry Gilliam The disorienting big-screen version of Hunter S. Thompson's controversial novel is not for everyone, but captures Vegas in a psychotropic vision that we've never seen before.

Leaving Las Vegas (1995) directed by Mike Figgis Figgis unflinchingly shows the best and worst of Vegas, painting it as an American mecca of glitz and greed where souls go to die.

Ocean's Eleven (2001) directed by Steven Soderbergh This calculatingly cool remake is nothing but good times.

Showgirls (1995) directed by Paul Verhoeven The sex, tales, lies, and exaggerations about showgirls, strippers, and hookers lure you in, but it's the overall badness of this train wreck that keeps you watching. Although Elizabeth Berkley being naked for a quarter of the movie doesn't hurt either.

Swingers (1996) directed by Doug Liman Liman's film (written by star Jon Favreau) has become a virtual hipster handbook. Lines like "Vegas, baby, Vegas," "Double down," and "They're going to give Daddy the Rainman suite," are embedded in the Gen-X lexicon.

Vegas Vacation (1997) directed by Stephen Kessler The lame John Hughes–less fourth installment of the tired *Vacation* franchise epitomizes the dark days of Vegas in the '80s to mid-'90s. The plot somehow manages to weave in Wayne Newton and Siegfried and Roy, and a majority of the scenes take place in the once "it" Mirage Hotel and Casino.

Viva Las Vegas **(1964) directed by George Sidney** Corny plot, cartoonish acting, and cheesy dialogue, but who cares when you get fast cars, the self-titled song, Ann-Margret in full pin-up form, and Elvis at his hip-shaking peak.

9 Celebrity Chefs

Tom Colicchio James Beard Award–winning chef Tom Colicchio illuminates his menu with dedicated observance of the natural flavors of great ingredients. His philosophy is "simpler is better," and it proves to be a perfect recipe for success at Craftsteak at MGM Grand.

Alain Ducasse This busy French superstar has restaurants around the globe, from Paris to New York and beyond. But quantity apparently doesn't make quality suffer. Ducasse's French-influenced menu at Mix in Las Vegas has already won the restaurant the prestigious Mobil Travel Guide Four-Star Award.

Thomas Keller Media has called him "America's Best Chef." Keller has brought his culinary skills from The French Laundry to Bouchon at The Venetian, and won a James Beard Award for his efforts.

Michael Mina James Beard Award–winning chef Michael Mina has three restaurants in Sin City: Nob Hill at MGM Grand has a San Francisco influence with organic produce and poultry flown in direct from the Bay Area; Seablue, also at MGM Grand, specializes in Mediterranean seafood; and his signature restaurant, Michael Mina, combines themes from both other menus at the sophisticated Bellagio.

Bradley Ogden The Bay Area has lent Vegas its prize chef, famous for "farm fresh" American comfort cuisine. Bradley Ogden at Caesars Palace was the first Las Vegas restaurant to be given the prestigious "Best New Restaurant" award by the James Beard Foundation.

Charlie Palmer He's well regarded for his "Progressive American" cuisine, and Charlie Palmer's culinary creations can be found at Charlie Palmer Steak at The Four Seasons and Aureole at Mandalay Bay. Aureole won the *Wine Spectator* Grand Award and *Wine Spectator* Award of Excellence three consecutive years, which is no surprise if you've seen its vertical cellar with flying wine angels.

Joël Robuchon France's "Chef of the Century," and the first chef to win three consecutive Michelin ratings, shows off his creations at two restaurants at the MGM Grand. L'Atelier de Joël Robuchon has a casual atmosphere where you can watch the counter preparations, while The Mansion is a formal dinner affair boasting elegant tasting menus.

Guy Savoy Three-star Michelin chef Guy Savoy and his son are creating magic on the second floor of the Augustus Towers at Caesars Palace. Culinary connoisseurs long awaited the opening of this restaurant.

Julian Serrano Formerly of Masa's in San Francisco, Serrano is one of the few celebrity chefs to actually work in his kitchen. At Picasso at The Bellagio, he turns out inspired French-Med cuisine that helped him win a James Beard Award, along with multiple years of AAA five-diamond awards.

8

Gambling Tips

Avoid casino slots in bars; they have some of the worst returns.

In blackjack, double down when the dealer shows a 6 and you have an 8, 9, 10, or 11.

Don't sit on the dealer's right if you are new to the game. This is called "third base," and the play in this seat affects the rest of the table. It's best if experienced players sit here.

The Hard Rock, Mandalay Bay, and the Palms have **poolside blackjack**, while the Tropicana is famous for its **swim-up blackjack**.

In roulette, look for a biased wheel. If you track the numbers being hit, and find that a particular number repeats within 100 spins, you might've found a biased wheel that is tipping the house edge in your favor.

In slots, play corner machines and "display" slot machines that can be found near entrances and buffets. Insiders think they're looser than the others.

Morning poker room tournaments are a better way for beginners to learn, rather than spending their money on cash games. They sell out early but only cost around $30 to $40. If you're really new, ask your hotel if it offers free tutorials.

Playing video poker at a bar will get you a free drink, but you're likely to have quite a few $20 Coronas over the course of an hour.

7

Songs

"Ain't That a Kick in the Head"—Dean Martin

"Big Spender"—Peggy Lee

"The Gambler"—Kenny Rogers

"Luck Be a Lady"—Frank Sinatra

"Pick Up the Pieces"—Average White Band

"Viva Las Vegas"—Elvis Presley

"With Plenty of Money and You"—Count Basie with Tony Bennett

HIT THE GROUND

6 Quotes

"Las Vegas is a society of armed masturbators/gambling is the kicker here/sex is extra/weird trip for high rollers ... house-whores for winners, hand jobs for the bad luck crowd."—Hunter S. Thompson, author

"Las Vegas is the only town in the world whose skyline is made up neither of buildings, like New York, nor of trees, like Massachusetts, but signs, neon nonetheless."
—Tom Wolfe, author

"Las Vegas looks the way you'd imagine heaven must look at night."
—Chuck Palahniuk, author

"Running a casino is like robbing a bank with no cops around. For guys like me, Las Vegas washes away your sins. It's like a morality car wash."
—"Ace" Rothstein in *Casino*

"What happens in Vegas, stays in Vegas."
—Manifesto for everyone and their grandmother

"Vegas, baby! Vegas!"—Trent (Vince Vaughn) in *Swingers*

5 Outrageous Suites

Hardwood Suite at Palms This 10,000-square-foot space has an indoor basketball court, a locker room, a poker table, a Jacuzzi, and a dance floor complete with a stripper pole.

Napoleon Suite at Paris Las Vegas It's a Palace of Versailles re-creation that overlooks the hotel's replica of the Eiffel Tower, and the staff, which includes a butler and a private masseuse, is required to speak French.

Penthouse Suite at The Hard Rock This spot comes with a bowling alley, a pool table, a fashion mini-bar stocked with couture, and a six-person hot tub with Strip views.

Presidential Suite at The Venetian The $10,000-a-night suite has two bedrooms and a pool hall, movie theater, kitchen, grand piano, and gymnasium with steam room.

Villa One at The Bellagio Enter this estate via a private tunnel with an Italian garden. Amenities include a private gym and a salon with on-site hairdressers.

4 Books

Bringing Down the House: The Inside Story of Six M.I.T. Students Who Took Vegas for Millions by Ben Mezrich

Fear and Loathing in Las Vegas by Hunter S. Thompson

The Money and the Power: The Making of Las Vegas and Its Hold on America by Sally Denton and Roger Morris

One of a Kind: The Rise and Fall of Stuey "The Kid" Ungar by Nolan Dalla and Peter Alson

3 Pro Sports Teams

Las Vegas 51s—Minor League Baseball The Las Vegas 51s (formerly the Las Vegas Stars) is a minor league baseball team that has called Vegas home since 1983. It's the AAA affiliate of the Los Angeles Dodgers and plays at Cashman Field (capacity 9,334). The team takes its name from the infamous Area 51 (located about 80 miles north of Las Vegas), and its logo jokingly depicts a gray-colored, beady-eyed alien. 702-798-7825, lv51.com

Las Vegas Gladiators—Arena Football League Pigskin purists might shun the AFL for its short field, thin goal posts, and no-name talent. But football fanatics have taken to the rock-'em, sock-'em indoor sport, as evidenced by the 20-plus-year-old league's rising attendance and recent expansion. 702-731-4977, lvgladiators.com

Las Vegas Wranglers—East Coast Hockey League The Las Vegas Wranglers began as an ECHL expansion team during the 2003-2004 season and play in the National Conference's West Division. The Wranglers' affiliation with the NHL's Calgary Flames allows numerous Flames prospects to develop and showcase their skills before heading to the NHL. 702-471-7825, lasvegaswranglers.com

2 Prerequisites for a Wedding

$55 dollars That's the cost of a marriage license. How much you spend on the ceremony is up to you.

Valid identification You'll need a photo ID and a social security number to go with it.

1 Singular Sensation

The Strip Maybe there are other streets in town, but for all intents and purposes, this is Vegas. Because the resorts are so large, they look closer than they truly are. Walking up and down the Strip is great, but rest assured it's quite a hike from the Luxor to Wynn. A trip between MGM Grand and The Venetian could easily take more than 30 minutes. When temperatures rise, remember to hydrate. After all, you're in a desert.

HIT THE GROUND

Just for Business and Conventions

Of the 38.5 million people that visited Las Vegas in 2005, 6.5 million came for a convention. Those "business" tourists make a big impact on the city and who you'll find wandering around at any given moment. If it's Rodeo week, the place turns Wild West. When the Magic show is in town, it's all about fashion. Conventions happen close to the Strip, so no need to worry about missing any of the action— most gatherings include events in off-site casinos, restaurants, and clubs to make sure it's equal amounts of work and play.

Business and Convention Hotels

Most of the large hotels host conventions, with the MGM Grand, The Mirage, and Mandalay Bay usually accorded top honors for their facilities.

Las Vegas Hilton Its just-off-the-Strip location gives a less-touristy feel ideal for business. $$$ 3000 Paradise Rd. S., 702-732-5111, lvhilton.com

Marriott Suites Las Vegas Midway between the Strip and the convention center. $$ 325 Convention Center Dr., 702-650-2000, marriott.com

Renaissance It's the largest non-gaming hotel in Nevada and very close to the convention center, making it a favorite with exhibitors. $$$ 3400 Paradise Rd., 702-733-6533, renaissancelasvegas.com

Addresses to Know

Convention Centers

- Cashman Center
  850 North Las Vegas Blvd.,
  702-386-7100

- Las Vegas Convention Center
  3150 Paradise Rd.,
  702-892-071 / 877-847-4858,
  lvcva.com

- Sands Expo & Convention Center
  201 E. Sands Ave.,
  702-733-7556

City Information

- The Nevada Commission on
  Tourism, 800-638-2328,
  travelnevada.com

Business Entertaining

Networking? Trying to seal a deal? Your business plans should include these places.

The Bar Tucked inside Daniel Boulud at Wynn Las Vegas, this is a plush and quiet bar for a private conversation before the dinner crowd gets buzzing. Wynn, 3131 S. Las Vegas Blvd. (E. Desert Inn Rd.), 702-770-7100, wynnlasvegas.com

Four Seasons Verandah Comfortable sophistication in a quiet setting. Four Seasons, 3360 S. Las Vegas Blvd. (Mandalay Bay Rd.), 702-632-5000, fourseasons.com/lasvegas

Mix at THEhotel Take your meeting while dining at Alain Ducasse's Mobil Four-Star Restaurant, or entertain over drinks with a sweeping view of Las Vegas. Mix is divided into both a fine dining room and a first-class lounge. Private rooms available. THEhotel, 950 S. Las Vegas Blvd. (Mandalay Bay Rd.), 702-632-7777, mandalaybay.com

Prime Steakhouse Grand and impressive yet reminiscent of an old speakeasy, it's located at The Bellagio, with some tables offering views of the fountains. The Bellagio, 3600 S. Las Vegas Blvd. (Flamingo Rd.), 702-693-7111, bellagio.com

Tao Nightclub For throwing a party your clients will never forget, book a VIP skybox with European bottle service at Tao Nightclub located in The Venetian. The Venetian, 3355 Las Vegas Blvd. (Flamingo Rd.), 702-388-8588, venetian.com

Also see: **Best Fine Dining** (p.24)
Best Trendy Tables (p.45)

Ducking Out for a Half-Day

Shut off your laptop, step out of the booth, and put the glitter in Glitter Gulch.

Red Rock Canyon Take the 13-mile scenic drive, or get outdoors with a short hike in Red Rock Canyon. It's just 17 miles and about 30 minutes from the Strip. Take Charleston Blvd. north of Sahara to 159, then take that till you see the entrance gates. $ *6am-dusk; gift shop 8am-dusk.* redrockcanyonlv.org

SuperCar Tours of Las Vegas Drive five sleek sports cars all in one day. A Ferrari, Viper, Corvette, AMG Mercedes, and Porsche are waiting for you. $$$$ 5021 Swenson St., 800-372-1981, supercartour.com

Also see: **Best Celebrity-Spotting Hotels** (p.21)
Best Destination Spas (p.23)
Best Golf Courses (p.27)

Gifts to Bring Home

Las Vegas souvenirs abound. Avoid them. Here are some better options.

Gambler's General Store From customized poker chips to your very own slot machine, it's here. *Daily 9am-6pm.* 800 S. Main St., 702-382-9903, gamblersgeneralstore.com

MGM Grand If you need to bring something home for the kids, select stuffed animals and other toys from either the MGM Lion Habitat or the Rainforest Café Retail Village. 3799 S. Las Vegas Blvd., 702-891-1111, mgmgrand.com

World's Largest Gift Shop If you're after kitsch, this is it. *Daily 8am-midnight.* 2440 S. Las Vegas Blvd., 702-385-7359, worldslargestgiftshop.com

Also see: **Cool Shopping Blocks** (p.56)
Bachelor(ette) Shopping Blocks (p.84)
Luxe Shopping Blocks (p.112)

HIT THE GROUND

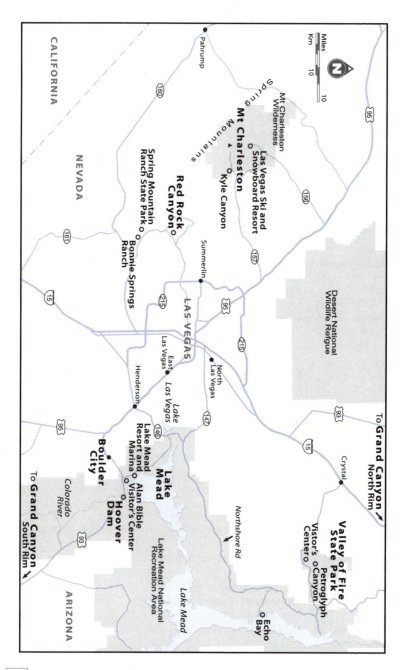

LEAVING LAS VEGAS

Once you're inside a casino, the proprietors really, really don't want you to leave—at least while you've got cash. But the reality is, there's only so long you can gamble, shop, golf, swim, spa, and party—then repeat the whole affair. Most people who've never been to Las Vegas are unaware of the fun to be had off the Strip. From the jaw-dropping vistas of Hoover Dam to a scenic drive in Red Rock Canyon, from skiing on Mt. Charleston to looking for petroglyphs in the Valley of Fire State Park, the list of attractions is as compelling as it is varied. Rent a car, or sign up for a tour, and see for yourself—there's more to Nevada than Vegas.

Area Resorts

Best

Hot Tip: Combine the best of a serene desert getaway with the excitement of the Strip by staying at one of these out-of-town spots—but be sure to rent a car to make it easy to get back and forth (although most hotels do run shuttles).

The Lowdown: In recent years, the desert around Las Vegas has seen a surge of high-end hotels and resorts filling up what was once a barren landscape. From the lush surrounds of Lake Las Vegas to the trendy Green Valley Ranch in Henderson, these spots are becoming destinations in and of themselves, with great clubs, restaurants, spas, and golf courses. Of course, there's a casino or two as well.

Green Valley Ranch • Henderson • Trendy (495 rms)

Green Valley Ranch is the crown jewel of the Station Casinos family, as well as the ultimate destination in Henderson, just 15 minutes and seven miles from the Strip. It's an elegant hotel with rooms spread between two towers. The standard ones are spacious at 510 square feet and decked out with Frette linens and goose-down comforters and pillows. All rooms have high-speed internet access, and include evening turndown service. Executive suites are the better rooms because of an extra sitting room with a desk. If you're a gambler, ask for a Strip view from the new East tower, but if you're coming to relax, the West tower has a better view of the mountains. A-list celebs and hip baby boomers come to the Ranch to get spoiled away from the Strip, or to party at Rande Gerber's The Whiskey. In the summer, Whiskey Beach flutters with beautiful people coming for the Friday night pool parties. George Clooney, Bill Clinton, and Kevin Spacey have made this a regular stop on their visits to Vegas. $$$$ 2300 Paseo Verde Pkwy. (Green Valley Pkwy.), 702-617-7777 / 866-617-7770, greenvalleyranchresort.com

Hyatt Regency Lake Las Vegas • Henderson • Moroccan (493 rms)

This Moroccan-flavored desert oasis stresses rest and relaxation over revelry. Designed to mirror a Moorish castle, the lovely hideaway is less than a 20-minute drive from the Vegas Strip, yet you would never know it from the serene surrounds. Nature, not neon, is the focal point of the $4.4 billion, 2,242-acre lakeside retreat. Two Jack Nicklaus–designed championship golf courses incorporate ten miles of the scenic shoreline that rims the 320-acre lake, where guests launch paddleboats, kayaks, and electric boats for fishing or sightseeing. The elegant earth-toned architecture offers sweeping views of the sparkling water and the surreal desert backdrop (needless to say, request a lake-view room, preferably one with a romantic Juliet balcony). Guests can bask in one of the resort's two cabana-lined pools or opt for a lakeside Mediterranean-style beach. The Pacific Rim–inspired Japengo restaurant has award-winning sushi, but the tacked-on casino and stodgy lounges seem more like an afterthought—plan on heading to the Strip to gamble. $$$ 101 Montelago Blvd. (Lake Las Vegas Pkwy.), 702-567-1234 / 800-233-1234, lakelasvegas.hyatt.com

Red Rock Resort Spa and Casino • Summerlin • Contemporary (462 rms)
This so-called "locals' casino" combines breathtaking views of the flaming Red Rock Canyon with a serene spa, sumptuous dining, hip nightlife, and state-of-the-art gaming. The boutique hideaway is located just 15 miles from the Vegas Strip and offers guests many of the same low-key, yet luxurious amenities as its sister resort, Green Valley Ranch. Red Rock's 414 guest rooms and 48 suites come fully equipped with 42-inch plasma TVs, iPod sound systems, high-speed wireless internet access, and in-room spa service. The spa is a sleek, ultra-modern retreat offering Ashiatsu massage, a boxing ring, personal trainers, and nutritional cooking classes. Excursions to the nearby Red Rock Canyon Conservation Area offer opportunities for hiking, horseback riding, rock rappelling, and white-water rafting. In-house amenities include three acres of poolside perfection, a 16-screen movie theater, nine restaurants, and five nightlife destinations, including Rande Gerber's red-hot Cherry nightclub. $$$ 11011 W. Charleston Blvd. (S. Pavilion Center Dr.), 702-797-7625 / 866-767-7773, redrockstation.com

Ritz Carlton Lake Las Vegas • Henderson • Timeless (349 rms)
This Tuscan-inspired luxury resort offers guests a true Vegas getaway. The Mediterranean-style lakeside spot includes a 30,000-square-foot spa and fitness center, world-class dining at the Medici Café, two outdoor pools, a white sand beach, 36 holes of championship golf designed by Jack Nicklaus, and access to lakeside recreational activities such as fishing, kayaking, hiking, boating, and gondola rides. A stone bridge, patterned after Florence's Ponte Vecchio, leads to a shopping village and the Casino MonteLago, a large but lifeless replica of a 16th-century Tuscan winery. Most of the 349 luxurious rooms and suites offer panoramic views of the high-desert mountains or Lake Las Vegas—it's a personal choice, but either way you'll be pleased. Couples and families might want to look into the Club Level package, which offers high-rolling perks for only $100 a night more, plus rooms on the bridge. The nightlife is nil, but if you're looking for action, the Vegas strip is only 17 miles away. $$$$ 1610 Lake Las Vegas Pkwy. (Lake Mead Pkwy.), 702-567-4700 / 800-241-3333, ritzcarlton.com/resorts/lake_las_vegas

LEAVING

The Grand Canyon

Hot Tip: Becky's Backyard is a website listing secret hikes and view spots that only insiders know. Find out where the best sunset is, the best place to see the river, how to get around, and the best short hike around the canyon (beckysbackyard-grandcanyon.com).

The Lowdown: The Grand Canyon is one of America's most treasured national parks, and a favorite among side trips from Las Vegas. To witness more than 2 billion years of geological history embedded in the earth is staggering. It is 275 miles from the Strip, and takes about 4.5 hours driving on U.S. 93 towards Henderson, and I-40E to Arizona 64N. The North Rim is open from mid-May to mid-October, while the South Rim is open year-round.

Best Attractions

Maverick Helicopters If you want to expedite the trip to this natural world wonder, take to the air. $$$$ 6075 S. Las Vegas Blvd., 702-261-0007, maverickhelicopter.com

River Rafting There are several providers to choose from on the National Park Service website (nps.gov/grca). OARS is a reputable company, and was founded in 1969 as the first small raft outfitter in the Grand Canyon. $$$ 209-736-4677, oars.com

Best Restaurants

The Canteen at Phantom Ranch Located inside the canyon, this friendly spot serves up breakfast (starting at 6:30!), lunch, and dinner. $ 303-297-2757, grandcanyonlodges.com

El Tovar Dining Room Considered one of the best restaurants in the area, Tovar is as good on atmosphere as it is with food. Its rustic Euro-lodge feel, complete with hewn beams on the ceiling, fits right in with the grandeur of the canyon. $$$ 928-638-2631, grandcanyonlodges.com

Best Hotels

El Tovar This is the most recognized hotel in the Canyon, and has hosted such notables as Theodore Roosevelt and Albert Einstein since its opening in 1905. It sits on the edge of the South Rim. Book way in advance. $$$ 303-297-2757 (to reach a guest or same-day reservations), 928-638-2631 (main reservation line), grandcanyonlodges.com

Phantom Ranch Sleep in the canyon—think cabins with bunk beds and indoor plumbing, which can only be reached by mule, foot, or raft. $$ 303-297-2757, grandcanyonlodges.com

Getting There: Go south on U.S. 93 (over the Hoover Dam) to Kingman, Arizona. Go east on I-40 to Williams. At the Arizona 64 junction, turn left (north) and proceed to the south entrance of Grand Canyon National Park. Driving time is about 5.5 hours.

29 miles S

Boulder City

Hot Tip: Feeling adventurous? Skydive Las Vegas is located in Boulder City, and will give you a tandem jump with views from the Las Vegas Strip to the Hoover Dam. (702-759-3482, skydivelasvegas.com)

The Lowdown: If you're thinking "Boulder Dam, Boulder City, there must be some connection," you'd be right. Boulder City sprung up within a year to house the 5,000-plus workers and their families who flocked to this desert town about seven miles from the dam. Despite the unbearable heat and the dangerous work, workers were lured by the dam's princely wages (50 cents an hour), unheard of during the Depression when most workers were being paid 5 cents to 30 cents an hour. Run by the federal government, the town was very conservative, and it is still the only place in Nevada that doesn't allow gaming. During construction, Boulder City was Nevada's third-largest city, but half the population decamped once the dam was complete. Today, with a population of about 15,000, Boulder City is known for its sleepy, small-town ambience, vintage 1930s-era homes, antique shops, jewelry stores, and galleries—all a welcome reprieve from the glitz of Las Vegas. Stroll over to Government Park, at the corner of Nevada Way and Colorado Street, where you can see one of the original 34-ton water wheels used in the turbines to generate electricity at the dam.

Best Attractions

Boulder City/Hoover Dam Museum The museum is on the second floor of the Boulder Dam Hotel and has displays of artifacts from the construction of Boulder City and Hoover Dam. Boulder Dam Hotel, 1305 Arizona St., 702-294-1988, bcmha.org

Government Park Check out one of the original 34-ton water wheels used in the turbines to generate electricity at the dam. Nevada Way and Colorado St., 702-293-9256

Best Restaurants

Coffee Cup This is a great '30s-era diner in a landmark '50s-era building. $ 512 Nevada Hwy., 702-294-0517

Matteo's Restaurant This eatery serves breakfast, lunch, and dinner. $ Boulder Dam Hotel, 1305 Arizona St., 702-293-0098, matteodining.com

Pit Stop A friendly, tasty bet for any meal of the day. $ 802 Buchanan Blvd., Ste. D, 702-293-7080

Best Nightlife

Stagecoach Saloon It ain't Vegas, but for a drink and a bit of karaoke, you won't go wrong. 1200 Nevada Hwy., 702-293-0926

Getting There: Take U.S. I-515S, continue on U.S. 93S-U.S. 95S, exit right, Buchanan Boulevard.

LEAVING

miles

S

Hoover Dam

Hot Tip: The line between the Pacific and Mountain time zones runs right down the middle of the dam, so you can gain an hour just by stepping over the line. If you want to drive across the dam (on Highway 93), be prepared for a search checkpoint and a wait between the hours of 10am and 6pm, when construction may delay traffic.

The Lowdown: It's easy to combine a day trip to Lake Mead with a tour of Hoover Dam, considered one of the seven wonders of the modern world—the American Society of Civil Engineers named it the Civil Engineering Monument of the Millennium. It's a well-earned distinction. Containing the powerful Colorado River, the dam created the largest artificial lake in the country (and the second-largest in the world), but it put an end to the massive flooding that used to occur whenever the Colorado overflowed its banks, and brought electric power and water to the arid Southwest. In fact, were it not for the Hoover Dam, many historians believe Las Vegas wouldn't exist on the scale it does today. Originally known as Boulder Dam, it was renamed for Herbert Hoover, who was president when Congress passed the funds to build it in 1928. Just walking across the top of the dam is awe-inspiring as you look down into Lake Mead on one side and the Colorado River on the other. Upwards of 2,000 to 3,000 people visit the dam each day. If you're not a fan of crowds, go in the early morning; seasonally, it's less crowded in January and February and gets progressively more crowded from spring break through Labor Day.

Best Attractions

The Discovery Tour Get a guided tour to see the massive power plant generators and other features of the dam. The staff will talk every 15 minutes at stopping points. Personal items are subject to an X-ray screening for security purposes. $ 702-494-2517, purchase tickets online at:
vegas.com/attractions/outside_lasvegas/hooverdamdiscovery.html

The Visitor's Center In addition to souvenirs and information about the Hoover Dam, there are feature films and exhibits about the construction of the dam. 702-293-1824

Winged Figures of the Republic The bronze Art Deco sculptures are a worthy additional photo stop. Free.

Getting There: Take U.S. I-515S, which automatically turns into U.S. 93S and takes you right to the dam.

172

38 miles E

Lake Mead

Hot Tip: There is a submerged town beneath the lake. St. Thomas, a farming community, was inundated in 1937. Some say that you can see some of what's left from the juncture that connects Overton Beach and the road to the Valley of Fire.

The Lowdown: The biggest artificial lake in the country and the second-largest in the world, Lake Mead was created in 1936 when the Hoover Dam put a stopper in the Colorado River at Black Canyon. The huge lake caters to boaters, swimmers, sunbathers, and fishermen, while its desert rewards hikers, wildlife photographers, and roadside sightseers. It's often a surprise to visitors, but there's a large scuba diving community in Las Vegas that enjoys exploring the underwater sights of Lake Mead.

Best Attractions

Alan Bible Visitor's Center This visitor's center has information about the lake and recreational services available. 702-293-8990

Echo Bay About 40 miles from the visitor's center, this beach has better sand and is less crowded than the other beaches, like Boulder Beach, which is only a mile from the visitor's center.

Lake Mead Cruises The Desert Princess is a 300-passenger stern-wheeler that cruises the lake. Passengers enjoy this for dinner cruises and dancing. Some weekends sightseeing cruises are available, too. 702-293-6180, lakemeadcruises.com

Best Accommodations

Forever Resorts Offers three- to seven-day rentals on houseboats that range from 56 to 70 feet and can sleep up to 12 people. $$ Locations vary. 800-255-5561, foreverresorts.com

Lake Mead Resort and Marina It has a floating restaurant, a beach, boat rentals, and camping facilities. $ 322 Lakeshore Rd., 702-293-2074, sevencrown.com

LEAVING

Getting There: From the Strip, it's a roughly 30-minute drive through the town of Henderson. Take I-215E (which turns into Lake Mead Boulevard) all the way to the Lake Mead National Recreation Area entrance. Entrance fee is $5 per car. To get to the park's front door, take I-215E to U.S. 93 through Boulder City. You'll end up on the west side of the lake, where you'll find boat rentals, fishing licenses, and supplies at Lake Mead Resort and Marina.

Mt. Charleston

Hot Tip: The temperature on the mountain can be 25 to 30 degrees cooler than that on the Strip, even in summer, so dress accordingly.

The Lowdown: Mt. Charleston is part of the Spring Mountain range, with an altitude of over 11,000 feet, and is just 35 miles northwest of Las Vegas, situated in the Toiyabe National Forest. The scenery changes from desert Joshua trees to towering pine trees along the drive up. It's hard for some people to believe that such a wilderness paradise exists so close to the Strip, but locals know only too well how much this area has to offer. In summer, the trails are filled (but not too full) with hikers, bikers, and nature lovers. You can even rent horses, and of course, there are great picnic spots. When the snow hits, it's a hot scene for skiing and snowboarding. Whatever season you come, be sure you take careful note of the weather—it gets cold up here, even in summer.

Best Attractions

Las Vegas Ski and Snowboard Resort This resort is located in Lee Canyon and has two campgrounds and a 40-acre ski area with ten runs. Located at end of Highway 156 in Lee Canyon, 702-645-2754, skilasvegas.com

Mt. Charleston Riding Stables It has horses for rent and horseback riding trails. 2 Kyle Canyon Rd., 702-387-2457, mountcharlestonridingstables.com

Best Restaurants and Nightlife

Mt. Charleston Hotel Turn left onto Kyle Canyon when you get to the intersection of Route 157 and U.S. 95. This hotel was built in 1984 and is known for its restaurant, large hearth, and bar. The mountain view is delightful. $ 2 Kyle Canyon Rd., 702-872-5500 / 800-794-3456, mtcharlestonhotel.com

Mt. Charleston Lodge Get here by taking Route 157 till it ends. This lodge is 7,717 above sea level and overlooks Kyle Canyon. Inside the lodge is a fireside cocktail lounge. $ 1200 Old Park Rd., 702-872-5408 / 800-955-1314, mtcharlestonlodge.com

Best Resources

General Contact Information 702-222-1597
Ski Information 702-872-5462
Snow Report 702-593-9500

Getting There: From Las Vegas, go north on U.S. 95, then left (west) on State Route 157 (alternate: Rte. 156).

17 miles W

Red Rock Canyon

Hot Tip: Pack a picnic lunch (or have the hotel do it) and enjoy it at one of Red Rock's many scenic spots.

The Lowdown: Red Rock Canyon sits in the midst of the Spring Mountains and is noted for its gorgeous red and orange limestone and sandstone highlights, which stand in stark contrast to the grays and browns of the surrounding mountains. For a quick tour, drive the 13-mile scenic loop—it's one way, so once you're driving, you're committed to the whole loop.

About five miles past Red Rock Canyon is Bonnie Springs Ranch/Old Nevada, a mock 1880s frontier town and old-style Western ranch. It's a bit like historic Williamsburg, but with cowboys and bison. About a mile from Bonnie Springs is Spring Mountain Ranch State Park, a rambling 1940s ranch house, once owned by Howard Hughes and designated as a park in 1974.

Best Attractions

Bonnie Springs Ranch There are plenty of activities at this kitschy Old West ranch, including guided horse trail rides, a small theme park with an opera house and wedding chapel, a miniature train that runs between the parking lot and the entrance on weekends, and simulated gunfights and hangings. $
1 Bonnie Springs Ranch Rd., 702-875-4191, bonniesprings.com

Escape Adventures Bike rentals for full or half day, to enjoy Red Rock's trails. $
8221 W. Charleston Blvd., 702-596-2953, lasvegascyclery.com

Hiking and Rock Climbing The visitor's center has information and maps on the various hiking and rock-climbing areas open to guests. 702-515-5350, nv.blm.gov/redrockcanyon.com

Lost Creek Discovery Trail Keep your eye out for the Willow Springs–Lost Creek turnoff 6 1/2 miles past the vista pullouts. This road leads to the Lost Creek Discovery Trail, a 3/4 mile trail with a seasonal waterfall, Native American pictographs, and a picnic area near the rocks.

13-Mile Scenic Loop When you get to Red Rock Canyon, there will be road signs leading you on a scenic loop. It opens at 6am every day and closes at nightfall. Note that it's a one-way loop, so if you start it, you're committed. If you'd like to bike the paved road, just park your car at the visitor's center.

LEAVING

Getting There: From Las Vegas Boulevard (the Strip), go west on Charleston Boulevard for 17 miles. You will see a sign on your right that says Red Rock Scenic Drive. Entrance to the park is $5 per car.

Valley of Fire State Park

Hot Tip: There is a Lost City Museum eight miles between the entrance to the Valley of Fire and Overton. Lost City disappeared around 1150, but the museum has a fine collection of artifacts from the Moapa Valley and its ancient Puebloan culture. There are also photographs of the evacuation of the Lost City in 1924.

The Lowdown: Nevada's oldest and (at nearly 35,000 acres) largest state park is a very easy half-day or full-day trip. There are two campgrounds with water, restrooms, showers, and grills for longer stays. Shifts in the earth's terrain 150 million years ago (along with continued erosion) have created some far-out sandstone formations that somewhat resemble beehives, a piano, an elephant, a duck, a dome—and they're named as such. Oxidized iron in the sand gives the rocks their reddish color, and when the sunlight hits just right, they give off a fiery glow. Tip: You can combine this with a trip to the Overton area of Lake Mead just six miles away.

Driving the Bitter Springs Trail, which you can pick up off I-15 at Glendale, will take you on a 30-mile scenic excursion through the park to the lake. If you're keen to explore Valley of Fire on foot—and there are some beautiful hikes of varying lengths and terrain here—it's best to visit in the spring or fall (or in the very early morning or late afternoon in the summer). Otherwise you'll be seeing the sights from your air-conditioned car in summertime temperatures that often reach 120.

Best Attractions

Bitter Springs Trail This trail can be found at 1-15 at Glendale. It is a 30-mile scenic excursion through the park to the lake.

Petroglyph Canyon Self-Guided Trail This is an easy half-mile hike with parking at the trailhead. It ambles along a sandy path through some remarkable rock formations. There is also detailed signage so that you don't miss the petroglyphs carved into the sandstone by the Anasazi Indians.

Two-Mile Scenic Loop Road Stay in your car and enjoy the scenery as you pass Arch Rock and Piano Rock. There is an alternate 11-mile drive that takes you past the White Domes formation. These routes are great when it's hot out.

Valley of Fire State Park Visitor's Center This center has plenty of information on ecology, archaeology, and how to best see the area today. It is open year-round. 702-397-2088, parks.nv.gov/vf.htm

Getting There: Take I-15 to Highway 169 (55 miles northeast of the Strip). It costs $5 per car to enter, $13 if you plan to camp. Note: There are no gas stations in the park, so fill up before you head out. There aren't any snack bars in the park either, so bring plenty of water and consider packing a lunch—there are numerous places to picnic.

Appendix: Gambling Tips

There are two reasons that people travel to Sin City: to party and to gamble. Granted, there are also business meetings, conventions, and more than enough quickie weddings presided over by Elvis impersonators to make "The King" roll over in his grave, but in the end, Las Vegas is all about carousing and wagering.

Anywhere you look, you'll find a slot or video poker machine, table game, sporting proposition, or some other wild wagering option that's just ready and waiting to take your hard-earned cash. Striking it rich is the goal, breaking even is the backup plan, but for many people, visiting the ATM—on more than one occasion—is the reality.

That's the nature of the beast. Casinos give you the opportunity, 24/7/365, to walk away with some of their cold, hard cash. So it goes without saying that they're going to have some sort of edge to make certain that the vast majority of gamblers don't succeed. In some cases the edge is small, just enough to tip the scales in the house's favor over the long run, making that particular game or wager a viable part of the casino. In others, the edge is so severe that you'd be much better off tearing your money into tiny pieces.

What's the key to leaving Las Vegas with a small fortune *without* having started with a larger one? Be wary of all of those magical systems and formulas that promise to make you filthy rich provided you follow their instructions to the letter—there is *no way* to guarantee that you will win at gambling in Las Vegas. But that doesn't mean you can't *improve* your chances of winning. By understanding exactly how each game works, and avoiding the traps and pitfalls associated with many of them, you can often decrease your chances of losing, leaving you more money to gamble.

Baccarat

Widely considered to be the most glamorous game in the casino, baccarat carries cachet largely because of the wealthy jet-setters who are forever linked to the game (think James Bond). Surprisingly, baccarat is a very easy game to play. In addition, it's also a good game for the low-stakes player as the casino's edge is relatively small. Today, many casinos offer smaller baccarat tables—called mini-baccarat—because its popularity among the masses has increased considerably. Baccarat is fast, easy, and takes no skill whatsoever to play.

Players have but three choices to make: They can bet on the player, bet on the banker, or bet for a tie. Once the bets are made, the dealer deals a pair of two-card hands from an eight-deck shoe—one for the player, the other for the banker. The object is to get as close to 9 as possible. As no total can be greater than 9, if 10 or more is reached, you must subtract 10 to determine the hand's value.

All 10s and face cards count as zero (the name baccarat comes from *baccara*, the Italian word for zero), while other cards represent their true value. For example, a 2 and a 5 would equal 7. A queen and an 8 would equal 8. A 6 and a 9 would equal 5 (15 minus 10 equals 5).

After the pair of two-card hands are dealt, a third card can be drawn by the player, the banker, or both. However, the decision to draw the card is not made by anyone at the table—it is predetermined by the rules of the game.

Players who win will pay a 5 percent commission (50 cents for every $10 bet) when they win by betting on the "banker" because the odds for the "banker" are better than those for the "player." Ties are paid at a rate of 8 to 1.

Blackjack

Blackjack, or 21, is the most popular casino table game in America by landslide proportions. It's also one of the easiest to understand. Using two or more cards, get as close to 21 as possible without going over. To win, you must beat the dealer's hand. That's it. Piece of cake, right? Unfortunately, there's a lot more to it than that. But the good news is, with proper play, blackjack is not only one of the best games (odds-wise) to play in the casino, it's perhaps the *only* game that can actually be beaten.

There are many variations of casino blackjack. Most involve the use of multiple decks (usually six), dealt from what is known as a shoe. The more decks in play, the greater the house's advantage. Whenever possible, play at a single-deck table as the advantage (albeit a small one at +.01 percent) is actually with the player. Also, there are some individual game features that can give the house an extra edge or, conversely, give you more of a chance against the house. But before we get into those, here's a quick 21 tutorial, just so you're completely familiar with the lingo.

First, you place a bet—anywhere from $1 to *sky's the limit*. After your first two cards are dealt, you'll be given the option of drawing more cards (called *hitting*) or staying with what you've got (called *sticking*). Your total, in addition to the dealer's *up-card* (the card he is showing), will determine your course of action. If you've already got 21, or blackjack—an ace and any 10 or face card—and the dealer doesn't also have a natural 21, you win and the dealer pays you 3 to 2 (one and a half times your bet). Assuming you don't have 21, the game goes on and the hit-or-stick option comes into play.

If your cards total 17 or more (and one of your cards is not an ace, which would give you a *soft* hand), you should stick. Always, and without question. Don't listen to what anyone else tells you. Seventeen or more without an ace, sit tight. Now, if you've got an ace (which can be either 1 or 11), and your cards total 19 or 20, same thing—just chill out and let the dealer do his thing. Nineteen and 20 are strong hands and often win.

But other soft hands should be played differently, again based on what the dealer is showing. If the dealer has a 5 or a 6 exposed (trouble cards, which often lead to *busting* or going over 21), this may be a good time to *double down* (doubling your original bet). Again, check the rules of the table before you sit down as some casinos only allow you to double down on 10 or 11. The ability to double on any total gives the player more of an advantage. However, if the dealer is showing a high up-card (8, 9, 10, or an ace), and your soft total is less than the dealer's up-card plus 10 (for multi-deck blackjack games, always assume the dealer has a 10 in the *hole* (the card that is face down), you may just want to hit.

Another important aspect of soft hands is a dealer's soft 17 (an ace and a 6). Many casinos require dealers to stay on soft 17, but others call for the dealer to hit. You want to play at casinos where dealers *stick* on soft 17. Casinos that hit soft 17s have an extra .20 percent edge against you and, believe me, this is war—you'll need every fractional advantage that you can find.

If your two cards are the same, you may want to *split* them (create two separate hands of the same original bet). Here's something easy to remember: *Always* split aces and 8s, regardless of what the dealer is showing, and *never* split 5s or 10s, again no matter what the dealer's up-card is. Every now and then you will see someone at the table splitting 10s. He's either a drunk or an idiot or a drunken idiot. If this happens, pick up your chips and move to a different table because he will undoubtedly cost the table money with his foolish play. Other pairs should be split based on what the dealer is showing. After cards are split, the hands proceed normally, unless you are splitting aces. Splitting aces only allows you one card per ace—unless it's another ace, in which case you can split them again. Some casinos do not allow you to split aces a second time in the same hand. Again, stay away from these venues. It's just another house edge—to the tune of .14 percent.

Insurance is another blackjack situation that you'll be forced to deal with sooner or later. Whenever a dealer has an ace as his up-card, he will offer the players insurance. By making a separate bet—a maximum of half your original bet—if the dealer has 21, you win the insurance bet and are paid at a rate of 2-to-1, essentially breaking even with the first bet you just lost. However, if you have blackjack and the dealer is showing an ace, you can request *even money*—an even money payoff instead of the usual 3-to-2.

Surrender is another feature that provides a player with more outs. If you don't like your starting hand, you can surrender half your bet. Only surrender when you have a very large bet and a total of 15 or 16 pitted against a powerful dealer up-card, such as a 10 or an ace.

Some more good tips for blackjack: If the dealer is showing a 2 through 6 and you have 13 or more, stick. If the dealer has a 2 or a 3 up and your total is 12, you may want to try hitting, as there are more cards in the deck that can help you than can hurt you (32 as opposed to 20). Subsequently, the card that you declined to take may help the dealer make his hand against you and the rest of the table.

Craps

At first glance, craps may look extremely complicated, but it is actually a very easy game to play. Don't be intimidated by the fast-paced action and excitement, and all the yelling and screaming that is commonly associated with a happening dice table—if you can count to 12, then you can play this game.

The game of craps begins with the *come-out* roll. The *shooter* (dice pass in turn, clockwise, around the table) rolls the dice and, if the total is 7 or 11 (a *natural*), anyone who bet on the pass line (the line directly in front of where he or she is standing) is a winner and receives even money for his or her wager. If a 2, 3, or 12 is rolled (*craps*), anyone who bet on the pass line loses. Bets are then replaced and the same shooter rolls again until a *point* (any number other than 2, 3, 7, 11, or 12) is established. The pass line bet is one of the best bets in the casino. After the point has been established, line bettors can place an additional bet behind their line bet and get the correct odds for that number if that number is rolled again (aka *making the point*). The house has absolutely no edge on any odds bets.

After the point is established, in addition to the odds bets, players can make a variety of other wagers. The smartest and safest bets available are on the numbers 6 or 8. Ten combinations of the dice will yield a 6 or 8, resulting in a payoff of $7 for every $6 wagered. Betting on 5 or 9 would be the next step down as there are only eight combinations for those two numbers, but the payoff is slightly higher at $7 for every $5 wagered. The 4 and 10 have only six combinations between them, but the payoff is an even greater $9 for every $5 wagered. All of these bets are relatively safe, in a matter of speaking, as only a 7 will hurt you. Anything else is of no consequence. Once the point has been established, if a 7 is rolled before the point is made, all pass line bets, and all placed number bets (4, 5, 6, 8, 9, and 10) lose. But if the point is made before a 7 is rolled, all pass line bettors are paid and the process starts over again. Players then have the option of leaving their place bets up or taking them down. Pretty simple, right?

Although it contains many numbers (2, 3, 4, 9, 10, 11, and 12), the *field* is widely regarded as a sucker's bet and should be avoided like the plague. Any time a casino is willing to pay you double (for the roll of a 2 or a 12), alarm bells should go off. Ditto for the *hardways* bets. Granted, there are some attractive odds associated with doubles combinations for the

Terminology

Whatever game you play, start with a rudimentary understanding of casino terminology and you can swim with the sharks, if not the whales.

Boxman: a craps dealer who sits over the drop box and supervises bets and payoffs

Casino boss: a person who oversees the entire casino

Comp: short for complimentary or free

Drop box: a locked box on tables where dealers deposit paper money

Eye in the sky: surveillance equipment, usually ceiling mirrors that conceal people assigned to watch the action to prevent cheating by players or dealers

Limit: the minimum or maximum bet accepted at a gambling table

Marker: an IOU owed to the casino by a gambler the hotel is allowing to play on credit

Pit boss: a person who oversees table dealers

RFB comp: free room, food, and beverage

Shooter: a gambler who is rolling the dice on a craps table

Stickman (stick chick): a dealer who moves the dice around on a craps table with a hooked stick

Excerpted from
"A Whale of a Good Time,"
The Fun Seeker's North America

numbers 4, 6, 8, and 10, but don't risk more than a few dollars—if any—on these propositions. If the number is rolled and it isn't a double, you lose. The same goes for all the single roll bets like 2 (snake eyes), 3, 11, or 12 (boxcars). Again, the high odds associated with them should be enough of a warning to steer clear.

You can also bet against the shooter. This is called *betting the don't*. Essentially, after the point has been established, you're rooting for a 7 to come before the point is made. It's definitely not as fun and, although it can be profitable at a cold table, it's not recommended for new players.

Race and Sports Books

The vast majority of Las Vegas casinos have race and sports books and will accept action on any number of sporting events taking place throughout the world. Depending on the sport, odds or a point spread (or a combination of the two) is used to even out the wagering. Bear in mind that just because one team is favored over another—even by a substantial amount—doesn't mean that team is any better than the other. Point spreads move based on where the majority of the action is going. If many people are betting on one team, the spread widens, giving the underdog more points in the hopes of swaying more bettors to that side of the proposition.

Forget what you see in the movies—professional sports bettors, aka *handicappers*, spend countless hours poring over information and statistics in their quest to pick the winners.

The only safe strategy is to avoid betting with your heart. Just because you're a die-hard Dallas Cowboys fan doesn't mean you should risk your rent money on them. But if you absolutely must bet on a sporting event to make the game "interesting" (famous last words), try to pick an underdog as it is always better to take the points, especially with today's free-agency market where any team can beat any other team on any given day.

Roulette

Developed in Europe, roulette involves betting on the numbers 1 through 36, plus 0 and 00, along with the colors red and black; half of the numbers are red, the other half black. Of the four major table games (blackjack, craps, roulette, and baccarat), roulette offers the worst odds to the player. Sure, hitting your number pays an impressive 35 to 1, but again, high payoffs should tell you all about your realistic chances of making money (or more importantly, *losing* money) at that game. Betting on either of the colors, which offer even money returns, is still not a great wager, as you have those two nasty green spots (0 and 00) to contend with, accounting for the house edge. But if you're undeterred in your plan to play roulette, try to find a casino that offers European-style roulette, which contains only one 0. At single-0 tables, the house edge is cut nearly in half—from 5.26 percent to 2.70 percent.

Slot Machines

First, the obvious: Slot machines are mechanical devices utilizing three or more circular reels—or, in the case of video slots, video mock-ups of those reels—adorned with a wide variety of colored symbols. Inserting coins (or bills) into the machine allows the player to spin the reels, with the pull of a lever (arm) or the push of a button, in the hopes of getting certain symbols to line up along the pay-line, resulting in a payoff. Many of the newer multicoin machines feature multiple pay-lines, which, while offering you more chances to win on each spin, also require you to pay more for that privilege, in some cases up to 45 coins per spin (as is the case with many of the latest high-tech nickel machines).

The most important thing to understand about all slot machines is that these babies are the real moneymakers in any casino. Ever wonder why your favorite property has 30 black-jack tables, three or four craps tables and roulette wheels, a smattering of other table games, and a whopping 2,000 slot machines? Consider that a busy 25-cent slot machine produces a yearly profit of more than $100,000. Two thousand of those bad boys would amount to a $200 million profit. The joke in Sin City is that slot machines pay the electric bill—for the entire Strip.

All modern slot machines contain a random number generator, or RNG, which controls the payback percentage. In Nevada, 75 percent is the minimum, although the actual number is approximately 95 percent. Basically, it means that for every $1 you insert into a slot machine you'll get back 95 cents. Any way you slice it, it's a winning proposition—*for the casino*. Sooner or later, you'll go broke. But jackpots get hit all the time—the big progressive jackpots get hit far less frequently than the others—and that's precisely what keeps people coming back: the lure of the big win.

The most important rule to remember playing any slot machine: Never spin the reels unless you're playing with maximum coins in. This may require you to rethink which machine you play, in terms of total investment per spin, but playing the slots is all about hitting the jackpot, which cannot be done unless you play the maximum coins allowed.

It's a fairly straightforward card game generally played with two to ten people. The dealer deals from a standard 52-card deck. As in most variants of poker, the objective is to win pots (the sum of the money bet by oneself and other players in a hand). A pot is won either at the showdown by forming the best five-card poker hand out of the seven cards available, or by betting to cause other players to fold.

Texas Hold 'Em is played using small and big blind bets. A dealer button is used to represent the player in the dealer position. The dealer button rotates clockwise after each hand, changing the position of the dealer and the blinds. The small blind is posted by the player to the left of the dealer and is usually equal to half of the big blind. The big blind, posted by the player to the left of the small blind, is equal to the minimum bet. Players are dealt two hole or pocket cards facedown. The player to the left of the big blind can fold, call (match the bet in front of you), or raise the bet. Betting proceeds clockwise around the table.

Crapese

Craps, whether played in the Runyonesque *Guys and Dolls,* or in billion-dollar resorts, is the fastest and liveliest casino game. Money moves quickly—it's fun for novices to simply watch dealers move the chips around—and it takes a fair amount of familiarity and comfort to play it well. To have fun, however, you only need to understand the language of the game. Start by learning how to count in crapese:

Two: aces or low
Three: ace-deuce
Four: little Joe
Five: fever
Six: sex
Seven: seven, seven out, or lucky seven
Eight: eighter from Decatur
Nine: Nina from Pasadena
Ten: ten on the end or Big Ben
Eleven: yo or yo-lev
Twelve: boxcars or high

Get the counting down and you'll next pick up terms such as "Two rolls, no coffee!" "Hands high, they fly!" "Too tall to call!" and "Pause is the cause!" Pretty soon you'll be kissing the dice (or letting the good-looking gamer next to you kiss them) and shouting, "C'mon, dice, baby needs a new pair of shoes!" or the ever-popular "Rent money!" as you throw the bones across the felt. After that, you're just a slippery slope away from calling out bets such as "Section eight press and a high-low with the cheese!" When you want to roll an eight, you'll call out "How do you spell relief?" and get the response "Roll eight!" When you win, you'll hear the stickman say, "Winner, winner, chicken dinner" and get high-fives all around. This sure beats pushing buttons and waiting for a bunch of cherries.

Excerpted from "A Whale of a Good Time," *The Fun Seeker's North America*

The dealer then deals a flop (three face-up community cards). Players can now check (pass the action to the next player), unless there's a bet ahead of them—then they have to call, fold, or raise the bet. After the flop betting round ends, a single community card (called the turn or fourth street) is dealt, followed by a third betting round. A final single community card (called the river or fifth street) is then dealt, followed by a fourth betting round and the showdown, if necessary.

If a player bets and all other players fold, then the remaining player is awarded the pot. If two or more players remain after the final betting round, a showdown occurs. The winner in a heads-up showdown is the player with the best five-card hand he can make from the seven cards comprising his two hole cards and the board (the five community cards).

In essence, Texas Hold 'Em is a game of chance, but when played correctly, it's a lot like investing. You bet heavily on hands that you have a better than average chance of winning, and you minimize your bets on those that you don't. As the old poker adage goes, "If after the first 20 minutes you don't know who the sucker at the table is, it's probably you."

Video Poker

The most important thing to understand about video poker machines is that they are *not* slot machines. Unlike slots, video poker machines require you to make decisions about your play. Essentially, video poker machines are just like regular five-card-draw poker games (based on a 52-card deck like real poker), except there are no other players to beat and you wager only at the beginning of the hand, before the cards are dealt. Once they are dealt, you try to make the best hand possible by replacing (drawing) cards—from just one to all five. A specific "minimum" hand must be attained to win, or at the very least recoup your original wager; higher hands yield higher payoffs.

If you don't understand all the ins and outs of poker, you can still enjoy video poker provided you know the hand rankings.

Although video poker machines are not slot machines, the vast majority still use a random number generator (RNG) to shuffle the deck. Without wild cards, there are 2,598,960 different five-card poker hands possible. Most video poker machines offer a higher payback percentage than slot machines. Some even offer a greater than 100 percent return on your money, provided perfect play strategy is utilized.

Just what is perfect play strategy? Way too intensive to cover here, but there are numerous books on the subject should anyone considering playing video poker want to read one to unlock the secrets.

Another important aspect of video poker is machine selection. Certain machines, while almost identical in appearance, have a slightly different pay table. This means that for the same hand, one machine would pay you more. Obviously, that's the machine you want to play. The best examples of these are the 9/6 machines versus the 8/5 machines. Look at the pay table on the machine's main screen: Royal flush, straight flush, and four-of-a-kind payoffs are all the same. But on one variant, a full house pays nine coins for every coin played versus eight on the other. The very same higher-paying machine returns six coins per coin wagered for a flush while the other only yields five. You might not think the minuscule difference warrants the extra time to look for the machine with the higher return, but trust us, over extended hours of play, those single-coin differences can factor into a considerable sum.

A Word About High Rollers and Comps

Casinos are happy to comp you all sorts of goods and services. All they ask is that you risk your money.

Your comps are determined by the amount you gamble. Perks include anything from hotel rooms and spa visits to show tickets, jewelry, and hookers (although you're probably not going to get anyone at the casino to admit that). The biggest comps are reserved for the biggest gamblers, known as "whales," who will wager seven-digit sums in a weekend. Even wagering less can earn perks, though.

Once you establish credit and get your player's card, you're allowed markers (an IOU) at the tables, and the casino begins to monitor your betting. Casinos value each game according to what they expect to win, and approximately 25 percent of their expected winnings are allocated for comps. One example is the "RFB" (room, food, beverages), available by placing an average bet of $300 over four hours per day (amount varies by casino) at such games as blackjack, craps, and roulette. Casinos expect to win your average bet each hour, or $1,200 per day, so they'll happily allow 25 percent of that to comp you an RFB. The value of your comp varies with your betting, but at any reasonable level you can land some truly nice perks. Whether VIP service at check-out, admission to the hottest restaurant and nightclub, or a limousine to the airport, it might just be enough to keep you smiling as you write another check to cover your markers.

LAS VEGAS BLACK BOOK

You're solo in the city—where's a singles-friendly place to eat? Is there a good lunch spot near the museum? Will the bar be too loud for easy conversation? Get the answers fast in the *Black Book*, a condensed version of every listing in our guide that puts all the essential information at your fingertips.

A quick glance down the page and you'll find the type of food, nightlife, or attractions you are looking for, the phone numbers, and which pages to turn to for more detailed information. How did you ever survive without this?

Las Vegas Black Book

Hotels

NAME TYPE (ROOMS)	ADDRESS (CROSS STREET) WEBSITE	AREA PRICE	PHONE 800 NUMBER	EXPERIENCE	PAGE
The Bellagio Timeless (4,348)	3600 S. Las Vegas Blvd. (Flamingo Rd.) bellagio.com	CS $$$	702-693-7111 888-987-7111	Luxe	113
Caesars Palace Classic (3,348)	3570 S. Las Vegas Blvd. (Flamingo Rd.) caesars.com	CS $$$$	702-731-7110 800-634-6001	Cool	58
Four Seasons Contemporary (424)	3960 S. Las Vegas Blvd. (Mandalay Bay Rd.) fourseasons.com/lasvegas	SS $$$$	702-632-5000 877-632-5000	Luxe	113
Green Valley Ranch Trendy (495)	2300 Paseo Verde Pkwy. (Green Valley Pkwy.) greenvalleyranchresort.com	VA $$$$	702-617-7777 866-617-7770	Leaving	168
The Hard Rock Hotel & Casino Modern (644)	4455 Paradise Rd. (Harmon Ave.) hardrockhotel.com	EF $$$	702-693-5000 800-693-7625	Bachelor(ette) Celebrity-Spotting	85 21
Hyatt Regency Lake LV Moroccan (493)	101 Montelago Blvd. (Lake Las Vegas Pkwy.) lakelasvegas.hyatt.com	VA $$$	702-567-1234 800-233-1234	Leaving	168
Luxor Theme (4,473)	3900 S. Las Vegas Blvd. (Tropicana Ave.) luxor.com	SS $$	702-262-4000 888-777-0188	Bachelor(ette)	85
Mandalay Bay Resort & Casino Contemp. (3,200)	3950 S. Las Vegas Blvd. (Mandalay Bay Rd.) mandalaybay.com	SS $$$	702-632-7777 877-632-7000	Cool	58
MGM Grand Modern (5,034)	3799 S. Las Vegas Blvd. (Tropicana Ave.) mgmgrand.com	SS $$	702-891-1111 800-929-1111	Cool	58
The Mirage Contemporary (3,039)	3400 S. Las Vegas Blvd. (Buccaneer Blvd.) mirage.com	CS $$	702-791-7111 800-374-9000	Bachelor(ette)	85
Palms Casino Resort Trendy (606)	4321 W. Flamingo Rd. (Arville St.) palms.com	WF $$$	702-942-7777 866-942-7777	Bachelor(ette) Celebrity-Spotting	86 21
Paris Las Vegas Theme (2,916)	3655 S. Las Vegas Blvd. (Flamingo Rd.) parislasvegas.com	CS $$	702-946-7000 888-796-2096	Bachelor(ette)	86
Red Rock Resort Spa & Casino Contemp. (462)	11011 W. Charleston Blvd. (S. Pavilion Ctr. Dr.) redrockstation.com	VA $$$	702-797-7625 866-767-7773	Leaving	169
Ritz Carlton Lake Las Vegas Timeless (349)	1610 Lake Las Vegas Pkwy. (Lake Mead Pkwy.) ritzcarlton.com/resorts/lake_las_vegas	VA $$$$	702-567-4700 800-241-3333	Leaving	169
Skylofts at MGM Modern (51)	3799 S. Las Vegas Blvd. (Tropicana Ave.) skyloftsmgmgrand.com	SS $$$$	702-891-3832 877-646-5638	Luxe	113
THEhotel Modern (1,117)	3950 S. Las Vegas Blvd. (Mandalay Bay Rd.) mandalaybay.com	SS $$	702-632-7800 877-632-7800	Cool	59
The Venetian Classic (4,027)	3355 S. Las Vegas Blvd. (Flamingo Rd.) venetian.com	CS $$$	702-414-1000 877-883-6423	Luxe	114
Wynn Las Vegas Contemporary (2,719)	3131 Las Vegas Blvd. S. (E. Desert Inn Rd.) wynnlasvegas.com	NS $$$$	702-770-7000 877-320-7123	Luxe Celebrity-Spotting	114 21

Neighborhood (Area) Key		
CS = Center Strip	**NS** = North Strip	**VA** = Various
DT = Downtown	**SS** = South Strip	
EF = East Flamingo	**WF** = West Flamingo	

Restaurants

NAME	ADDRESS (CROSS STREET)	AREA	PHONE	EXPERIENCE	PAGE
TYPE	WEBSITE	PRICE	SINGLES/NOISE	99 BEST	PAGE
Ah Sin!	Paris Las Vegas	CS	702-946-4593	Bachelor(ette)	87
Asian Fusion	parislasvegas.com	$$$	B ≡		
AJ's Steakhouse*	The Hard Rock Hotel & Casino	EF	702-693-5500	Bachelor(ette)	82, 87
Steakhouse	hardrockhotel.com	$$$$	- ≡		
Alex at Wynn	Wynn Las Vegas	NS	702-770-3300	Luxe	110, 115
French (G)	wynnlasvegas.com	$$$$	- ⊟	High-Roller Dining	29
Alizé	Palms Casino Resort	WF	702-951-7000	Luxe	115
French	alizelv.com	$$$$	- ≡		
Andre's	401 S. 6th St. (Chef Andre Rochat Pl.)	DT	702-385-5016	Luxe	115
French	alizelv.com/original	$$$$	- ≡		
Augustus Café	Caesars Palace	CS	702-650-5920	Cool	60
Continental	caesars.com	$$	- ≡		
Aureole	Mandalay Bay Resort & Casino	SS	702-632-7401	Luxe	109, 116
Continental (G)	aureolelv.com	$$$$	B ⊟	Fine Dining	24
Bartolotta, Ristorante	Wynn Las Vegas	NS	702-770-9966	Luxe	109, 116
Di Mare Italian	wynnlasvegas.com	$$$	B ≡		
BOA Steakhouse	Caesars Forum Shops	CS	702-733-7373	Cool	60
Steakhouse	boasteak.com	$$$	B ≡		
Border Grill	Mandalay Bay Resort & Casino	SS	702-632-7403	Cool	52, 60
Mexican	bordergrill.com	$$$	- ≡	Mexican Rests.	33
Bouchon	The Venetian	CS	702-414-6200	Luxe	107, 116
French	frenchlaundry.com	$$	B ≡	Brasseries	19
Bradley Ogden*	Caesars Palace	CS	702-731-7731	Cool	53, 61
American (G)	larkcreek.com	$$$$	B ≡	Fine Dining	24
The Buffet	Wynn Las Vegas	NS	702-770-3340	Luxe	110, 117
Buffet	wynnlasvegas.com	$$$	- ≡	Gourmet Buffets	28
The Buffet at Bellagio	The Bellagio	CS	702-693-7111	Luxe	110, 117
Buffet	bellagio.com	$$$	- ≡	Gourmet Buffets	28
Burger Bar	Mandalay Bay Resort & Casino	SS	702-632-9364	Cool	52, 61
American	fleurdelyssf.com	$$	B ≡		
California Pizza Kitchen	The Mirage	CS	702-791-7357	Bachelor(ette)	80, 87
American	cpk.com	$	B ≡	All-Night Eats	17
Canaletto	The Venetian	CS	702-733-0070	Cool	61
Italian	venetian.com/dining/canaletto.cfm	$$$	- ≡		
Charlie Palmer Steak*	Four Seasons	SS	702-632-5120	Luxe	109, 117
Steakhouse	charliepalmersteaklv.com	$$$	- ⊟	Steakhouses	40

Restaurant and Nightlife Symbols

Restaurants	Nightlife	Restaurant + Nightlife
Singles Friendly (eat and/or meet)	Price Warning	Prime time noise levels
⊡ = Communal table	C = Cover or ticket charge	⊟ = Quiet
B = Food served at bar		≈ = A buzz, but still conversational
(G) = Gourmet destination		≡ = Loud

Venues followed by an * are those we recommend as both a restaurant and a destination bar.

Note regarding page numbers: Italic = itinerary listing; Roman = description in theme chapter listing.

BLACK BOOK

Restaurants (cont.)

NAME / TYPE	ADDRESS / WEBSITE	AREA PRICE	PHONE SINGLES/NOISE	EXPERIENCE 99 BEST	PAGE PAGE
China Grill Chinese	Mandalay Bay Resort & Casino chinagrillmgt.com	SS $	702-632-7404 B ≡	Cool	61
Chinois Chinese	Caesars Palace wolfgangpuck.com	CS $$$	702-737-9700 B ≡	Bachelor(ette)	87
Le Cirque French	The Bellagio bellagio.com	CS $$$$	702-693-8100 B ▭	Luxe	117
Commander's Palace Creole	Aladdin/Planet Hollywood commanderspalace.com	CS $$$$	702-892-8272 B ≡	Cool Regional Dining	54, 62 37
The Country Club Continental	Wynn Las Vegas wynnlasvegas.com	NS $$$	702-770-3315 B ▭	Luxe	110, 117
Craftsteak Steakhouse (G)	MGM Grand mgmgrand.com	SS $$$$	- 702-891-7318	Cool	62
Daniel Boulud Brasserie French	Wynn Las Vegas wynnlasvegas.com	NS $$$$	702-770-3300 B ≡	Luxe Brasseries	110, 118 19
Delmonico Steakhouse Steakhouse (G)	The Venetian emerils.com	CS $$$$	702-414-3737 B ≡	Luxe Steakhouses	107, 118 40
Diego* Mexican	MGM Grand mgmgrand.com	SS $$	702-891-3200 - ≡	Bachelor(ette) Mexican Rests.	81, 88 33
Drai's* French	Barbary Coast drais.net	CS $$$	702-737-0555 - ▭	Luxe	118
Eiffel Tower Restaurant French	Paris Las Vegas eiffeltowerrestaurant.com	CS $$$$	702-948-6937 B▯ ≡	Luxe	118
808 Fusion	Caesars Palace caesars.com	CS $$$	702-731-7604 B	Cool	53, 62
Emeril's New Orleans Fish House Cajun	MGM Grand emerils.com	SS $$$	702-891-7374 B ≡	Cool Regional Dining	63 37
Fadó Irish Pub & Rest.* Irish	Green Valley Ranch fadoirishpub.com	VA $$	702-407-8691 - ≡	Bachelor(ette)	88
Fiamma Trattoria Italian	MGM Grand mgmgrand.com	SS $$$$	702-891-7600 B ≡	Bachelor(ette)	81, 88
Fin Asian Fusion	The Mirage mirage.com	CS $$	702-791-7353 - ≡	Bachelor(ette)	80, 88
FIX* Continental	The Bellagio fixlasvegas.com	CS $$$	702-693-8400 - ≡	Luxe	118
Fleur de Lys French	Mandalay Bay Resort & Casino fleurdelyssf.com	SS $$$$	702-632-9400 B ≡	Luxe	109, 119
Gallagher's Steakhouse Steakhouse	New York-New York gallaghersnysteakhouse.com	CS $$$$	702-740-6450 B ≡	Bachelor(ette)	89
Garduño's/Blue Agave Oyster & Chili Bar* Mexican	Palms Casino Resort palms.com	WF $$	702-942-7777 - ≡	Bachelor(ette)	79, 89
Grand Lux Café Continental	The Venetian grandluxcafe.com	CS $$	702-414-3888 B ≡	Bachelor(ette) All-Night Eats	80, 89 17
House of Blues* Cajun	Mandalay Bay Resort & Casino hob.com	SS $$$	702-632-7600 - ≡	Bachelor(ette)	81, 89

NAME TYPE	ADDRESS (CROSS STREET) WEBSITE	AREA PRICE	PHONE SINGLES/NOISE	EXPERIENCE 99 BEST	PAGE PAGE
Isla Mexican Kitchen Mexican	Treasure Island treasureisland.com	CS $$	702-894-7349 B =	Cool Mexican Rests.	63 33
Jasmine Chinese	The Bellagio bellagio.com	CS $$$$	702-693-7111 - =	Luxe	119
Jean-Philippe Pâtisserie Cafe/Dessert	The Bellagio bellagio.com	CS $	702-693-7111 - =	Luxe	110, 119
Joe's Seafood, Prime Steak & Stone Crab Seafood	Caesars Palace icon.com/joes	CS $$$	702-792-9222 B =	Cool	63
Joël Robuchon at The Mansion French Fusion (G)	MGM Grand mgmgrand.com	SS $$$$	702-891-7358 - =	Luxe High-Roller Dining	108, 119 29
Kokomo's Continental	The Mirage mirage.com	CS $$$	702-791-7350 B =	Bachelor(ette)	90
L'Atelier de Joël Robuchon French (G)	MGM Grand mgmgrand.com	CS $$$$	702-891-7358 B =	Luxe	120
La Creperie French	Paris Las Vegas parislasvegas.com	CS $	702-946-7147 - =	Bachelor(ette)	90
Le Village Buffet Buffet	Paris Las Vegas parislasvegas.com	CS $$	702-946-7000 - =	Bachelor(ette)	90
Little Buddha* Asian Fusion	Palms Casino Resort littlebuddhalasvegas.com	WF $$$	702-942-7778 - =	Bachelor(ette)	79, 90
Lutèce French	The Venetian arkvegas.com/lutece	CS $$$$	702-414-2220 B =	Luxe	120
Luv-It Custard Ice Cream	505 E. Oakey Blvd. (S. Las Vegas Blvd.) luvitfrozencustard.com	SS $	702-384-6452 - =	Luxe	120
Mesa Grill Southwest	Caesars Palace mesagrill.com	CS $$	702-650-5965 B =	Cool Regional Dining	53, 63 37
Michael Mina Seafood	The Bellagio michaelmina.net	CS $$$$	702-693-8100 B =	Luxe	108, 121
Mix in Las Vegas French	Mandalay Bay Resort & Casino alain-ducasse.com	SS $$$$	702-632-9500 - =	Cool Trendy Tables	54, 63 45
Mon Ami Gabi French	Paris Las Vegas monamigabi.com	CS $$	702-944-4224 - =	Cool Brasseries	53, 64 19
Mr. Lucky's 24/7 American	The Hard Rock Hotel & Casino hardrockhotel.com	EF $	702-693-5000 - =	Bachelor(ette) All-Night Eats	82, 91 17
N9NE* Steak House	Palms Casino Resort n9negroup.com	WF $$$$	702-933-9000 B =	Cool Trendy Tables	51, 64 45
Nob Hill Seafood (G)	MGM Grand michaelmina.net	SS $$$$	702-891-7337 B =	Cool Fine Dining	54, 64 24
Nobu Sushi (G)	The Hard Rock Hotel & Casino hardrockhotel.com	EF $$$$	702-693-5090 B =	Cool Sushi Restaurants	64 42
Okada Japanese	Wynn Las Vegas wynnlasvegas.com	NS $$$	702-770-3320 B =	Luxe	121
Olives Mediterranean	The Bellagio toddenglish.com	CS $$$$	702-693-8181 B =	Luxe	108, 121

BLACK BOOK

Restaurants (cont.)

NAME TYPE	ADDRESS WEBSITE	AREA PRICE	PHONE SINGLES/NOISE	EXPERIENCE 99 BEST	PAGE PAGE
Osteria del Circo Italian	The Bellagio osteriadelcirco.com	CS $$$$	702-693-8150 B ☰	Luxe	121
Palm Restaurant Steakhouse	Caesars Palace thepalm.com	CS $$$$	702-732-7256 B ☰	Luxe	122
Pharaoh's Pheast Buffet Buffet	Luxor luxor.com	SS $$	702-262-4000 - ☰	Bachelor(ette)	91
Picasso French Fusion (G)	The Bellagio bellagio.com	CS $$$$	702-693-8105 - ☐	Luxe	122
Pink Taco* Mexican	The Hard Rock Hotel & Casino pinktaco.com	EF $	702-693-5525 - ☰	Bachelor(ette)	80, 91
Postrio Fusion	The Venetian wolfgangpuck.com	CS $$	702-796-1110 B ☰	Cool	65
Prime Steakhouse Steakhouse (G)	The Bellagio bellagio.com	CS $$$$	702-693-8484 B ☰	Luxe Steakhouses	108, 122 40
R Bar Café* Seafood	Mandalay Bay Resort & Casino rmseafood.com	SS $$	702-632-9300 - ☰	Cool	53, 65
Red Square* Continental	Mandalay Bay Resort & Casino mandalaybay.com	SS $$$	702-632-7407 - ☰	Cool	51, 65
Restaurant Guy Savoy French (G)	Caesars Palace caesars.com	CS $$$$	702-731-7286 B ☐	Luxe High-Roller Dining	110, 122 29
Restaurant RM Seafood	Mandalay Bay Resort & Casino rmseafood.com	SS $$$$	702-632-9300 B ☰	Cool	65
Samba Brazilian Steakhouse Brazilian	The Mirage mirage.com	CS $$$	702-791-7337 - ☰	Bachelor(ette)	91
Seablue Seafood	MGM Grand michaelmina.net	SS $$$$	702-891-3486 B ☰	Cool	54, 65
Sensi Asian Fusion	The Bellagio bellagio.com	CS $$$$	702-693-8800 B ☰	Luxe	108, 123
Shanghai Lilly's Asian	Mandalay Bay Resort & Casino mandalaybay.com	SS $$$$	702-632-7409 - ☰	Bachelor(ette)	82, 91
Shintaro Sushi (G)	The Bellagio bellagio.com	CS $$$	702-693-8141 B☐ ☰	Luxe Sushi Restaurants	123 42
Simon Kitchen and Bar Continental	The Hard Rock Hotel & Casino simonkitchen.com	EF $$$$	702-693-4440 B ☰	Bachelor(ette)	82, 92
Spago Continental	Caesars Palace wolfgangpuck.com	CS $$$$	702-369-6300 B ☰	Luxe	109, 123
Spice Market Buffet Buffet	Aladdin/Planet Hollywood aladdincasino.com	CS $$	720-785-9005 - ☰	Bachelor(ette)	92
STACK Continental	The Mirage stacklasvegas.com	CS $$	702-792-7800 B ☰	Bachelor(ette)	79, 92
Sterling Brunch Buffet	Bally's caesars.com/Ballys/LasVegas	CS $$$	702-967-7999 - ☰	Luxe Gourmet Buffets	123 28
Sushi Roku Japanese	Caesars Palace sushiroku.com	CS $$$	702-733-7373 B ☰	Cool Sushi Restaurants	66 42

NAME TYPE	ADDRESS WEBSITE	AREA PRICE	PHONE SINGLES/NOISE	EXPERIENCE 99 BEST	PAGE PAGE
SW Steakhouse Steakhouse	Wynn Las Vegas wynnlasvegas.com	NS $$$$	702-770-9966 B	Luxe	124
Tao Asian Bistro* Asian Fusion	The Venetian taolasvegas.com	CS $$$	702-388-8338 -	Cool Trendy Tables	51, 66 45
3950 Steakhouse	Mandalay Bay Resort & Casino mandalaybay.com	SS $$$$	702-632-7417 B	Cool	66
The Verandah American	Four Seasons fourseasons.com/lasvegas	SS $$$	702-632-5121 -	Luxe	124
Zeffirino Ristorante Italian	The Venetian venetian.com	CS $$$	702-414-3500 B	Luxe	124

Nightlife

NAME TYPE	ADDRESS (CROSS STREET) WEBSITE	AREA COVER	PHONE FOOD/NOISE	EXPERIENCE 99 BEST	PAGE PAGE
AJ's Steakhouse* Martini Bar	The Hard Rock Hotel & Casino hardrockhotel.com	EF -	702-693-5500 -	Bachelor(ette)	93
Aladdin Theater Live Shows	Aladdin/Planet Hollywood aladdincasino.com	CS C	702-785-5000	Bachelor(ette)	93
Alesium after-hours Nightclub	3724 S. Las Vegas Blvd. (Flamingo Rd.) sevenlasvegas.com	CS C	702-739-7744 -	Bachelor(ette)	81, 93
Bar at Times Square Bar	New York-New York nynyhotelcasino.com	CS -	702-740-6969 B	Bachelor(ette)	81, 93
Battle Bar Bar	Treasure Island treasureisland.com	CS -	702-894-7330 B	Bachelor(ette)	79, 93
The Beatles: Love Show	The Mirage mirage.com	CS C	702-792-7777 -	Cool Cirque	54, 67 22
Big Apple Bar Bar	New York-New York nynyhotelcasino.com	CS -	702-740-6969 B	Bachelor(ette)	93
Blue Man Group Show	The Venetian blueman.com	CS C	702-414-1000 -	Bachelor(ette) Shows	94 38
Body English Nightclub	The Hard Rock Hotel & Casino bodyenglish.com	EF C	702-794-3623 -	Bachelor(ette) Nightclubs	82, 94 34
Bradley Ogden* Bar/Restaurant (G)	Caesars Palace larkcreek.com	CS C	702-731-7731 B	Cool	53, 67
Caramel Lounge	The Bellagio lightgroup.com	CS -	702-693-8300 -	Luxe Ultra Lounges	108, 125 46
Céline Dion: A New Day Show	Caesars Palace celinedion.com	CS C	702-731-7110 -	Luxe	110, 125
Center Bar Bar/Lounge	The Hard Rock Hotel & Casino hardrockhotel.com	EF C	702-693-5000 -	Bachelor(ette) Meet Markets	82, 94 31
Centrifuge Bar Bar	MGM Grand mgmgrand.com	SS C	702-891-1111 -	Bachelor(ette) Meet Markets	81, 94 31

BLACK BOOK

Nightlife (cont.)

NAME	ADDRESS (CROSS STREET)	AREA	PHONE	EXPERIENCE	PAGE
TYPE	WEBSITE	COVER	FOOD/NOISE	99 BEST	PAGE
Charlie Palmer Steak* Restaurant/Lounge	Four Seasons charliepalmersteaklv.com	SS -	702-632-5120 - ⊟	Luxe Quiet Bars	*109*, 125 36
Cherry Nightclub	11011 W. Charleston Blvd. (215 W. Frwy.) redrocklasvegas.com	VA C	866-767-7773 - ≣	Cool	67
Chippendales, The Show Show	The Rio chippendales.com	WF C	702-777-7776 - ≣	Bachelor(ette)	*80*, 94
Cleopatra's Barge Nightclub	Caesars Palace caesars.com	CS -	702-369-6300 - ≣	Luxe	*110*, 125
Club Paradise Strip Club	4416 Paradise Rd. (Flamingo Rd.) clubparadise.net	EF C	702-734-7990 - ≣	Luxe	*109*, 125
Coyote Ugly Bar	New York-New York coyoteuglysaloon.com/vegas	CS C	702-740-6330 - ≣	Bachelor(ette)	*81*, 95
Diego* Nightclub	MGM Grand mgmgrand.com	SS C	702-891-3200 - ≣	Bachelor(ette)	*81*, 95
Drai's* Nightclub	Barbary Coast draisafterhours.com	CS C	702-737-0555 - ≣	Bachelor(ette) After-Hours Clubs	*82*, 95 16
Drop Bar Bar/Lounge	Green Valley Ranch Resort greenvalleyranchresort.com	VA -	702-617-7777 - ⊟	Cool	67
Elton John: The Red Piano Show	Caesars Palace caesars.com	CS C	702-866-1400 - ⊟	Luxe Shows	*110*, 126 38
Empire Ballroom Nightclub	3765 Las Vegas Blvd. S. (S. Las Vegas Blvd.) empireballroom.com	SS C	702-415-5283 - ≣	Bachelor(ette) After-Hours Clubs	*80*, 95 16
Fadó Irish Pub & Rest.* Bar/Restaurant	Green Valley Ranch Resort fadoirishpub.com	VA -	702-407-8691 - -	Bachelor(ette)	95
La Femme Topless Revue	MGM Grand mgmgrand.com	CS C	702-891-7777 - ⊟	Luxe Shows	*108*, 126 38
FIX* Bar/Lounge	The Bellagio fixlasvegas.com	CS -	702-693-8400 - ≣	Luxe	126
Folies Bergère Topless Revue	The Tropicana tropicanalv.com	SS C	702-739-2222 - ⊟	Luxe	126
Fontana Bar Lounge	The Bellagio bellagio.com	CS -	702-693-7989 Ⓑ ⊟	Luxe Quiet Bars	*108*, 126 36
Foundation Room (at the House of Blues) Lounge	Mandalay Bay Resort & Casino hob.com	SS C	702-632-7601 - ≣	Cool	*51*, 68
Freezone Gay Club	601 E. Naples (Paradise Rd.) freezonelv.com	VA -	702-794-2300 - ≣	Bachelor(ette) Gay Bars and Clubs 26	96
Garduño's/Blue Agave Oyster and Chili Bar* Bar/Rest.	Palms Casino Resort palms.com	WF -	702-942-7777 - ⊟	Bachelor(ette)	*79*, 96
Ghostbar Nightclub	Palms Casino Resort n9negroup.com	WF C	702-938-2666 - ≣	Cool Bars with a View	*52*, 68 18
Gipsy Gay Club	4605 S. Paradise Rd. (Tropicana Ave.) gipsylv.com	VA C	702-731-1919 - ≣	Bachelor(ette) Gay Bars and Clubs 26	96
House of Blues* Nightclub/Live Music	Mandalay Bay Resort & Casino hob.com	SS C	702-632-7601 - ≣	Cool Live Music	*51*, 68 30

NAME	ADDRESS (CROSS STREET)	AREA	PHONE	EXPERIENCE	PAGE
TYPE	WEBSITE	COVER	FOOD/NOISE	99 BEST	PAGE
The Improv	Harrah's	CS	702-369-5000	Bachelor(ette)	96
Comedy Club	harrahs.com	C	- ≡		
Island Lounge	Mandalay Bay Resort & Casino	SS	702-632-7777	Cool	54, 68
Lounge	mandalaybay.com	-	- ≡		
Ivan Kane's Forty Deuce	Mandalay Bay Resort & Casino	SS	702-632-9442	Cool	52, 69
Nightclub	fortydeuce.com	C	- ≡	Burlesque	20
Jet	The Mirage	CS	702-792-7900	Bachelor(ette)	80, 96
Nightclub	jetlv.com	C	- ≡	Mega-Nightclubs	32
The Joint	The Hard Rock Hotel & Casino	EF	702-693-5066	Bachelor(ette)	82, 96
Live Music	hardrockhotel.com	C	- ≡	Live Music	30
Kà	MGM Grand	SS	702-796-9999	Cool	54, 69
Show	cirquedusoleil.com	C	- ≡	Cirque	22
KRAVE	Aladdin/Planet Hollywood	CS	702-836-0830	Bachelor(ette)	81, 97
Gay Club	kravelasvegas.com	C	- ≡	Gay Bars and Clubs	26
Le Rêve	Wynn Las Vegas	NS	702-770-7110	Luxe	126
Show	wynnlasvegas.com	C	- ≡		
Light	The Bellagio	CS	702-693-7111	Luxe	108, 127
Nightclub	lightgroup.com	C	- ≡	Nightclubs	34
Little Buddha*	Palms Casino Resort	WF	702-942-7778	Bachelor(ette)	79, 97
Bar/Lounge	littlebuddhalasvegas.com	-	- ≡		
Lure	Wynn Las Vegas	NS	702-770-3375	Luxe	110, 127
Ultra Lounge	wynnlasvegas.com	C	- ≡	Ultra Lounges	46
Mamma Mia!	Mandalay Bay Resort & Casino	SS	877-632-4700	Bachelor(ette)	97
Show	mandalaybay.com	C	- ≡		
MGM Grand Garden Arena	MGM Grand	SS	702-891-1111	Cool	69
Live Music	mgmgrand.com	C	- ≡	Live Music	30
Mist	Treasure Island	CS	702-894-7330	Bachelor(ette)	97
Lounge	mistbar.com	C	- ≡		
Mix Lounge	Mandalay Bay Resort & Casino	SS	702-632-9500	Cool	54, 69
Ultra Lounge	mandalaybay.com	C	- ≡	Bars with a View	18
Mystère	Treasure Island	CS	702-894-7111	Bachelor(ette)	80, 97
Show	cirquedusoleil.com	C	- ≡		
Napoleon's Champagne Bar	Paris Las Vegas	CS	702-946-7000	Cool	69
Bar/Lounge	parislasvegas.com	-	- ⊡	Quiet Bars	36
N9NE*	Palms Casino Resort	WF	702-933-9000	Cool	70
Restaurant/Bar	n9negroup.com	C	B		
O	The Bellagio	CS	702-693-7722	Luxe	108, 127
Show	cirquedusoleil.com	C	- ≡	Cirque	22
Olympic Gardens	1531 S. Las Vegas Blvd. (Oakey St.)	SS	702-385-8987	Bachelor(ette)	80, 98
Strip Club	ogvegas.com	C	- ≡		
Palapa Lounge	Palms Casino Resort	WF	702-942-7777	Bachelor(ette)	98
Bar/Lounge	palms.com	-	- ≡		
Palomino Club	1848 Las Vegas Blvd. N.	VA	702-642-2984	Bachelor(ette)	81, 98
Strip Club	(E. Owens St.)	C	- ≡	Strip Clubs	41

BLACK BOOK

Nightlife (cont.)

NAME TYPE	ADDRESS (CROSS STREET) WEBSITE	AREA COVER	PHONE FOOD/NOISE	EXPERIENCE 99 BEST	PAGE PAGE
Penn and Teller Show	The Rio pennandteller.com	EF C	702-777-7776 ⬛	Luxe	127
Peppermill Fireside Lounge Lounge	2985 S. Las Vegas Blvd. (E. Desert Inn Rd.) peppermilllasvegas.com	NS -	702-735-4177 ⬛	Cool	*52*, 70
Petrossian Bar Bar	The Bellagio bellagio.com	CS -	702-693-8100 ⬛	Luxe	*108*, 128
Phantom of the Opera Show	The Venetian phantomlasvegas.com	CS C	866-641-7469 ⬛	Luxe	128
Pink Taco* Bar	The Hard Rock Hotel & Casino pinktaco.com	EF -	702-693-5525 ⬛	Bachelor(ette)	98
Playboy Club Club	Palms Casino Resort palms.com	WF C	702-942-7777 ⬛	Cool	70
PURE Nightclub	Caesars Palace caesars.com	CS C	702-731-7873 ⬛	Cool Mega-Nightclubs	*53*, 70 32
Pussycat Dolls Lounge Nightclub/Lounge	Caesars Palace caesars.com	CS C	702-731-7110 ⬛	Cool Burlesque	*53*, 70 20
R Bar Café* Bar/Restaurant	Mandalay Bay Resort & Casino rmseafood.com	SS -	702-632-9300 ⬛	Cool	71
Rain Nightclub	Palms Casino Resort palms.com	WF C	702-938-9999 ⬛	Bachelor(ette)	*80*, 98
Red Square* Nightclub	Mandalay Bay Resort & Casino mandalaybay.com	SS C	702-632-7407 ⬛	Cool	*51*, 71
Risqué Ultra Lounge	Paris Las Vegas parislasvegas.com	CS C	702-946-4589 ⬛	Bachelor(ette)	*81*, 99
Rita Rudner Comedy Show	Harrah's ritafunny.com	CS C	702-369-5000 ⬛	Bachelor(ette)	99
rumjungle Nightclub	Mandalay Bay Resort & Casino mandalaybay.com	SS C	702-632-7408 ⬛	Bachelor(ette) Meet Markets	*82*, 99 31
Sapphire Gentlemen's Club Strip Club	3025 Industrial Rd. (E. Desert Inn Rd.) sapphirelasvegas.com	NS C	702-796-6000 ⬛	Luxe Strip Clubs	128 41
Scores Strip Club	3350 S. Procyon (Desert Inn Rd.) scoreslasvegas.com	VA C	702-367-4000 ⬛	Cool	*52*, 71
Seamless Nightclub	4740 S. Arville St. (W. Tompkins Ave.) seamlessclub.com	VA C	702-227-5200 ⬛	Cool After-Hours Clubs	*54*, 71 16
Shadow: A Bar Ultra Lounge	Caesars Palace caesars.com	CS -	702-369-6300 ⬛	Cool	*53*, 72
Spearmint Rhino Strip Club	3340 S. Highland Dr. (W. Desert Inn Rd.) spearmintrhino.com	NS C	702-796-3600 ⬛	Cool Strip Clubs	*53*, 72 41
Studio 54 Nightclub	MGM Grand mgmgrand.com	SS C	702-891-7254 ⬛	Cool Mega-Nightclubs	*54*, 72 32
Tabú Ultra Lounge	MGM Grand mgmgrand.com	SS C	702-891-7129 ⬛	Cool Ultra Lounges	*54*, 72 46
Tangerine Lounge/Nightclub	Treasure Island treasureisland.com	CS C	702-894-7580 ⬛	Bachelor(ette) Burlesque	99 20

NAME / TYPE	ADDRESS / WEBSITE	AREA COVER	PHONE FOOD/NOISE	EXPERIENCE 99 BEST	PAGE PAGE
Tao Lounge* / Restaurant/Lounge	The Venetian / taolasvegas.com	CS / C	702-388-8338 / - ☰	Cool	73
Tao Nightclub / Nightclub	The Venetian / taolasvegas.com	CS / -	702-388-8338 / - ☰	Cool / Nightclubs	52, 73 / 34
Thunder From Down Under / Show	Excalibur / thunderfromdownunder.com	CS / C	702-597-7600 / - ☰	Bachelor(ette)	80, 99
Tryst / Nightclub	Wynn Las Vegas / wynnlasvegas.com	NS / C	702-770-3375 / - ☰	Luxe	110, 128
V Bar / Lounge	The Venetian / venetian.com	CS / C	702-414-3200 / - ☰	Bachelor(ette)	100
Voodoo Lounge / Bar/Lounge	The Rio / harrahs.com	WF / C	702-252-7777 / - ☰	Cool / Bars with a View	53, 73 / 18
The Whiskey / Bar/Lounge	Green Valley Ranch Resort / midnightoilbars.com	VA / C	702-617-7777 / - ☰	Cool	73

Attractions

NAME / TYPE	ADDRESS (CROSS STREET) / WEBSITE	AREA PRICE	PHONE	EXPERIENCE 99 BEST	PAGE PAGE
Adventure Las Vegas / Tour	Various locations / adventurelasvegas.com	VA / $$$	702-869-9992	Bachelor(ette)	80, 101
Agent Provocateur / Shop	Caesars Forum Shops / agentprovocateur.com	CS / -	702-696-7174	Cool	53, 74
The Art of Shaving / Shop/Spa	Mandalay Place / theartofshaving.com	SS / -	702-632-9356	Cool	52, 74
Bear's Best / Golf	11111 W. Flamingo Rd. (Town Center) / bearsbest.com	WF / $$$	702-804-8500	Cool / Golf Courses	53, 74 / 27
Bellagio Fountains / Site	The Bellagio / bellagio.com	CS / -	702-964-7000	Luxe / Free Attractions	107, 129 / 25
Bellagio Gallery of Fine Art / Art Gallery	The Bellagio / bellagio.com	CS / $	702-693-7871	Luxe	108, 129
Bellagio Poker Room / Casino	The Bellagio / bellagio.com	CS / -	702-693-7290	Luxe / Texas Hold 'Em	108, 129 / 43
Bellagio Sports Book / Casino	The Bellagio / bellagio.com	CS / -	702-693-7111	Luxe / Sports Books	108, 129 / 39
The Big Shot / Ride	The Stratosphere / stratospherehotel.com	NS / $	702-380-7777	Bachelor(ette) / Thrill Rides	101 / 44
Binion's Gambling Hall & Hotel / Casino	128 Fremont St. (S. 1st St.) / binions.com	DT / -	702-382-1600	Luxe	109, 130
Caesars Palace Poker Room / Casino	Caesars Palace / caesars.com	CS / -	702-731-7110	Cool	54, 74
Caesars Palace Sports Book / Casino	Caesars Palace / caesars.com	CS / -	702-731-7110	Cool / Sports Books	54, 75 / 39

Attractions (cont.)

NAME / TYPE	ADDRESS (CROSS STREET) / WEBSITE	AREA / PRICE	PHONE	EXPERIENCE / 99 BEST	PAGE / PAGE
Canyon Ranch SpaClub / Spa	The Venetian / canyonranch.com	CS / -	702-414-3600	Cool / Destination Spas	52, 75 / 23
Desert Passage / Shops	Aladdin/Planet Hollywood / desertpassage.com	CS / -	888-866-0710	Bachelor(ette)	80, 101
Eiffel Tower / Site	Paris Las Vegas / parislasvegas.com	CS / $	702-946-7000	Luxe	107, 130
Exotic Car Rental / Car Rental	5021 Swenson St. (Tropicana Ave.) / exoticcarrentalslasvegas.com	VA / $$$	702-736-2592	Luxe	108, 130
Fifty Five Degrees / Shop/Wine Bar	Mandalay Place / 55degreeslasvegas.com	SS / -	702-632-9355	Cool	53, 75
Flyaway Indoor Skydiving / Ride	200 Convention Cntr. Dr. (Las Vegas Blvd. S.) flyawayindoorskydiving.com	NS / $$$$	702-731-4768	Bachelor(ette) / Thrill Rides	81, 101 / 44
The Forum Shops / Shops	Caesars Palace / forumshops.com	CS / -	702-893-4800	Cool	53, 75
Four Seasons Spa / Spa	Four Seasons / fourseasons.com/lasvegas	SS / -	702-632-5300	Luxe	110, 130
Fremont Street Experience / Shop/Site	Fremont St. (Main St.) / vegasexperience.com	DT / -	(no phone)	Luxe / Vintage Vegas	109, 130 / 47
Gambler's Book Shop / Shop	630 South 11th St. (Charleston St.) / gamblersbook.com	DT / -	702-382-7555	Bachelor(ette)	101
Grand Canal Shoppes / Shops	The Venetian / venetian.com	CS / -	702-414-4500	Bachelor(ette)	80, 102
Guggenheim Hermitage Museum Art Gallery	The Venetian / venetian.com	CS / $	702-414-2440	Cool	52, 75
The Gun Store / Shop/Sport	2900 E. Tropicana Ave. (McCloud St.) / thegunstorelasvegas.com	VA / -	702-454-1110	Bachelor(ette)	81, 102
IMAX Theater / Theater	Luxor / luxor.com	SS / $	702-262-4400	Bachelor(ette)	102
In Search of the Obelisk / Ride	Luxor / luxor.com	SS / $	702-262-4400	Bachelor(ette)	81, 102
King Tut's Tomb & Museum / Museum	Luxor / luxor.com	SS / $	702-262-4400	Bachelor(ette)	81, 102
Liberace Museum / Museum	1775 E. Tropicana Ave. (Spencer Ave.) / liberace.com/museum.cfm	VA / $	702-798-5595	Luxe / Vintage Vegas	131 / 47
Little Church of the West / Wedding Chapel	4617 S. Las Vegas Blvd. (W. Russell Rd.) littlechurchlv.com	SS / -	702-739-7971	Wedding Chapels	48
Little White Wedding Chapel / Wedding Chapel	1301 S. Las Vegas Blvd. (Sahara Ave.) alittlewhitechapel.com	NS / -	702-382-5943	Wedding Chapels	48
Madame Tussaud's Wax Museum Museum	The Venetian / mtvegas.com	CS / $$	702-862-7820	Bachelor(ette)	103
Mandalay Beach / Pool	Mandalay Bay Resort & Casino / mandalaybay.com	SS / $$	702-632-7777	Bachelor(ette) / Pool Scenes	103 / 35
Manhattan Express / Ride	New York-New York / nynyhotelcasino.com	CS / $	702-740-6969	Bachelor(ette) / Thrill rides	91, 103 / 44

NAME TYPE	ADDRESS (CROSS STREET) WEBSITE	AREA PRICE	PHONE	EXPERIENCE 99 BEST	
Maverick Helicopter Tours Tour	6075 Las Vegas Blvd. (S. Russell Rd.) maverickhelicopter.com	NS $$$	702-261-0007	Cool	
MGM Grand Spa Spa	MGM Grand mgmgrand.com	SS -	702-891-3077	Cool Destination Spas	
Mirage Poker Room Casino	The Mirage mirage.com	CS -	702-791-7291	Bachelor(ette) Texas Hold 'Em	
Moorea Beach Club Pool	Mandalay Bay Resort & Casino mandalaybay.com	SS $	702-632-7777	Cool	52
Neon Museum Site	Fremont St. (Main St.) neonmuseum.org	DT -	702-387-6366	Luxe	109, 13
9/11 Memorial Site	New York-New York nynyhotelcasino.com	CS -	702-740-6969	Luxe	131
Palms Casino Resort Pool Pool	Palms Casino Resort palms.com	WF $$	702-942-7777	Bachelor(ette) Pool Scenes	79, 104 35
Paris Spa by Mandara Spa	Paris Las Vegas mandaraspa.com	CS -	702-946-4366	Bachelor(ette) Destination Spas	80, 104 23
Playboy Store Shop	Palms Casino Resort palms.com	WF -	702-942-7777	Bachelor(ette)	104
Reflection Bay Golf Club Golf	Lake Las Vegas Resort lakelasvegas.com/golf_reflection.asp	VA $$	702-740-4653	Bachelor(ette) Golf Courses	80, 104 27
Rehab at Hard Rock Pool	The Hard Rock Hotel & Casino hardrockhotel.com	EF $$	702-693-5000	Bachelor(ette) Pool Scenes	82, 104 35
Richard Petty Driving Exp. Sport	6975 Speedway Blvd. Unit D-106 (Hwy. 15) 1800bepetty.com	VA $$$$	702-643-4343	Cool	54, 77
Rock Spa at Hard Rock Spa	The Hard Rock Hotel & Casino hardrockhotel.com	EF -	702-693-5554	Bachelor(ette)	105
Royal Links Golf Club Golf	5995 E. Vegas Valley Rd. (S. Sloan Ln.) waltersgolf.com	VA $$$	702-450-8123	Cool	53, 77
Shadow Creek Golf	3 Shadow Creek Dr. (Loose St.) shadowcreek.com	VA $$$$	702-791-7161	Luxe Golf Courses	109, 131 27
Shark Reef Aquarium	Mandalay Bay Resort & Casino mandalaybay.com	SS $	702-632-7800	Cool	54, 77
Sirens of TI Show/Site	Treasure Island treasureisland.com	CS -	702-894-7111	Bachelor(ette) Free Attractions	79, 105 25
Spa at the Palms Spa	Palms Casino Resort palms.com	WF -	702-942-6937	Bachelor(ette)	105
Spa Bellagio Spa	The Bellagio bellagio.com	CS -	702-693-7472	Luxe	110, 132
Spa Mandalay Spa	Mandalay Bay Resort & Casino mandalaybay.com	SS -	702-632-7220	Cool	52, 77
Stratosphere Observation Deck Site	The Stratosphere stratospherehotel.com	NS $	702-380-7791	Bachelor(ette)	105
Sundance Hellicopters Tour	5596 Haven St. (E. Sunset Rd.) helicoptour.com	VA $$$$	702-736-0606	Luxe	109, 132

Las Vegas Black Book by Casino

Code: H-Hotels; R-Restaurants; N-Nightlife; A-Attractions. Blue page numbers denote listings in 99 Best. Black page numbers denote listings in theme chapters. The Las Vegas Neighborhoods Map is on p.207.

BLACK BOOK

BLACK BOOK

The Venetian (cont.)

Wynn Las Vegas

Las Vegas Unique Shopping Index

NAME	(702) PHONE	AREA	PRODUCTS	PAGE
Agent Provocateur	696-7174	CS	Sexy lingerie	74
Ancient Creations	938-6755	CS	Unique jewelry made of coins	84
The Art of Shaving	632-9356	SS	Men's grooming products and spa	74
Bose	384-4067	VA	Electronics	84
Brioni	791-3440	NS	Stylish men's clothes	112
Chocolat	770-3475	NS	Chocolates and other sweets	112
The Chocolate Swan	632-9366	SS	Chocolates and coffee	57
Desert Passage	866-0710	CS	Aladdin/Planet Hollywood shopping	101
Diesel	696-1055	NS	Stylish clothes for men and women	56
Fifty-Five Degrees Wine+Design	632-9355	SS	Wine shop and tasting bar	75
Five Little Monkeys	632-9382	SS	Children's clothes and toys	57
Fornarina	215-9300	SS	Hipster clothes and shoes	57
The Forum Shops	893-4800	CS	Caesars upscale shops	75
Fred Leighton	693-7050	CS	High-end jeweler	112
Fremont Street Experience	(no phone)	DT	Downtown souvenir shops	130
Gambler's Book Shop	382-7555	DT	Books and gambling accessories	101
Grand Canal Shoppes	414-4500	CS	Venetian's canal-side shops	102
The Gun Store	454-1110	VA	Guns and firing range with rentals	102
Hermès	893-8900	CS	Designer clothes and accessories	112
Houdini's Magic Shop	314-4674	CS	Props for magic tricks	84
Jo Malone	770-3485	NS	Perfumery	112
L'Occitane	384-3842	VA	Candles, lotions, and grooming aids	84
Manolo Blahnik	770-3477	NS	Shoes for collectors	112
Nanette Lepore	893-9704	CS	Flirty, feminine women's clothes	56
Oscar de la Renta	770-3487	NS	Designer clothes for women	112
Playboy Store	942-7777	VA	Sex toys, lingerie, and other products	104
Prada	866-6886	CS	Designer goods	112
Puma	366-9921	VA	Trendy sneakers	84
Showcase Slots	733-6464	CS	Gambling goods	84
Talulah G	737-6000	NS	Trendy women's fashions	56
Taryn Rose	732-2712	CS	Designer shoes	77
TeNo	735-8366	CS	Watches and jewelry	84
Theory	386-5022	VA	Sleek women's clothes	84
Thomas Pink	696-1713	CS	Men's shirts and ties	56
Via Bellagio	693-7722	CS	Bellagio's very exclusive shops	133
Wynn Esplanade	770-7000	NS	Wynn's shopping arcade	133
Yves Chantre	732-8138	CS	Women's grooming products	84
Wolford	387-9626	CS	Women's undergarments	84

For Neighborhood (Area) Key, see p.188.

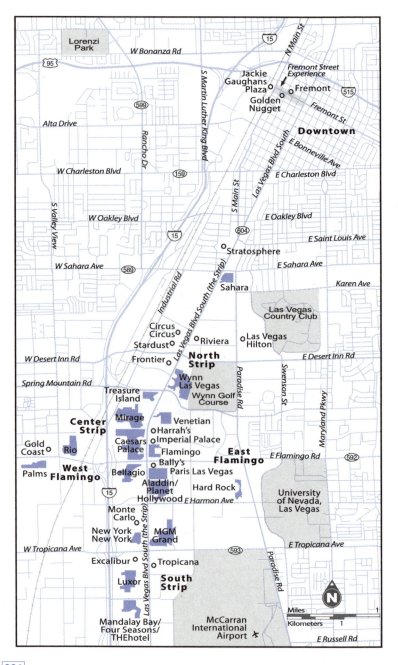

Lorenzi Park

W Bonanza Rd

95

Jackie Gaughans Plaza

Fremont Street Experience

Fremont

515

Golden Nugget

Fremont St

Alta Drive

599

Rancho Dr

S Martin Luther King Blvd

Downtown

E Bonneville Ave

Las Vegas Blvd South

W Charleston Blvd

159

E Charleston Blvd

S Valley View

W Oakley Blvd

S Main St

604

E Oakley Blvd

15

E Saint Louis Ave

Stratosphere

E Sahara Ave

W Sahara Ave

589

Industrial Rd

Sahara

Karen Ave

Las Vegas Country Club

Circus Circus

Las Vegas Blvd South (the Strip)

Stardust

Riviera

Las Vegas Hilton

Frontier

North Strip

E Desert Inn Rd

W Desert Inn Rd

Spring Mountain Rd

Wynn Las Vegas

Wynn Golf Course

Paradise Rd

Swenson St

Maryland Pkwy

Treasure Island

Center Strip

Mirage

Venetian

Harrah's

Imperial Palace

Gold Coast

Rio

Caesars Palace

Flamingo

East Flamingo

E Flamingo Rd

592

Palms

West Flamingo

Bellagio

Bally's

Paris Las Vegas

15

Aladdin/ Planet Hollywood

E Harmon Ave

Hard Rock

University of Nevada, Las Vegas

Monte Carlo

New York New York

MGM Grand

W Tropicana Ave

593

E Tropicana Ave

Excalibur

Tropicana

Las Vegas Blvd South (the Strip)

Luxor

South Strip

Paradise Rd

Miles

Kilometers

1

1

N

Mandalay Bay/ Four Seasons/ THEhotel

McCarran International Airport

E Russell Rd

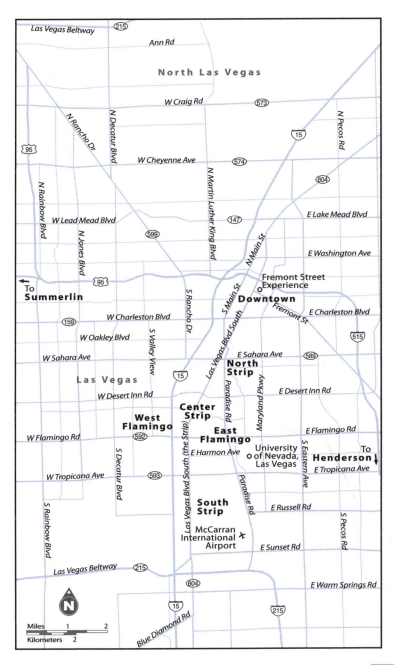

It's New. It's You.
Night+Day online
@ pulseguides.com

a travel web site designed to
complement your lifestyle

Today's urbane, sophisticated traveler knows
how fast things change in the world. What's hot,
and what's not? Now you have access to the
insider information you need, whenever you
need it—**Night+Day**—at pulseguides.com.

We're committed to providing the latest, most
accurate information on the hottest, hippest,
coolest and classiest venues around the world,
which means keeping our listings current—
even after you've purchased one of our
Night+Day guides.

Visit pulseguides.com and browse your way to any
destination to view or download the most recent
updates to the **Night+Day** guide of your choice.

Online and in print, **Night+Day** offers independent travel advice tailored to suit your lifestyle,
capturing the unique personality of each city.
From uptown chic to downtown cool, our guides
are packed with opinionated tips, and selective,
richly detailed descriptions geared toward the
discerning traveler.

Enhance your travel experience online:
- Zero in on hot restaurants, classic
  attractions and hip nightlife
- Print out your favorite itinerary to keep
  in your purse or pocket as you travel
- Update your **Night+Day** guide with
  what's new
- Read news and tips from around the world
- Get great deals on all the titles in our Cool
  Cities series

Night+Day—online now at pulseguides.com.